Applications of Computer Science and Technology in Different Fields

Applications of Computer Science and Technology in Different Fields

Edited by

Adele Kuzmiakova

ARCLER PRESS

www.arclerpress.com

Applications of Computer Science and Technology in Different Fields

Adele Kuzmiakova

Arcler Press
224 Shoreacres Road
Burlington, ON L7L 2H2
Canada
www.arclerpress.com
Email: orders@arclereducation.com

ISBN: 978-1-77407-743-6 (Hardcover)

ABOUT THE EDITOR

Adele Kuzmiakova is a computational engineer focusing on solving problems in machine learning, deep learning, and computer vision. Adele attended Cornell University in New York, United States for her undergraduate studies. She studied engineering with a focus on applied math. While at Cornell, she developed close relationships with professors, which enabled her to get involved in academic research to get hands-on experience with solving computational problems. She was also selected to be Accel Roundtable on Entrepreneurship Education (REE) Fellow at Stanford University and spent 3 months working on entrepreneurship projects to get a taste of entrepreneurship and high-growth ventures in engineering and life sciences. The program culminated in giving a presentation on the startup technology and was judged by Stanford faculty and entrepreneurship experts in Silicon Valley. After graduating from Cornell, Adele worked as a data scientist at Swiss Federal Institute of Technology in Lausanne, Switzerland where she focused on developing algorithms and graphical models to analyze chemical pathways in the atmosphere. Adele also pursued graduate studies at Stanford University in the United States where she entered as a recipient of American Association of University Women International Fellowship. The Fellowship enabled her to focus on tackling important research problems in machine learning and computer vision. Some research problems she worked on at Stanford include detecting air pollution from outdoor public webcam images. Specifically, she modified and set up a variety of pre-trained architectures, such as DehazeNet, VGG, and ResNet, on public webcam images to evaluate their ability to predict air quality based on the degree of haze on pictures. Other deep learning problems Adele worked on include investigating the promise of second-order optimizers in deep learning and using neural networks to predict sequences of data in energy consumption. Adele also places an emphasis on continual education and served as a Student Leader in PyTorch scholarship challenge organized by Udacity. Her roles as the Student Leader were helping students debug their code to train neural networks with PyTorch and providing mentorship on technical and career aspects. Her hobbies include skiing, playing tennis, cooking, and meeting new people.

TABLE OF CONTENTS

LIST OF FIGURES

have sensors that are able to direct them as well as collect data

Figure 10.7. It uses electricity to move in the water as it collects data on the water quality. It is able to note any unwanted materials in the water such as heavy metals

Figure 10.8. Wind energy is a clean and safe way of providing electricity to a large area. It is also safe for the environment and very effective. It's efficiency however, depends on the condition of the weather

Figure 10.9. There are simulation kits that have been developed to ensure the better prediction and decision making when it comes to wind energy

Figure 10.10. Above are the urban energy systems. So as to ensure that is it sustainable, it needs to meet the needs of the growing population

Figure 10.11. Conserving energy in the cities is important in lowering the high costs that are spent annually on electricity

Figure 10.12. It is important for cities to look for alternative sources of energy that are renewable. This will help in cleaning up the environment, which is very important if we are going to stop climate change

Figure 10.13. Drones are being used to survey forests, so as to catch situations on time, so as to be able to reverse them before they become irreversible

Figure 10.14. Google maps is able to provide a satellite view of certain areas which can help in the visualization of habitat that occupy endangered species. This will help in noticing any changes that may affect they survival

Figure 10.15. Above are the components of the remote monitoring system that can be used for the monitoring of wildlife

Figure 10.16. SMART hooks are helping in preventing ghost fishing as well as fishing unwanted species. This helps in protecting endangered species that may get trapped on long lines, such as sharks

Figure 10.17. Drones are becoming very popular, despite the fact that they are quite expensive. They are being used to observe animals and take photos so as to avoid having a researcher going to the field themselves

Figure 10.18. Above is an example of an application that is used to educate the population on different monkey species, including those that are endangered

Figure 10.19. Above is an illustration on the manner in which predictive analytics occur

Figure 10.20. Cyber security is at the top with climate change in the issues that are a major threat in the world today

Figure 10.21. Donation can be done online with the click of a button on your mobile phone. Technology has made it easier for us to give back to the environment that has given us so much

LIST OF ABBREVIATIONS

AI	artificial intelligence
AORs	application owning regions
API	application program interface
AR	augmented reality
CASA	computers as sociological actors
CSC	computer-supported collaborative
CSCWS	computer-supported collaborative working systems
DSS	decision support structures
ELC	electronic line calling
ELT	extremely large telescope
ESO	European Southern Observatory
ESS	executive support structures
FOR	file ownership region
GDSS	group decision support structures
GPS	global positioning system
HCI	human-computer interaction
HRI	human-robotic interaction
ICT	information communication technology
IT	information technology
JWST	James Webb Space Telescope
KWS	knowledge work structures
LIGO	Laser Interferometer Gravitational-Wave Observatory
MIS	management information structures
ML	machine learning
MS	Microsoft
MVS	multi-virtual storage
OAS	office automation structures

OASIS TC	Organization for Advancement of Systemic Information Standards Technological Committees
OS	operating system
OSLC	open solutions for lifecycle collaboration
PCs	personal computers
RDF	resource definition framework
SD	software development
SKA	square kilometer array
SQL	systemic query language
TORs	terminus owning region
TPS	transaction processing structures
UCD	user-centered development
UI	user-interface
UX	user experience
VMS	variable message sign
VR	virtual reality

PREFACE

Computer science and technology is a field that contributes a lot in this day to day life and age. It has different types of sub-fields of study under this particular field e.g. software engineering, computer graphic and visualization, network, and operating systems, artificial intelligence one could major in any particular field. With this field of computer science and technology it comes with a lot of benefits from studying it especially in this ever-changing world it constantly evolves as new form of technology are introduced daily, becoming a great choice if one wants to create a dynamic career that will keep one learning and gaining new skills. The new skills developed will also benefit with the learning of logic, design, and also engineering. With good foundation in these disciplines will greatly help to write code and also de-bug software helping in other areas of life and studies too.

When one majors in this field of computer science and technology one has the opportunity to be involved in innovation and to do work which has real impact in the society.

Studying computer science and technology is a great choice no matter what field one is interested in. Whether one wants to develop software that powers successful businesses, or create new hot mobile application apps, or create digital effects for blockbuster films, specialized computer, and technology skills will be indispensable. Even if one is not sure on what to do a degree in computer science and technology can put one in a position which has many openings like law, finance, engineering, and even entertainment fields have serious demand for this field of study with computer and technology skills.

This volume extends previous work by examining how computer science and technology can be applied in different fields. The importance of this volume cannot therefore be overemphasized. It is hoped that this volume will provide an understanding of the actual technologies used in day to day activities.

The volume has 10 chapters, and each chapter discusses about a specific topic under computer science and technology. Chapter 1 introduces the concepts of human-computer interaction; Chapter 2 offers basic information on how computer science and technology have revolutionized the medical sector;

Chapter 3 discusses the applications of computer science in business; Chapter 4 discusses where computer science and linguistics meet; Chapter 5 discusses how astronomical field benefited from computer science and technology; Chapter 6 focuses on computer science and robotic technology; Chapter 7 discusses the applications of computer science and technology in agriculture; Chapter 8 discusses how computer science and technology changed the sport sector; Chapter 9 tackles how the transportation sector benefited from computer science and technology; and lastly, Chapter 10 looks at how has computer science and technology changed the environment.

These 10 chapters were lengthily prepared for the readers to have a preview of how computer science and technology relate to other fields. The author paid more emphasis on the simplicity of the content in order to make the book comprehensible and understandable to all readers.

CHAPTER

1

Human-Computer Interaction

CONTENTS

1.1. INTRODUCTION

Human-computer interaction or HCI is a multidisciplinary area that focuses on computer technology designing, especially, the contact between people and computers. Though originally concerned with computers, this discipline has since grown to cover nearly all types of information technology (IT) design. It combines skills from computing, behavioral science, cognitive psychology and design to comprehend and facilitate improved interactions between individuals and machines.

The discipline is subdivided into three parts which include: the individual, the computer, and interaction. A user is anybody or group that handles the machine, considering various factors which may affect their communication with the machine, such as sensory systems, education levels, socio-cultural differences and age.

Generally, the computer refers to a comprehensive term indicating any set of technology, applications, or digital systems. Interaction, on the contrary, is the design factor. Its key objectives are usability and practicality, which are always exclusive to every unique project. For instance, a designer working on a set of software to support students to get into programming, may have rather different HCI considerations compared to the designer operating a system for an expert coder.

Figure 1.1: In the 21st century humans and computers are more interlinked than before.

Source: https://store.hp.com/us/en/tech-takes/exploring-human-computer-interaction.

1.2. ORIGINS OF HCI

HCI first appeared in the 80s as a response to the creation of the PC. For the initial time in history, workstations were accessible to general users, which resulted in a new range of design problems. The problem wasn't what a workstation could do, but rather how it can be done. Having this right was a crucial aspect of making PCs a commercial success, since they had to attract and satisfy each type of consumer, right from the most practiced to the total novice. Therefore, the first mainstream technology companies restructured the relationship between people and machines into a product that was much more meaningful rather than mere utility value (Kim, 2015).

Instead, they saw it as a liberal dialogue, a dynamic relationship that is continuously evolving in reaction to new technology and consumer demands. It is how the world has moved from the traditional devices to hand-held technologies which seem to understand where we are, what the things we do, and might predict what we do next. Unsurprisingly, HCI has grown to become among the most significant considerations for any IT or tech provider. Finally, this relatively fresh field provides a range of career choices for tech-savvy pupils.

Machines like Apple Macintosh and IBM PC started appearing in offices and homes in large quantities. Now, sophisticated electronic machines were available to the general public for uses similar to word processors, accounting aids and games units. Accordingly, as processors weren't too large, the requirement for creating HCI which was also simple and resourceful. This was beneficial for less experienced operators. Right from its onset, HCI would extend to incorporate various disciplines, such as computer science, human-factors mechanics and cognitive science (Kim, 2015).

1.3. INCREASE IN POPULARITY AND ADOPTION ACROSS VARIOUS SECTORS

HCI soon rose to become a topic of intense research and investigation. Experts who studied and operated in HCI viewed it as an essential tool to promote the notion that the interface between a processor and the user must resemble a typical human-to-human, flexible dialogue. Originally, HCI scholars focused on refining the practicality of desktop computers. That is, practitioners focused on how simple workstations can be understood and used. Nevertheless, with the meteoric rise of technologies, including the Web and mobile phone, computer use would gradually go away from desktop units to cover the smartphone world. Furthermore, HCI has progressively included more fields to cater to every member of the society.

Nowadays, it is no longer feasible to consider HCI as a branch of computer science, but rather HCI has developed to be a broader, bigger, and much more varied field than CS itself. HCI transformed from its original focus on personal and general user behavior to comprise of social and administrative computing, availability for the elderly, mentally or physically impaired, and just about anybody, plus for the broadest possible range of human experiences as well as activities (Kim, 2015).

It further developed from desktop office software to include games, commerce, education, health, and medicine among other applications. It grew from preliminary graphical user layout to include a variety of interaction methods and devices, multilevel interactions, device support for prototype-based user interface specification, plus a host of emergent universal, portable, and context-aware interactions.

1.4. USER EXPERIENCE (UX) IMPACT OF HCI AND OTHER RELATED FIELDS

HCI is a diverse field which relates with areas like user experience (UX) model, user-centered development (UCD) and user-interface (UI) design. In some ways, HCI was a forerunner to UX model. In spite of that, some variances still remain between the UX and HCI design. Some practitioners of HCI are generally more academically involved. They are concerned with scientific research and promoting empirical knowledge for users. Alternatively, UX designers are nearly invariably business-focused and concerned with building various products or services—such as, smartphone programs and websites. Despite this divide, the feasible considerations for items that UX experts concern themselves with have immediate links to the resolutions of HCI professionals about users' mindsets.

With the wider span of subjects that HCI covers, the UX designers possess a rich resource from which to draw from, even though much research still remains suitable to academic audiences.

For designers, they may also lack luxury of time that HCI experts usually enjoy. Therefore, developers must stretch beyond the regular industry-based constraints to include these more research findings. By doing that well, you may leverage vital insights into attaining the best models for your users. Through "collaborating" in this manner with the HCI field, designers can drive significant changes in the industry and society (Preece, Sharp, and Rogers, 2015).

1.5. SIGNIFICANCE OF HUMAN-COMPUTER INTERACTION

Usability is the important term in HCI. While HCI deals with a variety of highly technical factors of computing, it is fundamentally a people-centered technology. After all, what benefit is technology if people can't really use it? Practicality is redefined based on the design goals. Safety and functionality usually are primary, however, there are other matters to consider, such as effectiveness, efficiency, plus, in some occasions, enjoy ability. Besides, in today's very competitive virtual markets, HCI development can be the gap between achievement and failure.

Great HCI design shall encourage individuals to use particular mobile apps over others, or buy a certain smartphone or tablet. Equally, it can considerably improve industry productivity rates. A customer service practitioner who has to traverse server-based structures to achieve a particular request, is highly likely to make certain mistakes than a person who operates with an integrated structure. It further takes longer. A clever HIC system design may enhance sales and service rates, including boosting customer satisfaction by eliminating (or at least decreasing) those hindering call waiting times (Preece, Sharp, and Rogers, 2015).

1.6. HCI WILL DETERMINE THE FUTURE – FOR GOOD OR BAD

HCI is more involved in our day-to-day lives now than ever before. As a matter of fact, it is present everywhere. People use it to discover relevant information, handle their finances, make friendships, progress their professions or studies, plus find new types of entertainment. Furthermore, it has grown to become a vital part of the current experience that many individuals struggle to envision living without these modern devices (Kim, 2015).

Plus, when they do, they may sometimes encounter a low-level anxiety or dread which researchers refer to as nomophobia, which is a combination of the terms 'no,' 'mobile' and 'phobia.' This is a modern factor highlighting the new kind of relationship that exists between people and machine. Nomophobia also addresses some of the rather negative features of HIC. Researchers established that certain apps or games can promote compulsive behavior through activating the brain's dopamine compensation system. Dopamine is basically a neurotransmitter which transfers messages between nerves, neurons, and different cells within the body.

Furthermore, it plays a crucial role in improving mood and basically rewarding users with feel-good hormones which motivate them to take certain actions which meet their needs and desires. Basically, this is what causes some people to refer to their social media pages around 50 times per day, or even more. After all, every time they click, there is likelihood that they see a new like, retweet, or even positive comment. This is yet another type of validation that doesn't occur by accident.

Social media is among the best examples of how HCI may impact human behavior. Additionally, it may also trigger other less desirable types of communication, like internet trolling. Hence, it is important to recall that HCI isn't only about interactions between humans and computers but it also has an important

ethical dimension which relates to people's mental health, online communications, and the quality of political discussions. HCI shall continue shaping our experiences many years into the future, besides those operating in this field have the responsibility of ensuring that it drives out the best from us, not the worst of us (Kim, 2015).

1.6.1. HCI Promotes Lots of Career Prospects

In case you seek a broad range of job options, studying HCI can become a great starting point. The field is largely about solving issues and innovation. HCI teaches you to identify sectors of improvement and later create high quality services and products. Besides, if you can showcase these abilities to prospective employers, you can considerably increase your probability of becoming more visible in the highly-competitive jobs markets.

HCI programs (particularly at postgraduate level) typically have close bonds with established or emergent tech companies. Therefore, there are plenty of chances for networking, such as internships and appointments at prestigious institutions. Many HCI learners end up being employed at various successful and powerful tech giants, such as Google, Samsung, and Microsoft. Some particular career paths are software engineering, computer programs, UX designer, system engineering, and project management, whereas others even advance on to create their own technology businesses or work freelance.Largely, HCI is a sector for the future. With technology continuing to develop and becoming more extensively available, there would be a growing demand for HCI developers and designers. This essentially means extensive job security, and a very practical opportunity for earning a good income – the typical salary for any HCI engineer is roughly $96,000 per year. Moreover, you'll be operating at the frontline of innovation, assisting to create and formulate the next big thing in technology that may considerably improve the livelihoods of millions of individuals (Kim, 2015).

1.6.2. It Solves Some of the Prevalent Threats to Society

A study from the University of Bristol established that HCI design may help technology companies to minimize their carbon footprint. Scientists focused on YouTube, a video platform that streams roughly 1 billion hours of video content each day. Within 12 months, this produces around 10 million tons of carbon dioxide – which is roughly the same amount generated by a city like Baltimore. Nevertheless, with only a few basic design tweaks which minimize digital waste, it may be reduced by roughly 100–500Kt of carbon dioxide per year – which is the carbon emission equivalent of roughly 30,000 UK homes.

Even though various studies show how tech may become more ecofriendly, the Bristol study has been the first effective attempt at measuring the environmental impacts of HCI design. People are increasingly getting aware of the great amounts of energy expended by this technology, plus data centers and companies are becoming more aware of the requirement to adjust their practices in consideration of the challenges which climate change brings to humanity as well as the universal ecosystem.

Various researchers developed a new HCI off-shoot known as Sustainable Interaction Design or SID. SID creates a form of digital service that includes user behavior, data usage plus further identifies various aspects of digital waste. Furthermore, following the models of HCI, both developers and engineers can execute design changes which considerably reduce carbon emissions without affecting the overall quality of the item or service (Kim, 2015).

As of now, SID is already getting implemented by various large businesses and organizations, plus looks ready to play a vital role in the shaping of ecofriendly digital industries. Learners who are interested in studying HCI will be placing themselves in a good position within the modern and future job markets. It is an exciting chance to contribute to a unique industry which shall shape individuals lives for many generations to come.

1.7. TYPES OF COMPUTER INTERACTION SYSTEMS

Information structures are formed for varying reasons, based on the specific needs of human operators and the business. Likewise, transaction processing systems or TPS work at the operational rank of the institution; office automation structures (OAS) and knowledge work structures (KWS) support processes at the knowledge context. Other higher-level models might include management information structures (MIS) and decision support structures (DSS).

Professional systems apply the knowledge of decision makers for solving specific, structured issues. On the tactical level of management there are executive support systems (ESS). Equally, group decision support structures (GDSS), including the more commonly described computer-based collaborative work systems or (CSCWS) promote group-based decision making of unstructured or semi-structured varieties (Kim, 2015).

1.7.1. Transaction Processing Structures

Transaction processing structures (TPS) are automated information systems which were formed to process huge volumes of data for regular business transactions like payroll and inventory. In essence, TPS removes the burden of necessary operational exchanges and limits the time once needed to perform them physically, although people may still input information to computerized systems.

Similarly, TPS are boundary-spanning components that allow the organization to network with external environments. Since managers checkup the data produced by TPS for detailed information regarding what's happening in their businesses, it's vital to the daily processes of a business that these structures work smoothly and without any interruption.

1.7.2. Office Mechanization Systems and Insight Work Systems

At the knowledge basis of the organization there are two types of systems. The first is Office Automation Systems (OAS) which support data workers, mostly those who don't typically create fresh knowledge but instead assess information to transform information or operate it in some forms before allocating it with, or officially circulating it throughout, the company and, sometimes, even further. Some familiar elements of OAS comprise of spreadsheets, desktop publishing, word processing, electronic scheduling, as well as voicemail communication, teleconferencing, and email.

On the other hand, Knowledge Work Systems (KWS) promote professional workers like scientists, engineers, and physicians by supporting them in their endeavors to create fresh knowledge, and from allowing them to add it to their business or the society at large.

1.7.3. Management Information Systems

Management information systems or MIS don't replace transaction operating systems (OSs); rather, all MIS cover transaction processing. MIS, basically, are automated information systems which work due to the purposeful collaboration between individuals and computers. Through requiring people, applications, and hardware work in conjunction. Management information systems promote users in achieving a wider scale of organizational duties than TPS, including decision examination and decision making.

To access data, operators of management information systems (MIS) share a standard database. This database stores both information and models which assist the user to interact with, understand, and apply that information. Management information systems furthermore output information that is applied in decision-making. A management information system might also help in integrating a couple of automated information roles of a business.

1.7.4. Decision Support Structures

A higher-level category of hi-tech information systems is the decision support systems or DSS. These are quite similar to the conventional MIS since they both are reliant on the database which is a key source of data. The decision support system moves away from conventional management information applications, since it highlights the importance of decision-making in its different phases, even though the real decision still remains to be the exclusive realm of the decision-maker. Likewise, DSS are very closely personalized to the individual or group that's using them compared to a conventional management information system. Occasionally, they are deliberated as systems which concentrate on business intelligence.

1.8. ARTIFICIAL INTELLIGENCE AND SPECIALIST SYSTEMS

Figure 1.2: AI helps to simplify daily human work and activities.

Source: https://www.emarsys.com/resources/blog/real-ai/.

Artificial intelligence (AI) may be regarded as an overarching project for expert structures. The overall push of AI has largely been to promote machines which behave logically. Two methods of AI research include (I) comprehending natural language and (II) examining the capacity to reason out an issue to its logical end. Professional systems use the techniques of AI logic to solve the issues presented to them through business (as well as other) users (Sutcliffe, 2013).

Professional structures are a very unique group of information system which have been made feasible for use by industry, because of extensive availability of hardware including software systems like expert system shells and personal computers (PCs). An expert structure (also known as knowledge-based system) successfully captures and utilizes the understanding of human experts, or professionals for solving any particular issue experienced in an institution. Consider that unlike DSS that leaves the final resolution to the decision-maker, for expert systems they choose the ideal solution to an issue or a particular class of problems.

The basic modules of an expert structure are the information base, an interpretation engine connecting the operator with the structure by processing inquiries through languages like systemic query language (SQL), plus the user interface. Individuals called knowledge mechanics capture the professionalism of experts, create a computer system which includes this specialist knowledge, and then execute it (Sutcliffe, 2013).

1.9. GROUP DECISION SUPPORT STRUCTURES (DSS) AND COMPUTER-SUPPORTED COLLABORATIVE (CSC) WORK SYSTEMS

Organizations are becoming progressively dependent on groups or lineups to make decisions mutually. When teams make semi-structured or unstructured choices, a team decision support structure may provide a solution. Team decision support systems, which are applied in special rooms fitted in a variety of different configurations, allow group members to interrelate with electronic support—typically in form of specialized application—and a unique group facilitator.

The group DSS are designed to bind a group together for purposes of solving community problems, with assistance from various supports like polling, brainstorming, questionnaires, and scenario creation. Likewise, GDSS software may be designed to reduce typical unconducive group behaviors like lack of participation because of fear of rejection for conveying an unpopular or disputed perspective, authority by vocal group participants, and "group thinking" decision making. Occasionally, GDSS are deliberated under the more widespread term of computer-supported collaborative working systems (CSCWS), which may comprise of software support known as groupware for group collaboration through networked computers. Additionally, group DSS can be utilized in virtual settings (Sutcliffe, 2013).

1.10. EXECUTIVE SUPPORT STRUCTURES

When managers turn to the computer, mostly they're looking for methods of helping them to make decisions on a strategic level. The executive support structures (ESS) assist executives to manage their connections with the external setting by offering image and communications technologies within accessible places like boardrooms or private corporate offices. While ESS depends on the information produced by MIS and TPS, ESS assist their users to address formless decision problems, which aren't software specific, by developing an environment which helps them to think about strategic issues in a knowledgeable way. Furthermore, ESS extend and promote the functions of executives, allowing them to derive sense from their environments.

1.11. MODERN ADVANCEMENTS IN HCI

There is no hesitation that the way people interact with workstations has changed considerably over the past decade. Besides, if you're contemplating becoming a UI developer, you're probably aware how much mobile phones and tablet devices have opened the way for loads of new and creative interactions between people and computers (Sutcliffe, 2013).

The ratio of computing power found in modern smartphones is truly amazing. For instance, your smartphone possesses more computing power than the computers NASA used back in 1969, during the time it landed astronauts onto the moon. These portable instruments have allowed for all kinds of remarkable new human-computer connections, which are in your palms.Voice is yet another form of interaction that is rising exponentially. Programs such as Apple's Siri are now making it feasible to set appointments, research the web, install timers and perform other simple duties using just your voice. The possibilities of this form of human-computer interface is absolutely huge, though society still has a long path to go ahead (Kim, 2015).

Going into the future, user interfaces will no longer be trapped inside a screen but rather incorporated into your daily activities. Consider a future where digital interfaces are tailored to your own needs and may appear anywhere. Technology also promises a future where you can actually communicate with computers, instead of just poking letters onto the screen. It is promise that many of today's exciting technologies are trying to deliver. And as people who have contributed in UI Design with the last decade, software developers are excited to see just how technology is evolving to a more engaging and interactive future.

1.12. WHAT THE FUTURE LOOKS LIKE

Currently, we are on the edge of some remarkable advancements in VR. Technologies like The Oculus Rift that first emerged in 2012 are promising users an immersive virtual reality (VR) experience within a headset. The Oculus can be attached to a Leap-Motion controller, which allows users to literally move their hands in actual life, translating to moves in the virtual gaming world for a more immersive experience. Equally, wearable's have been emerging into the spotlight. With devices like the Apple Watch emerging onto the scene, high levels of competition are bound to come up since these instruments are becoming portable, more equipped and stylish.

1.13. VOICE-BASED USER INTERFACE

Voice interaction will soon go past making appointments or browsing the web. It is expected that, in the coming 5 years, the adoption level of speech recognition shall be more than 80%. This truly makes sense when you contemplate how much lesser our screens are becoming. With less display size, interfaces may soon become much difficult to navigate.

Touch would likely still be popular in the mobile world for a lengthy period to come, nevertheless, voice definitely promises a much deeper and more universal technique for interrelating with our devices. For UI designers, the goal here would be staying updated with emerging voice-control apps and technologies entering the market.

1.14. VIRTUAL REALITY

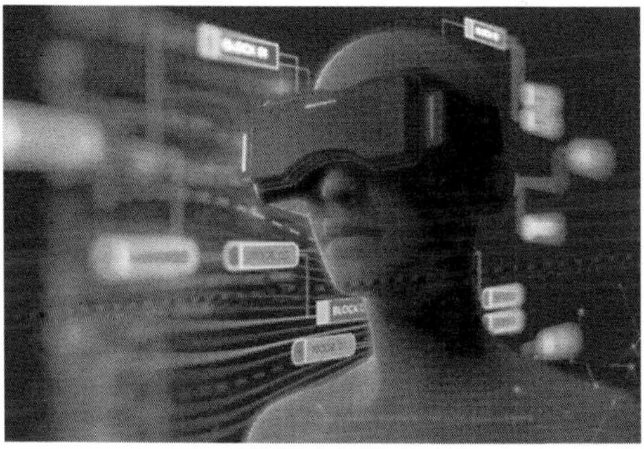

Figure 1.3: VAR headsets allow users to experience the digital world practically.

Source: .https://www.canterbury.ac.nz/engineering/schools/csse/research/hci/.

VR (virtual-reality) technology is going to become a lot more fascinating in the next few years. Moreover, with Facebook's acquisition of Oculus as well as Microsoft joining the VR field with HoloLens, the competition is heating up. Eventually these headsets may render the television outdated. After all, it is better to watch your preferred football team from a virtual projector in your living room, rather than a fixed rectangular box on the wall. This is definitely good news for designers, besides the new technology shall come with a totally new mix of HCIs.

Consider being in a packed coffee shop without having any laptop. Rather, everybody has a headset on. Plus, instead of tapping or clicking, they could actually be moving their hands around or pointing in air. It could seem somewhat silly at first, however, over time this might be fully normal. When these headsets become popular, augmented reality (AR) shall indeed come to the fore. Imagine checking a restaurant menu and looking up its menu in particular, then reading its Yelp rating in virtual form in the space next to it. Alternatively, imagine having Google Maps directives projected right on the car screen before your eyes (Kurosu, 2017).

The new VR systems will promote the rise of many innovative and unique interfaces, it will truly determine the way that people develop UIs and interrelate with computer networks. Interfaces shall no longer be caged in small screens, but rather exist in our real 3D world. As a matter of fact, the role of the interface developer and the tri-dimensional computer animator shall start to blend together. The evolution will be gradual, though it will be particularly important for UX and UI designers to get familiar with tri-dimensional design techniques in case they are to remain pertinent in this modern VR driven world (Kurosu, 2017).

1.14.1. Wearable Devices

The Apple Watch is a new invention that has introduced some really distinct HCIs, such as the virtual crown as well as ability to check another individual's pulse. In the near-term future, these devices shall become economical, more practical and less reliant on your smartphone, which shall consequently make them way more adoptable.

That being said, the wearable's industry as its known today may not actually exist in the coming 20–30 years. The modern wearable's market is packed with smart jewelry, watches, and also smart shoes. Plus, while these devices may have their role in history, still they are just a stopgap measure since more advanced technologies are expected to come up in the next few years. As per now, the wearable's industry is gradually gaining momentum, besides there are many new interfaces and design patterns which shall emerge from that. The world is heading towards a future where people and computers are linked more jointly than ever before.

As for designers, it shall become important for them to keep a keen eye on these industries as they develop. Matters are definitely going to be shifting big time, though the great news is that these major changes won't appear overnight. However, it doesn't mean that designers are now free to rest their heads. By staying ahead of these new design factors and going ahead to work with these modern computer structures and design patterns, developers will be able to future proof themselves for the impending digital world (Kurosu, 2017).

1.15. IMPACT OF AUGMENTED REALITY ON LEARNING AND EDUCATION

The application of AR or AR in learning is a crucial topic of research. It allows for the inclusion of virtual items into real-life environments in order to promote actual interactions. Studies on AR inclusion in the education sector are still in the preliminary stage. Additionally, there is a lack of proper research on the outcomes and effects of AR in the education sector.

Furthermore, the application of AR in school has become increasingly accessible, since it doesn't require any special equipment, but can instead be used on smartphone devices easily. Many people now possess mobile devices, besides their use has grown significantly, thus facilitating improved access to AR. The incorporation of mobile AR technology into education is increasing swiftly, besides the practicality of smartphone-based AR has improved due to progresses in mobile technology. This technology is applicable in different sectors of education not just the classroom.

In fact, it is estimated that AR usage will enhance student learning motivation as well as contribute to greater academic achievement. There is inadequate research on the effect of using portable AR in education, though room still exists for exploring the prospective of AR to drive student learning motivation, plus contribute to greater educational achievement and motivation to discover more in the world of computers and IT (Sutcliffe, 2013).

1.15.1. Definition of Augmented Reality

In its essence, AR integrates both real and simulated worlds, complementing the physical world with computer-generated digital objects in real-time. Based on recent commonly accepted descriptions, AR is thought to be an innovation with three primary requirements which are: merging of real and simulated objects in an actual environment, matching of real and simulated objects together, and practical interaction.

Mixed reality might be described as a situation whereby real and digital objects are combined. Equally, AR can be regarded as a mixed-reality innovation which features more reality, since this technology comprises of virtual items in the operator's real environment, facilitating interaction with simulated content.

In case of portable AR, the technology covers the addition of virtual components to the actual world via a smartphone camera. Some common examples of smartphone AR applications are Pokémon GO, a location-based portable AR game which allows users to catch different digital Pokémon characters around their region, as well as AR GPS DRIVE or WALK NAVIGATION that offers an AR-driven navigation system. Generally, VR differs greatly from AR, since in VR the physical world is completely shut out plus the operator steps into a virtual world through a VR headpiece like Samsung Gear VR and Oculus Rift (Sutcliffe, 2013).

AR no longer needs specialized tools and can easily be applied through computing or mobile appliances. A lightly AR complements the actual world with a comparatively small ratio of virtual information, whereas a heavily AR features frequently available virtual information.

The rate of virtuality in the physical world determines which type of technology would be needed to promote the AR, since various display and tracking systems result in different levels of immersion. The immersive technologies like head-mounted displays are utilized to promote heavily AR, while fostering more immersion compared to mobile devices that can promote lightly AR. A good example of the lightly AR technology is Pokémon GO smartphone application, which may be controlled through a smartphone. On the other hand, a heavily AR example is the popular Star Wars Jedi-Challenges, it is a mobile application that requires operators to put on a headset first.

Many individuals now own mobile phones and thus have access to AR. Furthermore, the use of AR for education has been made practical due to developments in mobile technology, including the heightened use of smartphones. Similarly, tablets and smartphones are suitable for facilitating AR experiences, because of quick processors, graphics firmware, and different onboard sensors (Sutcliffe, 2013).

1.15.2. Augmented Reality in School

The educational value of AR is closely associated with the method in which it was designed, executed, and assimilated into both formal and informal education environments. A significant consideration would be on how AR technology can support and provide meaningful learning.

Taking AR as a learning model instead of some form of technology can be productive for teachers. The participation of educators is vital in facilitating the growth of favorable AR systems for teaching, which improve the prospective for AR to be integrated in education. AR uses have further been built for different sectors of education.

A number of these AR use cases have been highlighted in various studies. Researchers have tested the impacts of AR enhanced science course books on lower-secondary school pupils. Including the use of AR-based mobile learning applications for natural science study activities on 4th grade students, this program guided learners towards target ecology disciplines and showcased the corresponding education tasks and other related education materials.

Furthermore, tests have been done on the application of AR improved laboratory guidebooks in science laboratories for first-year pupils. This particular study tested the effect of the Anatomical 4D mobile application towards the education motivation of students studying health sciences. These different cases show than AR can be applied in different learning environments, since it is a flexible technology (Preece, Sharp, and Rogers, 2015).

1.15.3. Benefits of Using AR in Education

AR provides inventive ways of interrelating with the physical world, and can generate experiences which wouldn't be conceivable in either a entirely real or simulated world. AR has the unique capacity to form immersive hybrid learning systems, which combine both real and virtual aspects. AR technologies allow users to experience modern scientific phenomena that aren't conceivable in the physical world, such as various chemical reactions, making unavailable the subject content available to students. Generally, the manipulation of simulated objects and scrutiny of phenomena which are not easy to perceive in the physical world can be expedited through AR (Kim, 2015).

This kind of learning experience may promote thinking skills and promote conceptual learning of phenomena which are either undetectable or hard to observe and correct any misconceptions. AR addresses learning problems which are typically experienced with visualizing unobservable objects.

The expertise and knowledge which students develop from technology-based learning environments can be nurtured more effectively with AR technology. Besides, the cognitive workload might be reduced through integrating several sources of data.

The immersion and interface features provided by AR might encourage learners to participate in learning activities, plus may improve pupils' motivation to learn.

AR provides highly interactive encounters and can generate practical learner activity, connectivity, and a high amount of realism. Similarly, interaction with the environment is significant in the learning process, plus, apart from reality, AR is among the best methods for enabling this interaction (Kurosu, 2017).

1.15.4. Problems of Using Augmented Reality (AR) in Education

The operators of AR technology might experience usability matters and technical problems, besides some pupils may find this invention complicated. Among the main problems of AR systems is usability; nevertheless, ease of use has also been mentioned as a benefit.

There is no evidence suggesting that usability matters are directly linked to AR technology, plus may instead arise from insufficient innovation experience, user face design errors, technical issues, or negative attitudes. Furthermore, the combination of concrete and virtual objects may lead to confusion as pupils may face problems navigating between simulated and reality (Sutcliffe, 2013).

Moreover, the application of AR technology in a school environment requires multitasking, since students must engage with huge amounts of data and multiple technological instruments to achieve complex tasks. Equally, this may cause a cognitive overload including a feeling of confusion or being overwhelmed. To prevent any adverse effects, schools can place restrictions on overuse of AR technology, besides educators might be hesitant to use AR since this technology often needs innovative teaching methods to be implemented.

The material available through AR applications is frequently inflexible, which restricts the educator's control over the material and prevents elasticity to accommodate learners' needs. The accessibility of authoring implements may resolve this problem by allowing operators to revise and develop AR applications. Another problem could be that the solidity of portable AR technology isn't guaranteed, besides difficulties may be faced if the innovation lacks well-designed user system and guidance since this may cause the technology to become a bit complicated. Operators may also require time to become familiar and contented with AR technology (Sutcliffe, 2013).

1.15.5. AR Mobile Application

In previous researches, the AR learning tools used were developed especially for the school courses. The AR portable application applied in education isn't designed specifically for classwork, instead systems like Anatomy 4D mobile programs can be applied in the health sector as well.

The practicality of this mobile software to university health sciences students was corroborated by a program conveyor before the study. Additionally, Anatomy 4D is an open application which uses AR to allow interaction with portraits of the whole human body. The program uses a target portrait, plus the mobile device camera to showcase an AR version of the human body. Similarly, the Anatomy 4D mobile app was picked based on its availability. All players used both the bodily anatomy notes and AR mobile learning application.

1.16. IMPACT OF IOT (INTERNET OF THINGS) ON DAILY ACTIVITIES

IoT apps promise to deliver great value in our lives. With modern wireless networks, advanced sensors and innovative computing capabilities, the IoT might be the next frontline in the technology race. Consider an intelligent device, such as a traffic camera. This instrument can monitor the roads for traffic congestion, weather conditions, accidents, and transfer this information to a shared gateway. This gateway further receives information from similar cameras and transmits the data further into a city-scale traffic monitoring system.

Take, for example, the Municipal Corporation deciding to repair a particular road. This could cause a traffic jamming on the path to a primary highway. This vision is directed to the city-wide transport monitoring system. Now, seeing that this is an intelligent traffic system, it promptly learns and forecasts patterns in traffic, through the application of Machine Learning (ML). Therefore, the smart system is capable of analyzing the situation, predicting its impact and transmitting the data to other metropolises that link to the same road through their own unique smart systems (Sutcliffe, 2013).

The Traffic Control System can examine data obtained and find routes around the scheme to prevent bottlenecks. The system can also convey live directions to motorists through smart tools and radio channels. In the meantime, places such as city schools and worksites near the project can also be referred to modify their schedules. Eventually, this forms a network of self-reliant systems that leverage real-time management. It's one of the popular examples of IoT Applications.

1.16.1. What Exactly Is IoT?

IoT is a platform through which embedded appliances are linked to the internet, meaning they can gather and exchange information with each other. This allows devices to network, cooperate, and, improve their functions by learning from each other's encounters just like people do. IoT systems are expected to improve billions of daily items with connectivity as well as intelligence. It is already being installed extensively, in different domains, such as Wearable's, Smart Home Applications, Smart Cities, Agriculture, Industrial Mechanization and Health Care (Kim, 2015).

For IoT applications, wearable innovation is the hallmark of IoT systems and perhaps is among the earliest sectors to have adopted IoT technology. Machines like heart-rate monitors and smartwatches are everywhere nowadays. One of the relatively unknown wearable devices is the Guardian glucose checking device. This device was developed to help individuals suffering from diabetes. The device can detect glucose levels inside the patient's body, by using a small electrode known as glucose sensor that is placed beneath the skin and transmits the information through Radio Frequency to a gauging device.

When talking about IoT Apps, Smart Homes is probably among the first things that most people think of. One good example is Jarvis, which is the AI home mechanization system adopted by Mark Zuckerberg. There is also Allen Pan's Residence Automation System in which various functions around the home are activated by using a sequence of musical notes (Kim, 2015).

IoT is also applicable in the Health Care sector. It can further turn responsive medical-based structures into proactive wellness-based structures. The resources to which current medical research applies, generally lack crucial real-life information.

It typically uses leftover information, organized settings, and practitioners for health examination. IoT has opened the doors to a variety of valuable information through analysis, real-life field information, and testing. The IoT also enhances the existing machines in terms of power, precision, and accessibility. IoT concentrates on developing systems instead of just equipment.

Furthermore, by now most people have heard about Smart Cities. The theory of the optimized transport system is among the many aspects which comprise a smart city. The benefit of smart city model is that it is specific to the city. For instance, the issues faced in a city like Mumbai are rather different from those in Delhi, whereas the problems faced by Hong Kong are distinct from New York.Likewise, global issues, such as universal clean drinking water, declining air quality and growing urban density, happen in different ratios across cities. Therefore, they affect every city uniquely. The State and engineers may use IoT for purposes of analyzing the usually-complex issues of metropolis planning specific to every city. The utilization of IoT applications may help in sectors such as waste control, water management and emergencies (Kim, 2015).

Agriculture is yet another field where IoT is applicable. Research shows that the ever-growing global population would reach around 10 billion come the year 2050. In order to feed this massive population, it is essential to combine agriculture and technology to obtain the best outcomes. There are various possibilities in this sector and among them is Smart Greenhouses. A greenhouse farming system improves the harvest of crops by managing environmental parameters.

Nevertheless, manual handling of processes results in production loss, labor cost, energy loss, and even making the procedure less effective. A greenhouse with implanted technological instruments not only makes things simpler to be supervised but also, allows operators to manage the climate within it. Sensors measure various parameters depending on the crop requirement and transfer it over to the cloud. Consequently, it processes the information and provides a control action.

Of great significance in IoT Applications is Industrial Automation. It is one of the sectors where both rapid developments, and the quality of items, are among the crucial factors for a greater Return on Investment. Additionally, IoT Systems can be used to re-engineer items and their packaging in order to deliver improved performance in terms of both price and customer experience. Similarly, IoT here may prove to be a game changer in terms of solutions towards various domains in its category (Kim, 2015).

For Industrial Automation functions, in only one-year web connected devices jumped from an estimated 5 million up to the billions. Furthermore, Business Insider Intelligence projects that roughly 24 billion IoT equipment would be connected come the year 2020, creating a revenue of well over 300 billion.

It's correct to say that IoT is dynamic, futuristic, and keeps improving. Its systems don't come pre-assembled, but rather grow or evolve with time. The IoT has combined hardware and software systems to the web to build a smarter world. It's been developing at a high pace and provides a wide range of opportunities that both government and business can benefit from. As a matter of fact, the amount of job openings for IoT experts is at an unparalleled high.

CHAPTER

2

How Computer Science and Technology Have Revolutionized the Medical Sector

CONTENTS

2.1. INTRODUCTION

Computer science has continued to be used widely in the medical sector. There are many different ways in which computer science has been integrated in the medical sector. This being said, there is a need for the professionals in the medical sector to understand the major benefits of using the different computers techniques in hospital services, health, and medicine.

Globally, computers are continuing to develop more and more, making them popular almost every single day. They can now be found in almost every home since their development in the early 1800s. They have led to a great revolution of our daily lifestyles. There are many techniques that can be applied in the medical field, and this is one of the greatest social impacts that computer science has provided. Very many hospitals, especially the larger ones, have incorporated computers into their daily routine.

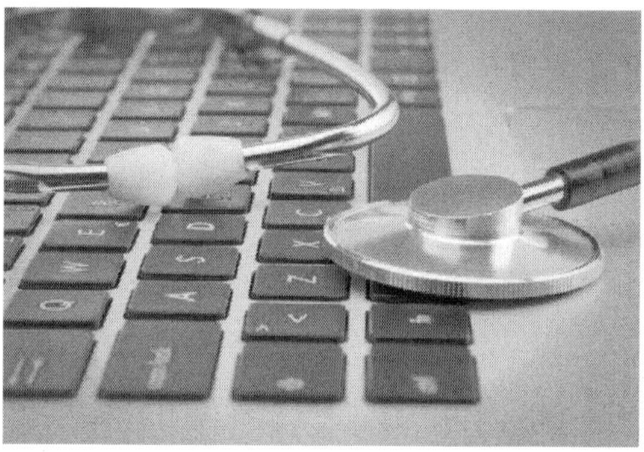

Figure 2.1: Computers have developed in a manner that has led to their integration in the medical field.

Source: http://news.mit.edu/2015/how-computer-can-help-your-doctor-better-diagnose-cancer-0423.

Computers are being used as diagnostic aids in hospitals and these have shown to be very integral. Some of the main ways in which computers are being used in hospitals include: analysis of data in the hospital, the information system of the hospital, medical decision making that is assisted by computers, taking care of the patients that are critically ill, medical imaging, therapy that is computer assisted, etc.

The healthcare industry of today has been able to use computers in a manner that is much more sophisticated. Lab scientists are not expected to make analyses of medical data in research laboratories anymore. There are now information portals that are based on the web that allow patients and doctors to have coordination of the plans of treatment, as well as doctor appointments. There are also mobile and wearable devices that allow the patients to keep track of their vitals such as blood pressure and heart rate. Below will be a discussion on the many different applications of computer science in medicine.

2.2. MEDICAL IMAGING

This is a technique and process that involves the creation of representation, that are visual, of the inner parts of the human body for purposes of analyzing in a clinical manner and making interventions medically. It also involves using the visual representations to see how the internal organs and tissues are functioning. It is done for the revealing of the internal parts of the body that are hidden by the bones and the skin. They are used to make diagnoses and come up with treatment plans for certain diseases and conditions (Shortliffe and Perreault, 2013).

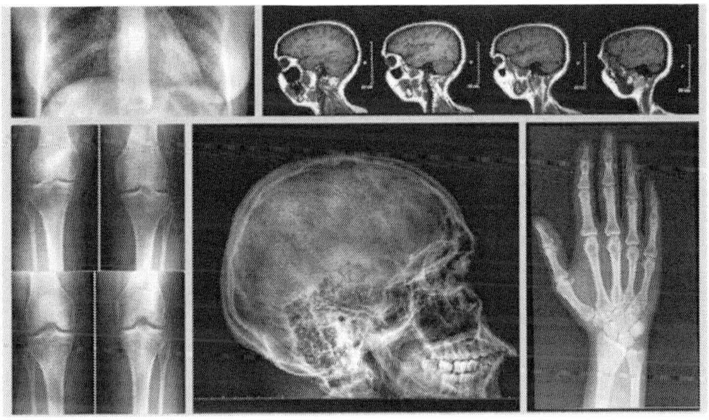

Figure 2.2: Above is an example of an image that was taken of a patient. They help us to see the parts of the body that are covered by the skin.

Source: https://openmedscience.com/medical-imaging-modalities/.

This technique also helps with the establishment of databases consisting of the normal anatomy and physiology of the human body. This enables users to check if there is any abnormal structure or function in the body. Despite the fact that it is also possible to have imaging of organs and tissues that have been removed from the body, this is normally referred to as pathology rather than medical imaging.

Pathology is a sub-field in biological imaging that uses radiology for imagining of magnetic resonance, ultrasounds, X-ray radiography, tactile imagining, medical photography, elastography, endoscopies, and positron emission tomography.

There are other techniques used to measure and record. These are representations of other technologies that are used for the production of data that can be represented in graphs or maps that have the information on the location of the measurements.

These are all forms of medical imaging which are achieved using computers (Shortliffe and Perreault, 2013).

There are so many studies that have been done on medical imagine since 2010. This is because some of them have high levels of radiation exposure. About 50% of the radiation in the United States is due to medical imaging.

This radiation is caused because most of these devices are created using technologies from the industry of semiconductors, which include Complementary metal-oxide semiconductor integrated circuit chips and even sensors like biosensors, and processors like microprocessors and system on chip devices.

Medical imaging has proven to be a solution to problems that are mathematically inverse, because they are created to be techniques that produce images of the inner body without invading the body.

This all means that there are no effects that are caused on the tissues or organs that are being imaged.

Medical ultrasonography has a probe that has pressure waves that are ultrasonic as well as echoes that are inserted into the tissue so as to show he inner parts of the tissue.

Projectional radiography has a probe that utilizes X-ray radiation that undergoes absorption at various rates by the different body tissues such as fat and muscle.

Most of the medical imaging techniques that are used are considered noninvasive, which means that they do not introduce any instruments into the body of the patient.

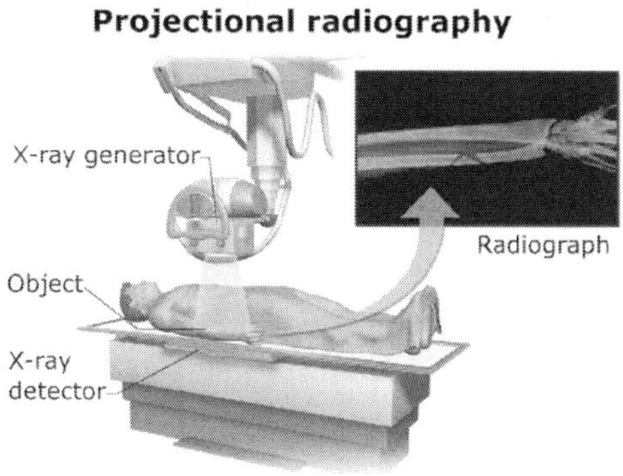

Figure 2.3: Above is an example of how an X-ray machine works to produce a radiograph.

Source: https://en.wikipedia.org/wiki/X-ray_machine.

There are many different processes and modalities that are used in medical imaging for making diagnoses and treatment plans. This means that the technology is very important in the improvement of public health for many different groups. They are also used after treatment for follow up on whether the condition has improved or not.

X-rays and ultrasound are some of the medical imaging techniques that have proven very useful over the past years across many medical industries. In preventative medicine, public health, palliative care, and curative care, there needs to be a correct diagnosis if we want to treat a patient. Despite the fact that the doctors can make a judgment before the condition is treated, using medical imaging techniques is important in confirming these judgments. This helps to ensure that the assessments are correct in terms of how respond to treatment (Anderson and Jay, 2012).

Considering that the policies in healthcare are improving, there is a major increase in the number of global procedures based on imaging. There is a need for effective and safe equipment to make correct decisions and avoid unnecessary procedures. For example, using ultrasounds can help in avoiding some surgical intervention. Ultrasounds are simple diagnostic imaging techniques.

Medical imaging involves a team of trained professionals including radiographers, radiologists, sonographers, nurses, biomedical engineers, and medical physicists, who have a great deal of knowledge on how to handle these machines. This means that computers not only make it easier for doctors to diagnose and suggest treatment plans but also provide more job opportunities due to the development of technology. Medical professionals use computers to optimize patients' wellbeing. It is considered a multidisciplinary approach (Consoli, Recupero, and Petković, 2019).

In conclusion, medical imaging refers to images for studying and making diagnoses on different conditions of the human body. All the devices that have been mentioned above are all controlled by computers. This is including techniques such as X-ray imaging which have been around for many years. They still require computers to adjust images and also to ensure that the images have been transferred.

2.3. MONITORING OF PATIENTS

Devices that are used for the monitoring of patients are some of the most important devices inside and outside of the hospital. If a hospital does not have reliable devices for patient monitoring, nurses and doctors can miss information about the patient that could have a huge impact on whether they stay alive or die. Medical monitoring involves being able to observe a certain condition or disease over a certain period of time.

Monitoring conditions and diseases involves the continuous measurement of body vitals using a medical monitor and/or the repetitive performance of medical tests such as blood glucose etc. Telemetry or Biotelemetry involves being able to transmit data from the medical monitors to the station that is dealing with the monitoring (Consoli, Recupero, and Petković, 2019).

Monitoring can be done in many ways, depending on what vitals or parameters are being targeted. Some of these include:

- *Cardiac Monitoring* – This mostly refers to doing electrocardiographs on a patient in a continuous manner, this including making assessments in the conditions of the patient when it come to their cardiac rhythm. An ambulatory patient can wear a small monitor called a Holtermonitor. This monitor helps in making sure that the patient's vitals (those mentioned above) are monitored. In addition to this, the patient can have a Swan-Ganz Catheter that helps in monitoring their cardiac output. The blood pressure and the flow of blood inside the circulatory system can be measure using hemodynamic monitoring. There are two ways to measure blood pressure in a patient. Either invasively using a blood pressure transducer assembly that is inserted, or in a manner that is not invasive using an inflatable cuff.

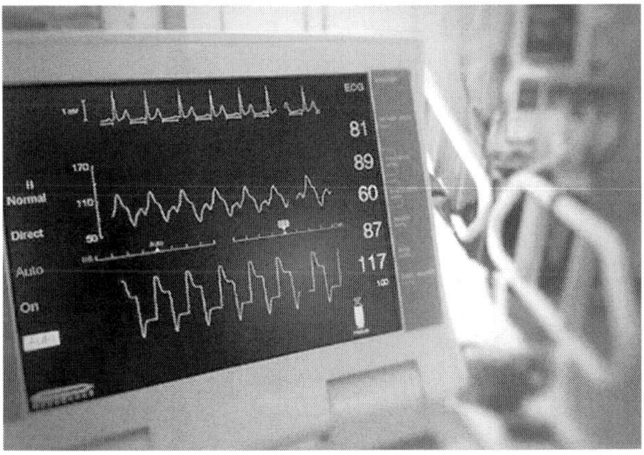

Figure 2.4: Above is an example of a cardiac monitor that helps in monitoring the heart vitals such as the heart rate.

Source: http://exclusive.multibriefs.com/content/cardiac-monitoring-in-the-emergency-department.

- *Respiratory monitoring* – there are different ways that the respiratory function can be monitored. Firstly, there is the pulse oximetry which deals with measuring the percentage of oxygen that is saturated. This is measured using an infrared finger cuff. Secondly, there is capnography which deals with measurement of the concentration of carbon dioxide in the blood. It is also used for the monitoring of the airway respiratory rate. The respiratory rate is monitored using a thoracic transducer belt or even capnography.
- *Neurological monitoring* – this is done for the monitoring of the intracranial pressure. Technology has also led to the development of other patient monitors that deal with the monitoring of the brain waves, bi-spectral index, the concentrations of the gas anesthetics, etc. They are normally used during surgeries and are incorporated into the machines that are used for anesthesia. Electroencephalophalography monitors have been used in the intensive care units of the neurosurgery sector, and they have

proven to have a high multichannel capability allowing them to also be able to monitor physiological aspects.

There are other parameters that can be monitored such as childbirth monitoring, blood glucose monitoring, monitoring of the body temperature using a thermoelectric transducer that is contained in an adhesive pad, and even using circulatory tumor cells to monitor cancer.

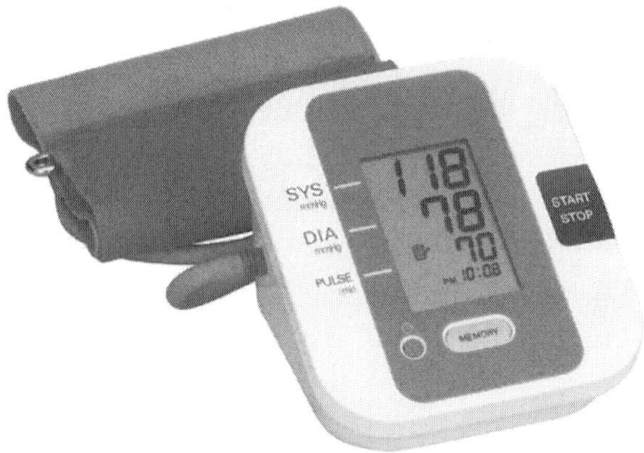

Figure 2.5: Above is a blood pressure monitor that shows the systolic and diastolic pressure.

Source: https://melsonmedical.en.made-in-china.com/product/heSJFvXxkKAs/China-Best-Blood-Pressure-Monitor-Blood-Pressure-Machine-Sphygmomanometer.html.

The main vitals that are monitored almost daily include blood pressure and heart rate, thus showing the importance of these machines. Some of the other vitals that can be monitored include the respiratory rate and the pulse oximetry. In critical care units, there is integration of multimodal monitors and anesthetic machines into the bedside monitors that help with the simultaneous measurement and displaying of the vital parameters. This allows for the patient to be monitored in a continuous manner, and also allowing for the medical staff to have continuous notifications on any changes in the patient's vitals. There are some monitors that are used in large hospitals that help in informing the staff on any fatal cardiac conditions that are pending before the physical signs can be seen by the medical practitioners (Shortliffe and Perreault, 2013).

Computer science has greatly helped the medical field in this aspect due to the major challenges in the hospitals. Some of these challenges include:

- *The lack of doctors and nurses* – There has been an increase in the demand for health care, thus causing overcrowding in the hospitals due to rising number of conditions that are complicated which leads to the lack of effective patient monitoring.
- *The importance of continuous monitoring* – there is proof that there is a reduction in the number of people who go to the intensive care unit due to clinical deterioration in hospitals due to continuous monitoring in the unit of surgery. Being able to monitor the vital signs of the patients in the surgical unit has also proven to be helpful in reducing the time that each patient stays in the hospital. This is because when you continuously monitor the patients, there is a higher chance of recognizing any early signs of the patient's health deteriorating.

One of the main benefits of having computer monitoring equipment includes: Having one main monitor for the side of the bed as well as during transportation helps get rid of a need for having monitors that are separate. These wireless monitors allow for a fully networked and easily exported. There are sections of the technology that allow for it to be well visible to those that are monitoring the data. It gives a huge opportunity to the health care workers when it comes to keeping their patients alive.

Technology has made it possible for us to use one monitor to cater for the patient's need from the beginning of the treatment process to the end. This means from the time they are admitted to the time they are discharged. Monitoring devices are used in both hospitals and clinics. They are also used at the homes to track the vitals of those who are critically ill and even athletes. Some of the vitals that are tracked in the household include body temperature, blood pressure, and heart rate. There are certain sensors that are inserted in the devices used for monitoring that help in the tracking of data (Shortliffe and Perreault, 2013).

Due to industrialization, changes in the climate, and progressions that are being made technically, there are many more health issues that are occurring in the recent days that have been a cause of the deteriorating health including diseases that are chronic, or even those that are related to the heart. It is important for one to understand that being able to detect any health issues early can help in extending lives as well as lowering the rate of morbidity in the world.

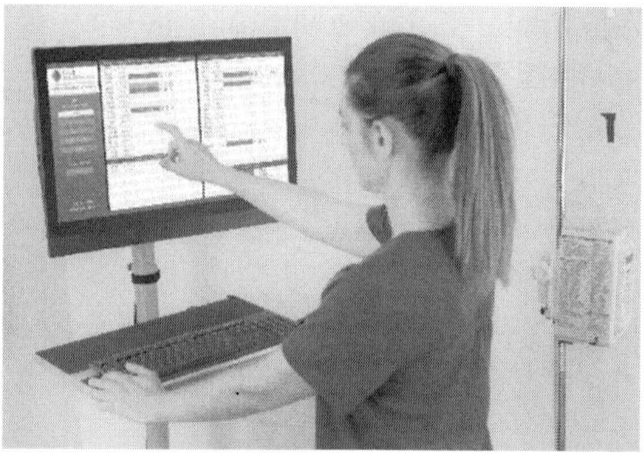

Figure 2.6: Nurses and doctors are able to input patient data immediately they get it, allowing it to also be stored immediately.

Source: https://www.prnewswire.com/news-releases/study-shows-wearable-leaf-patient-monitoring-system-promotes-early-mobility-improves-teamwork-enhances-workflow-300806221.html.

The monitoring software works by storing data in a database that helps in displaying the values of the voltage in real time, using graphics and metrics. It does all thus buy monitoring the condition of the patient's health and making sure they stay within the acceptable limits. If the values in the readings are out of the rage that is acceptable, there is a notification that is sent to the doctors or nurses on either the computer, tablets or mobile phones. This allows the professionals to take the specific steps that are expected of them to ensure the health of their patient. So as to make a multifunctional health monitoring system, it is possible for one to add additional sensors.

2.4. COMPUTER-ASSISTED SURGERY

Computer-enhanced surgery and robotically assisted surgeries can be incorporated in the medical scene for preoperative planning surgical navigation and assistance in surgical procedures. Computer-assisted surgery or CAS has become more closely linked to image guidance and an operation where imaging scans and computer programming is used to model an organ. In neurosurgery, for example, models are used as a guide to precisely navigate and treat a tumor or a vascular malformation and other lesions as well. Imaging guidance surgery has allowed surgeons to undertake complex operations without large intrusions being made in the body within confined areas of the body.

Figure 2.7. *Doctors are able to use this technology to practice outcomes before the main surgery.*

Source: https://opmed.doximity.com/articles/is-computer-assisted-surgery-the-future-of-orthopedics.

Computer-assisted surgery essentially has two components one being the robotically-assisted surgical device and the other being the human element, the surgeon himself (Bhatt et al, 2016). This means essentially that these devices are not really robots because they cannot function without direct human control. The robotically assistant surgical device operates using computer and software technology for a variety of surgical procedures anomaly would have the following constituents:

- A console from where the surgeon operates. Ordinarily, the console is the operation center of the device and allows the surgeon to have a full view of the surgical environment and equipment.
- Bedside cart with hinged mechanical arms and surgical instruments. The cart contains equipment which allows the surgeon have greater control over the whole procedure. The bedside cart also includes an endoscope, which is a special camera used in the operating room.
- A hardware and software cart that has other supporting equipment such as an electrosurgical unit suction and irrigation pumps and a light unit.

With these three components the general principles of computer-assisted surgery are met whereby the surgeon is able to create a virtual image of the patient, analyze the image, perform a diagnostic and make preoperative plans even with surgical simulations.

The Food and Drug Administration in the United States has robotically assisted surgical devices cleared for use and training by surgeons across the board, from general surgery to cardiac colorectal gynecological neurological thoracic and urological procedures (Bhatt et al, 2016).

2.4.1. Computer-Assisted Surgery for Patients

For patients, the biggest benefit of robotically assisted surgery is the element of minimal invasive surgery. Minimally invasive surgery allows the physician to utilize a number of techniques that limit the size and number of incisions made. This in extent also limits recovery time and is considered how much safer option than conventional open surgery. Patience considering treatment must openly communicate to the Physicians about the risks and benefits of computer-assisted surgery in comparison to other treatment options and should feel free to inquire about the devices and the surgeons experience with them.

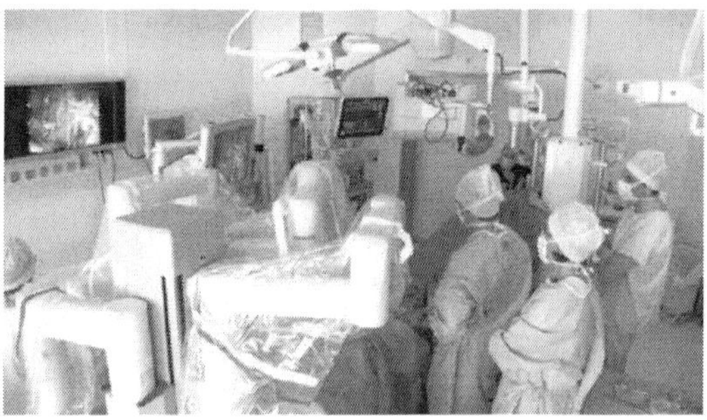

Figure 2.8: This technology will help in reducing human error and therefore lowering the mortality rate from surgeries.

Source: https://www.trtworld.com/news/computer-assisted-surgery.

Computer-Assisted surgery from healthcare providers: When used appropriately and with adequate training, computer-assisted surgery is a wonderful treatment option that is both safe and effective. However, it is important to understand that it is a responsibility of physicians, manufacturers, and health care providers to maintain and uphold training, development, and implementation of computer-assisted surgery devices. This is because they are no officiated medical bodies that regulate the training, supervision or provide accreditation to legally marketed medical devices.

Users of computer-assisted surgery devices should be aware that there are several different models which work very differently and may not have the same functions depending on the specified device.

By extent Physicians and healthcare facilities that have these devices must certify adequate training is finished before performing procedures with these tools.

Applications: Due to the fact that computer-assisted surgery is so flexible it has charged a revolution in the medical field and has made high-precision surgical domains easier to operate within.

2.4.2. Computer-Assisted Neurosurgery

A remote manipulator or a teller manipulator was the first computer-assisted surgical device used in neurosurgery.

It is a device the uses electronic hydraulic or mechanical linkages to move her hand like mechanism controlled by physician. The device initially was used to manipulate hazardous materials for safety reasons but in the 1980s it made its way into neurosurgery.

This happened when the instrumental scaled down allowing greater development in brain microsurgery where it compensated for the surgeons' physiology, improving accuracy.

The field includes spinal procedures where are the benefits of navigation and robotic systems have been felt. Examples of navigation systems and robotics systems used in computer-assisted neurosurgery include:

- Medtronic Stealth;
- BrainLab;
- 7D Surgical;
- Stryker;
- Mazor Renaissance;
- MazorX; and
- Globus Excelsior GPS.

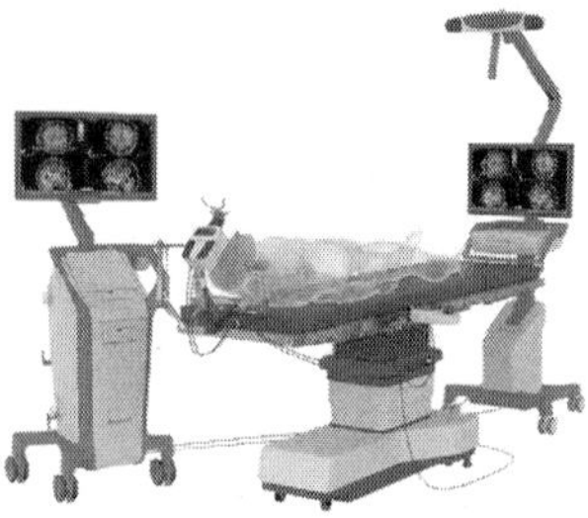

Figure 2.9: Above is the Medtronic Stealth which is a machine that helps in computer-assisted neurosurgery.

Source: https://www.bioworld.com/articles/431900-fda-gives-nod-to-medtronics-stealth-autoguide-system-for-cranial-procedures.

2.4.3. Computer-Assisted Oral and Maxillofacial Surgery

Othorgnatic surgery, simply known as jaw surgery, essentially makes corrections to the anomalies of the jaw and skull around the temporo-mandibular region. Computer imaging and simulations make preoperative planning and simulations possible. Additionally, osteotomies were planned on cast models but since the 19th pre-surgical planning is simulated in a virtual environment based on CT or MRI imaging. This is reduced to cost time it takes to make these cast models for each patient.

During the craniofacial surgery itself a bone fragment tracking system that uses infrared cameras and infrared transmitters are attached to the head of the patient. This allows a computer console to continually virtualize the position of the bone fragments using the position of the transmitters (Preim and Bartz, 2007).

2.4.4. Computer-Assisted Ear Nose and Throat Surgery

ENT specialists ordinarily used image-guided surgery and there has been some application of robotic surgery mostly because of high-precision movements around critical regions like the optic nerve.

2.4.5. Computer-Assisted Orthopedic Surgery CAOS

Orthopedic surgeons have been using robotics in a variety of procedures like hip replacements and computers have proved useful especially in the preoperational stage allowing the physician to have a good image of the anatomical positions of displaced bones. Examples of CAOS devices include:

- HipNav;
- OrothoPilot; and
- Praxis.

2.4.6. Computer-Assisted Visceral Surgery

Disorders and deformities in the viscera and mammary glands can be treated with minimal risks and minimal invasive approaches. Hysterectomies laparoscopies cardiac surgery and other operations have specialized surgical robots that perform a myriad of tasks.

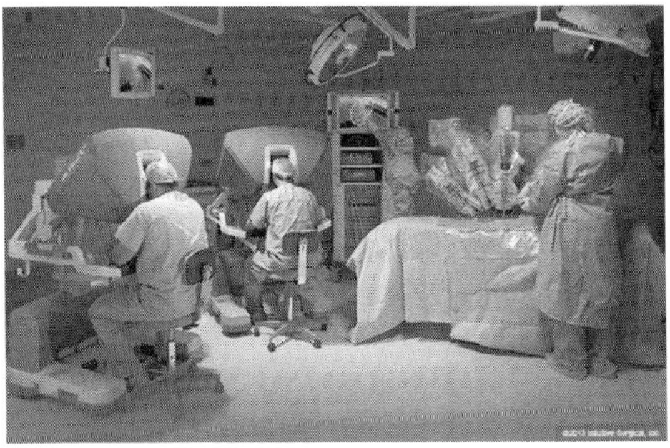

Figure 2.10: Robotic surgery has proven to make surgery less invasive in comparison to a doctor making the surgery.

Source: https://www.aarp.org/health/conditions-treatments/info-12–2013/robotic-surgery-risks-benefits.html.

Some of the advantages include:

- The biggest advantage is already being listed in the nature of robotic surgery being less invasive and by accident less traumatic where the patient experiences less pain and a quicker recovery time. Higher surgical accuracy is achieved when robotic surgery is implemented minimizing risk in situations where one slip of the scalpel or a misplaced set of forceps would have caused extensive damage or resulted in the death of the patient. There are surgeries that carry on for extensive periods of time and it can be exhausting for the surgeon. Fatigue reduces concentration and ability to focus increasing the element of risk. Computer-assisted surgery devices reduce fatigue for the surgeon allowing them to comfortably operate.

Some of the disadvantages include:

- The benefits of computer-assisted surgery do not come without some shortcomings. One major limiting factor is that of latency which is defined as the time delay between instructions given by the surgery and action movement of the robot. This is obvious real-time effects. Another disadvantage is that these systems go at the cost of millions of dollars rendering them a taxing investment even for very large well-funded hospitals. Finally, the size of some of these systems and their large footprints serve as a disadvantage, where it may be difficult to even fit both the surgical team and the surgical device into one operating room.

Ultimately computer-assisted surgery and robotically-assisted surgery have a bright future with medical technology becoming seamless and medical technology in the coming years will make surgeries easier and safer for the patient and the physician.

2.5. TELEMEDICINE

It is known that telemedicine and telehealth are used interchangeably but this is not exactly the case.

Telehealth refers to any distribution of services that are related to health as well as any data using technologies that allow for the distribution of electronic information and telecommunication.

It allows for there to be care, contact, education, monitoring, intervention, reminders, advice, etc. between clinicians and patients who are far from each other.

Telehealth is used in a sense that is much more limited in clinical services (monitoring and making diagnoses) that are much more remote. When there is lack of infrastructure such as transport, funding, and even staff, telehealth is what is utilized in ensuring that gap is bridged.

Telehealth also helps in providing learning opportunities to distant people. It helps in allowing for presentations, meetings, etc.

Figure 2.11: Doctors are able to schedule meeting with their patients using telemedicine.

Source:* *https://www.mobihealthnews.com/content/experts-debate-telemedicine-merits-and-myths.

Some examples, in which telehealth could be used include:

- Performing a robotic surgery through access that is remote;
- Using digital monitoring instruments to perform physical therapy;
- Forwarding of tests within one or more facilities so that the results can be interpreted by more than one specialist;
- Monitoring the vitals of a patient at their own home though continuously sending the information on the patient to the doctor or nurse;

During all times, the connection should be strong and reliable. There has been an improvement on the infrastructure of broadband, thus making the use of telemedicine much more effective and efficient. Health professionals are able to achieve this by first assessing the aspects in which a patient's health can be improved using telemedicine such as the time in which they travel, the time they have off of work and also the costs it takes for them to achieve this. Companies that deal with this technology are able to make the transition into telemedicine easier.

There are four main ways in which one can deliver these services:

- Using videos that is live;
- Storing and forwarding;
- Monitoring patients remotely;
- Engaging in mobile health.

Storing and forwarding deals with data acquisition to ensure the data is transmitted to a medical professional when it is convenient for them to assess. It is very beneficial considering the fact that it does not require both patients to be at the same place at the same time. Store and forward is mostly used by pathologists and radiologists. A component of this transfer should include medical records that a well-structured in a manner that is electronic. This normally asks the doctor to use the information that is provided, either in audio or video, to come up with a diagnosis and treatment instead of having to perform a physical examination (Preim and Bartz, 2007).

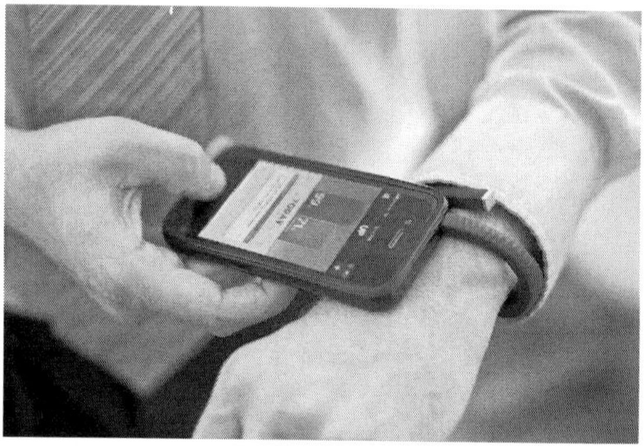

Figure 2.12: Smartphones are being used for the remote monitoring of patients. There are applications that are installed that are able to even measure the heart rate of the patient.

Source: https://www.pbs.org/newshour/health/doctors-monitor-patients-vitals-via-smartphones-fitness-trackers.

Through remote monitoring, a patient can monitor their own vitals while doctors and nurses can also monitor patient's vitals in a remote manner using computer devices. This is mostly used in the management of chronic diseases, such as heart diseases, asthma, and diabetes. These devices can provide health outcomes equivalent to in-patient encounters and are much more affordable.Real-time interaction involves having electronic consultations. These are done using interactive telemedicine services. They help with providing real-time interactions between the doctor and the patient. There are many different clinical disciplines that have integrated video conferencing in their daily routines. They have also been used in other aspects including diagnosis, to monitor the patients, counseling, and even in management (Anderson and Jay, 2012).

There are technologies that allow for the receiving and transmitting of signals that are in audio and video form. This is referred to as video-telephony. These signals can be transmitted by different people at different places so as to allow them to communicate in real time. This form of technology initially used image phones which would work by exchanging still images after every few seconds over a specific type of telephone line (POTS-type). This technology is mainly useful as of now to those who are deaf and speech impaired. They are able to use them while utilizing sign language. It is also useful to those who have issues with mobility or those who are far from the hospital and need medical services using telemedicine.

2.6. ELECTRONIC HEALTH RECORDS

These are versions of medical histories of patients that are stored in an electronic form. This is done so that the medical facility can maintain the information over a long period of time. It may have all the information on the patients' clinical state that are important to the nurses and doctors. This includes where they live, notes on their progress, any clinical issues they may have, any medicine that the patient may be taking, vital signs, any data from the laboratory, reports from radiology, any past medical history, allergies, body weight and height, billing records, age, vaccination records, etc.

This form of technology helps in automating the access to the data and helps in making sure that the workflow of the clinician is streamlined (Anderson and Jay, 2012). It also has the ability to ensure that other activities that are related to care are supported either in a direct or indirect manner through certain interfaces, including quality management, reporting of outcomes and decision support that is based on evidence.

Electronic health records are a major step in improving the relationship between the health providers and patients. They are a major aspect in continuing the upward progression of healthcare. The information that is stored in these records are readily available and this allows for the clinicians to come up with better diagnoses for any medical conditions that the patient may have thus promoting the provision of better care.

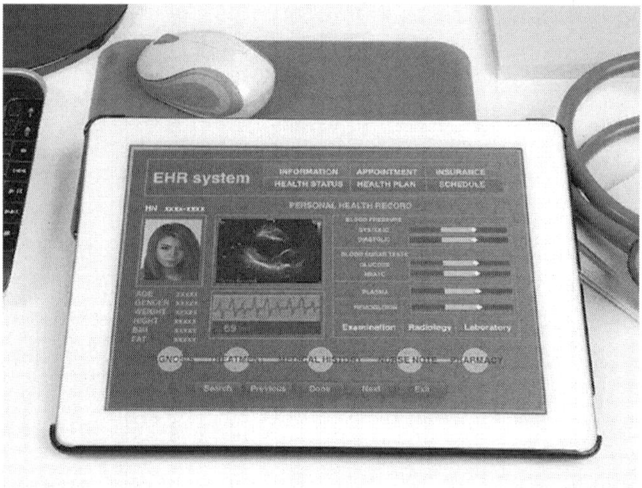

Figure 2.13: Electronic health records have made it easier to store patient data in a more accessible manner.

Source: https://www.medscape.com/viewarticle/887548.

Some of the ways in which electronic health records can improve the care of patients include:

- It reduces the incidence of medical errors by improving the accuracy and clarity of the records.
- It reduces the number of duplicated tests that are performed in the hospital due to the availability of all the patient's medical data.
- It reduces any delay in treatment and allows the patients to know their conditions better so as to have informed decision making.

This technology is a collection of the patient's information that has been systematized and stored in an electronic manner. This means that it is possible to share this information amongst different settings that provide healthcare. This information can be shared using network connections, information systems amongst enterprises, or even other networks of information.

It has been known that electronic health records are a major step into increasing the quality of care. Clinicians are able to use the information from the records of the patient to ensure quality outcomes using proper management programs for providing care.

Chronically ill patients can now be identified and stratified using the combination of the many different forma of clinical data from the health records in the system.

They have helped in preventing hospitalization of high-risk patients using the electronic health records which provide the analytics and data that is needed to achieve this.

These systems are designed to ensure that the data is stored in an accurate manner and also in a manner that can capture the patient's state over a long period of time.

It helps in getting rid of the need to look for the medical records of the patient as it makes sure the data is legible and highly accurate. It also helps in keeping the files up to date and therefore reducing the level of data replication.

It also avoids the loss of data by losing paperwork. Since it is digital, the information on a patient can be accessed by searching in the system by typing a keyword, thus making it much more effective when trying to extract medical information on a patient when trying to examine for any trends and changes that are long term. Being able to globally adopt electronic health records can help in performing population baes studies (Consoli, Recupero, and Petković, 2019).

There are many pros and cons of electronic health records and paper records. Firstly, there is an ease that is brought about by electronic health records especially when it comes to how transparent, portable, and accessible they are to the healthcare providers; however, this also means that there is a high possibility for medical records to be stolen by people who are not authorized or even users who are unscrupulous, when compared to paper records.

There is therefore a need for a strict security requirement for electronic health records which are stated in the act.

This is one of the main reasons that certain hospitals are still not adopting electronic health records (Consoli, Recupero, and Petković, 2019).

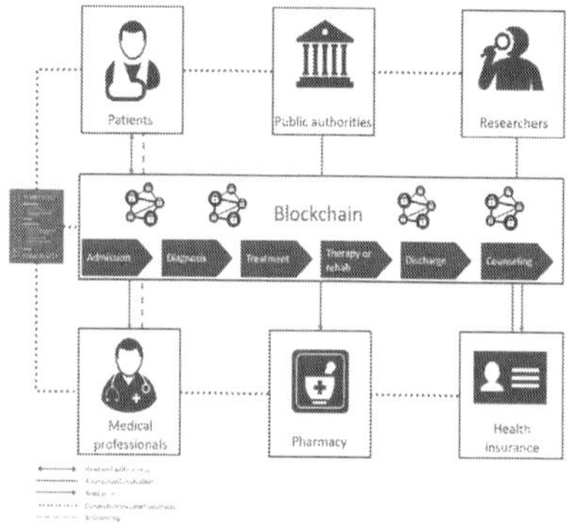

Figure 2.14: Above is an illustration of all the people who could have access to electronic medical records.

Source: https://www.jmir.org/2019/10/e13585.

Secondly, using paper medical records can lead to poor legibility thus contributing to medical errors. So as to improve the reliability of these records, hospitals have implemented standardized abbreviations, forms that are pre-printed, and a standard for penmanship. Electronic records have an advantage in this section because they are able to ensure standardization of forms, input of data, as well as terminologies. Having digitized forms has helped in the facilitation of data collection for clinical studies and epidemiology. All in all, there have been fewer cases of complications, mortality, and expensive costs in many hospitals due to the adoption of electronic health records (Consoli, Recupero, and Petković, 2019).

Within certain legal limitations, it is possible for electronic health records to be updated continuously. It is also possible to ensure the facilitation of the coordination of the delivery of healthcare in facilities that are not affiliated, if there was the ability to exchange records between various electronic medical records systems.

In addition, it is possible to anonymously use information from an electronic system to report statistics in issues that involve improving quality, management of resources and the surveillance of communicable diseases in public health. It is however, difficult to eliminate the data from its context.

Some of the technical features of this technology include:

- Using and sharing information over networks that are secure due to digital formatting;

- Tracking the progress of health care being delivered, such as medical prescription or outcome of the diagnosis;
- Providing warnings and reminders that have been triggered;
- Facilitating the life cycle of medical orders, reports, and results;
- Reducing the time it takes to bill the patient, leading to an accurate billing system;
- Promoting the exchange of health information in an electronic manner from one organization to another.

Not only is it possible to use an electronic medical record to write and read the records of the patient using a work station, but also is it possible to use handwriting capable mobile phone, a tablet or even smartphone, depending in the setting of the health care facility and the type of system it is using. Consumers are able to ready gain access to the individual notes from an electronic medical record due to the accessibility of personal health records.

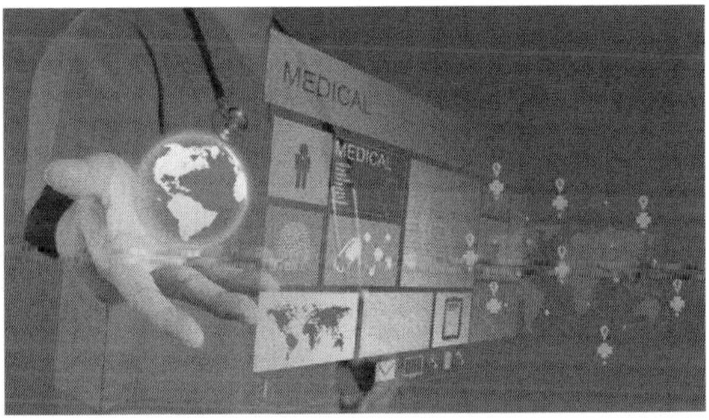

Figure 2.15: Electronic medical records have made it easier for hospitals to deal with large quantities of data.

Source: https://innovatemedtec.com/digital-health/ehr--emr.

Some electronic medical records are able to ensure the monitoring of any medical events by ensuring the analysis of the patient's information from the records so as to make predictions, detections, and prevention of events that may be potentially adverse. This may involve making orders on transfers and being discharged, making orders to the pharmacy, results from radiology, results from the laboratory, and other forms of services that are ancillary. This helps in reducing any chances of critical opportunities by informing the health care providers if the patient has missed medical care in a period longer than that which is acceptable.

2.7. MEDICAL DATABASES

It is evident that the healthcare industry is becoming digitalized at a fast rate. This is because we are moving from paper records to electronic records. This therefore leads to the healthcare database.

Many of them at that. Databases have been found to be a foundation in using any form of data. A database refers to a data collection that has undergone organization for the purpose of storing it, accessing it and retrieving it. There is many different forma of database.

The most common type, however, is the online transaction processing database. Databases have helped in the replacing of paper records which include folders, documents, and even filing cabinets. Using electronic data is now much more immediate and convenient.

An online transaction processing database refers to one that is running on a single computer. Electronic health records are an example of this. The online transaction processing database has a major advantage which allows for transactional processing that is quick and in real time. It is designed in a manner that allows it to be fast and it helps in delivering sub-seconds times of response.

An example can be seen when a patient goes to the hospital, searching the name of the patient in the electronic medical records can show a result for the search that is instant. At the same time, if her blood pressure it taken and inputted into the electronic records, it is stored there instantaneously. This is all thankful to the architecture of the online transaction processing database (Bhatt et al, 2016).

As of today, healthcare databases are used for many different functions. One of the most important functions of the medical database is as a foundation when it comes to being able to run the many systems that deal with transactions in the medical industry.

The structure of the online transaction processing database helps in accommodating the creation of many different applications that can be used for transactions such as lab systems, electronic health records, processing of bills and payments, human resources, education, research, ADT tracking, etc. Most of the applications that are used in hospitals are run by the online transaction processing database.

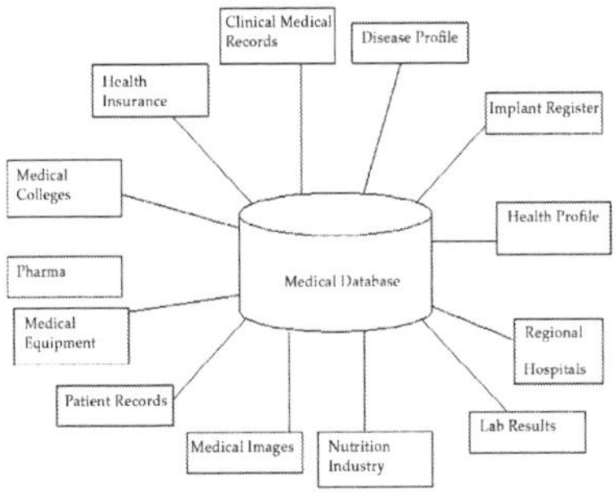

Figure 2.16: Above is an illustration of an integrated medical database system.

Source: https://www.researchgate.net/figure/ntegrated-Medical-Database_fig1_316989933.

One major point that needs to be understood is that each online transaction processing database deals with a single application. This means the electronic health records has its own online transaction processing database, the Human Resources system has its own online transaction processing database, etc. This then allows for one to understand that each organization that deals with healthcare, especially those large hospitals, depend on a great number of databases (Bhatt et al, 2016).

There are a couple of advantages of the online transaction processing database. The advantages of online transaction processing databases are similar to those of the applications that are running in them. These applications and databases are to thanks for the major advances in the automation and the standardization of processes that are made clinically and in business.

Using health databases also makes It is possible for data to be stored externally and also be backed up in a place that is secure so as to reduce the chances of losing data. It makes it possible for the back-end data to be much more accurate and standardized due to the front-end software being able to make provisions of tip texts and also enforcing the integrity of data. In addition to all this, it allows for faster processing of transaction that are typical because the information is stored in an electronic manner. This includes results from the lab, claims of payments, etc.

One of the greatest advantages that the online transaction processing database has is the ability to capture large amounts of data healthcare organizations. This means that they have massive stores of data that can be utilized to provide care that is much more effective and better.

Despite all these advantages, there are also a couple of disadvantages. Having this amount of data in the online transaction processing databases can also lead to major problems. There are about two major problems. They involve a large amount of raw data. This can be understood by making a comparison to searching for information on the internet. Just because you have access to a large amount of information, doesn't mean that you are able to immediately gain an understanding or knowledge (Bhatt et al, 2016).

The healthcare organizations now have a large amount of data to deal with. There is a need for every single person using the database to have a manner to turn all that information that is raw into knowledge that is actionable and targeted. It can be very overwhelming to make sense of that raw data without any access to the correct processes and tools for guiding the processes.

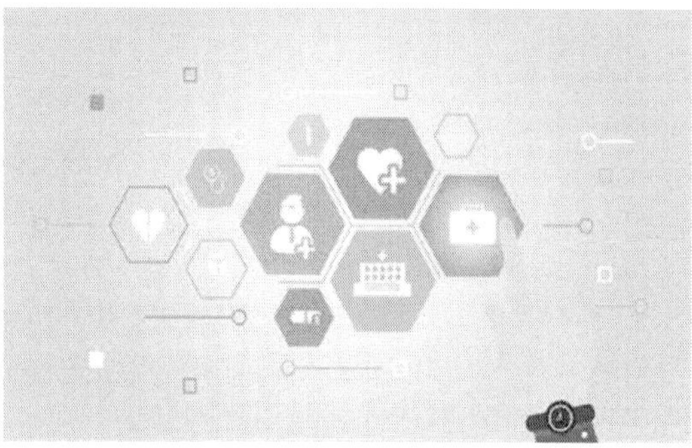

Figure 2.17: Medical database are different in different hospitals due to the different systems that they use.

Source: https://www.shutterstock.com/search/medical+database.

Another disadvantage is that data is siloed. The architecture of the online transaction processing database naturally produces data silos, considering the fact that each app uses its own database. The online transaction processing database are not designed in a manner that allows for the analysis of each database silo. This is complicated because the health care systems require analysis of all applications and systems so as to access the kind of information and insight that the organizations need for succeeding in these times that require care that is based on value.

Despite these problems, there are some solutions that have been invented to combat them. This solution exists in a different type of healthcare database: an online analytical processing database. This is also called an enterprise data warehouse (Preim and Bartz, 2007).

The online analytical processing database exists as a layer above other databases. They normally find themselves above the online transaction processing database. This database normally is found as a layer above all of the transactional application databases of the healthcare organization. It is designed in a way that allows for it to have the combination of data from the online transactional processing databases and promote the creation of a layer that has undergone optimization for and is dedicated to analytics.

This means that the healthcare organizations are able to do analysis on data in a sophisticated manner from many different sources: the electronic health records, patient satisfaction, costing, etc. These databases have made it possible for the many online transactional processing databases in the healthcare organizations to realize their full potential.

2.8. HEALTH INFORMATION SYSTEMS

Health information systems are very important in the health care system. They have a link to the informatics on health that mainly deals with the functioning of the administration in the hospitals and clinics. It is an formation system that is well integrated and comprehensive. It also has different implementations. It is mainly designed for the delivery of administrative operations that are early in this industry.

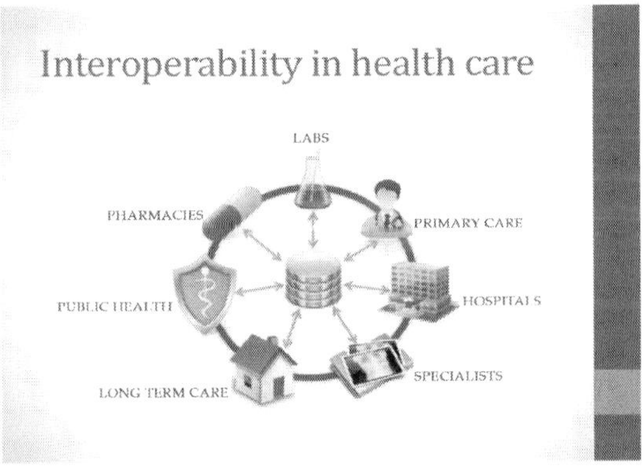

Figure 2.18: Above shows the interoperability in healthcare and health information systems. This is important in ensuring the proper running of any hospital.

Source: https://mentorhealthdotcom.wordpress.com/2015/08/07/understanding-interoperability-and-health-information-systems/amp/.

These systems have been made digital and they now mostly involve computers, as they phase out the paper records. Health information systems that are computerized comprise of sequences such as the input of data, the processing of data, any outputs, as well as boundaries. The system of the computer gains the data on the health of the patient, which undergoes processing to later on develop the expected output, and there are also boundaries that have been initially defined for the influencing of the outputs.

There are many aspects that involve memory functions and monitoring that are involved in processing. The health informatics that have been digitalized are in association with a great deal of aspects. Some parts of the health system include the medical professionals, the organizations, and the mortuary. All these sections of the health system have a boundary that is clearly defined. This means that it is not possible to consider a section such as a milk shop as a part of the health system.

How the computer inputs, processes, and outputs information is all based on the function of the system. This can also be influenced by the fact that specific system models can be based on the aspects of the input, therefore influencing the processing and output of the information. This however, is not common, because most of the health information systems are based on the outputs (Preim and Bartz, 2007).

2.8.1. Types of Health Information Systems

Health information systems that are based on the subject – These systems can either be based on the subject or the task at hand. Those that are based on the subject have a relation to any part of the organization that is dealing with health care, including patients and doctors. Those that are based on the task have an association with specific tasks such as the theatre for operations and admissions. It has been proved that those that are based in the subject tend to function better than those that are based on the task because they lower the chances of duplicating the data. This is due to the fact that those that are based on the task have similar subjects undergoing different tasks. This means that the main details of the subject would be recorded every single time for each different task. However, in the information systems that are based in the subject, the main data in the subject is only recorded once and this information can then integrate into the different tasks. An example of the health information system that is based on the subject includes the electronic medical records.

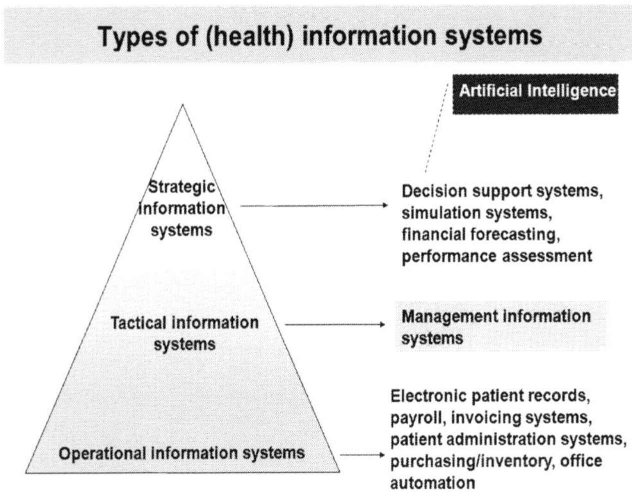

Figure 2.19: These are some of the types of health information systems including the strategic information system.

Source: https://slideplayer.com/amp/6915666/.

Strategic Health Information Systems – This is one of the most common methods of making classifications of the information on health. This specific information pyramid has different levels that have provisions that are designed for the systems of information that are dealing with a certain type of information. This information system has more pros than other information systems. Some of the main advantages include:

- It allows for an organization to be assessed in regards to spreading of digitization in the system of information. This is very easy to achieve because the systems that deal with the operations are mainly designed previous to the formation of information systems that are executive or those that deal with management.
- It allows for the giving of permission for any developments that are inappropriate or uneven to be highlighted. This can be achieved by making considerations on how dependent the hierarchical data is, for there to be a need for the management information systems to feed to the operational system.

So as to make an identification of the deficiencies of the individual system, it is important for one to consider the deficiencies. There are a couple of approaches that one can take to achieve this:

- There are certain digitized planning tools that can be used to provide output information that a hospital may need urgently. The disadvantage of this system is that is does not contain a feeder system that helps in keeping the information up to date.
- Most hospitals experience difficulties with cost management and most likely rely on a method called "top-down apportioning". This happens because they do not have a feeder system that helps in providing data on the per-client usage that is exact. However, exceptions exist and some hospitals that do not have this problem due to the existing feeder system.
- There are many hospitals equipped with management systems for nurses as well as a data collection approach that is manual so as to ensure proper maintenance of the system. It is however, important for an information system that is effective to get this information from the clinical system directly.

Administrative and clinical health information systems – These provide a representation for a different division of health information systems. It is however, not possible for the development of clinical systems that are independent on certain types of data that is administrative. The foundation of a health information system that is integrated is a major section that is created among the most important information on the patients, thus providing a link to the various clinical systems. There is therefore an allowance for healthcare systems that are departmental for individual patients for setting up extra research datasets for carrying forward certain activities. All of the clinical systems are equipped with electronic medical records that have the information on the patient. All hospitals are as of now equipped with a patient administrative system that helps in providing data in the form of episode statistics from the hospital. This can undergo regard as a system that is administrative due to its design to ensure that retrospective data entry is provided as well as any information on each care episode of the patient. At the same time, the data that has information on diagnoses, outcomes, and processing can be referred to as clinical.

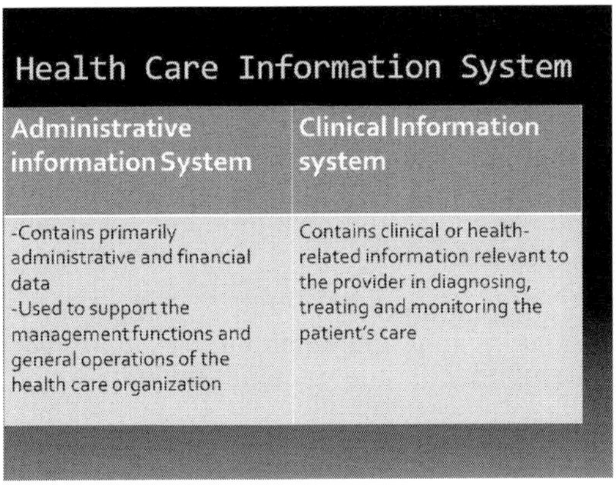

Figure 2.20: These are some of the differences between the administrative information system and the clinical information system.

Source: https://slideplayer.com/amp/10665365/.

Electronic Health Record – this is a major part of the health information systems. Different countries have different standards and different electronic medical records. It is therefore necessary to have a standard that is common and open. Electronic medical records need to be developed in an open manner. Open electronic medical records are equipped with certain sets of specifics within the architecture of the electronic medical records. This however, cannot be considered as an application software. It is created in a way that promotes the fulfilment of the purpose of being able to enable semantic interoperability of the information system in the health sector in and within the various electronic medical records. All of these systems are not in a proprietary format so as to prevent the lock in of information by the vendor. All of the concepts of information in the healthcare sector undergo storage in a manner that is well structured called the archetypes. These are stored outside the software. These types of archetypes store all the information concepts of healthcare and they also record all the main clinical activities. Some of the major sections of the archetypes have certain evaluations, instructions, actions, and observations. The data that is created from these sections undergoes storage in the electronic medical records in a composition structure that is larger and has its own archetypes (Preim and Bartz, 2007).

Clinical and financial health information systems – this is also a different division of the systems in healthcare. This system gives permission for patient costing to be easily accessed and also in helping the usage of different departments by the patients to be monitored.

This only occurs as the different deliverables are tagged with their prices that are associated. It is important to note that most of the billing and costing is normally done based on an estimation as per ensuring the whole costs are apportioned retrospectively. These systems also have the ability to invoice as well as follow up on any incident that involves the patient not paying. In this case, this system is very important for the smooth operation of the hospitals and clinics.

Decision Support Health information systems – this is also an important health system. This is a form of artificial intelligence (AI). This system works by getting the computer to attempt performance of sections that require to be processed by the user, after the conversion of the information into information that is clinically relevant.

Despite the fact that there are technical capabilities for the development of these systems, and this idea is very old, there has not been a large number of hospitals that have been able to adopt this system, due to both organizational and professional reasons.

This has led to many hospitals being able to deal more with professional decision support systems in healthcare organizations. This system is, however, more of a system that deals with procedure adherence instead of the decision support system that makes sure that the actions of the health providers are adhering to the set rules.

Decision support systems normally help in the following ways:

- Helps in presenting the information on the patient's health in a way that is advantageous to processing that is cognitive. This involves being able to flag, sort, and classify the information. This means that is deals with the facilitation of the decision making if the user. This means it can provide a list of blood pressure drugs instead of presenting those for every single condition. It makes is possible for the mimicking of processes that are cognitive.
- It gives results of manipulated data and can lead to a certain action that is suitable by creating a mimic of the process that is cognitive and also processing the output.

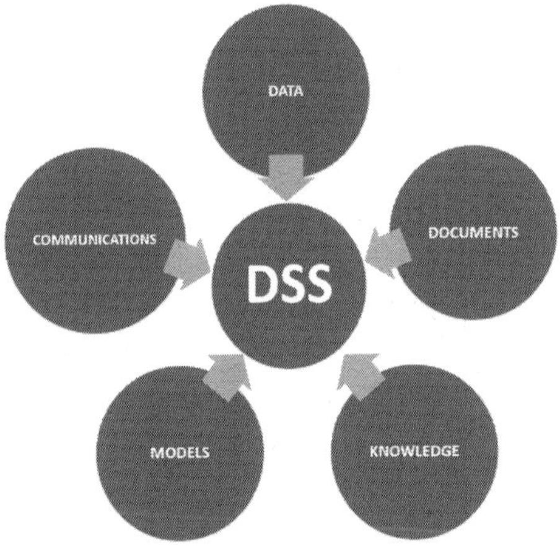

Figure 2.21: These are some of the classification of decision support system.

Source: https://www.semanticscholar.org/paper/Decision-Support-Systems-%28-DSS-%29-in-the-Process-of-Mantovani/81c2fae9fb185914fb1fc76035ef8b720dd7b654/figure/1.

All the health information systems have their pros and cons, direct, and indirect benefits, and provide an advantage that is competitive. They all help in the enhancement of the care that is provided to the patients. They also help in raising the level of profit that the organization can incur, due to the quality care, efficiency, and effectiveness, making mire patients much more confident in choosing the specific clinic or hospital.

2.9. MEDICAL LAB TECHNOLOGY

Computers that are being used in all medicine fields. They are used for many different functions in medical labs. They have helped in testing for diseases, making diagnoses, find out if drugs are safe and effective to use, etc. Below are some of the ways in which computers are used in the lab.

2.9.1. Drug Testing

Medical labs globally can test many different compounds to screen them for characteristics that could potentially save lives. There are so many plants and compounds that we have not explored. In addition to testing such compounds, the number of compounds that are being tested can undergo sorting and analysis in a short period of time in comparison to doing this work manually.

2.9.2. Being Able to Run Simulations

Running simulations on the computer has proven to be a very important advancement in the medical field. Computers have made it possible for the personnel in the lab to run many different simulations in a short period of time. They use these simulations to predict outcomes of how a drug will affect the user and whether it will be a suitable treatment for the specific user.

2.9.3. Doing Blood Work

One of the most important parts of working in a lab includes being able to take and analyze the results of blood samples. Computers have helped in making this job even easier. Computers that have been designed in a sophisticated manner are able to make quick determinations on the elements of the blood such as sugar, proteins, amino acids, and others. The computers are then able to generate results that the doctor can look at using his/her computer.

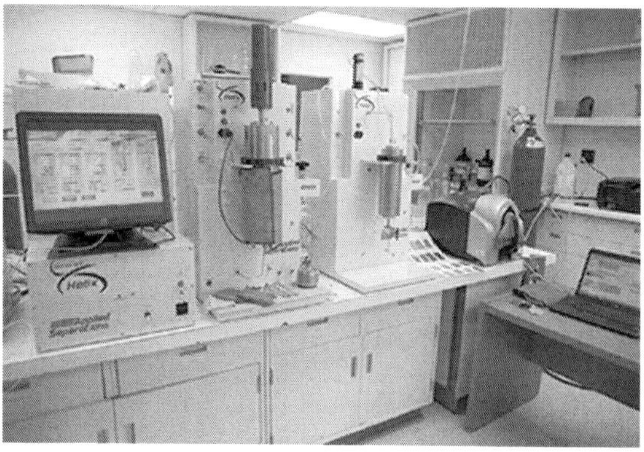

Figure 2.22: Computers have helped in making the work of scientists and researchers easier. They are able to do more work than any human being could do at a time with hardly any errors.

Source: http://www.eco2dye.com/lab-systems.html.

2.9.4. Generation of Research Data

Research is a very important job in the lab. Computers have it possible for the aggregation of many different individual records, allowing for them to be presented in. A format that is readily usable. This information is then used in many different ways.

2.9.5. Analysis of Patient Data

Computers have made it possible to ensure that patient data is kept up to date, and this is important in ensuring that a certain treatment plan is followed. These computers are able to keep track of the data on the patient and ensure that all the options for treating the patient are available.

2.9.6. Modeling Predictions

Medical lab personnel are able to utilize computers to find out how certain data may affect patients in the future. This is helpful in using patient data to foresee any future health problems, or how a certain drug will react with the patient. They can even be used to anticipate the rate of drug absorption in the body. This allows them to make any necessary adjustments in ensuring the components are safe for the end-user.

CHAPTER

3

Applications of Computer Science in Business

CONTENTS

3.1. INTRODUCTION

Business computing refers to the practice of using computer innovation to undertake a business function. These activities comprise of any action that either openly or indirectly supports financial, managerial, or any other data that is central to operating a business such as payroll or scheduling of meetings. Integration of computing into the corporate world should be seamless, ensuring that both hardware and software items interact appropriately and reliably with each other. Business computing and assimilation addresses the business problems – as well as technical conflicts – which arise when a large number of individuals in a huge enterprise work mutually on a range of tasks. Information, for example, that's gathered from a number of sources, may come with network-induced faults and should be made practical, or "application," across various enterprise systems.

Figure 3.1: A company executive making a presentation using modern computer technology.

Source: https://erau.edu/degrees/bachelor/business-analytics.

Computer science integration makes it possible for companies to manage data which could be fluctuating constantly. Another primary integration activity involves adapting information to one main format, so that connections between disparate information can be well described. Additionally, computing middleware forms the "connective tissue" which makes it conceivable to combine various structures built at distinct times or venues. The objective is to merge them with the slightest amount of effort plus the highest potential for synergy (Lin and Huang, 2011).

3.2. CUSTOMER INFORMATION CONTROL SYSTEM

CICS is a middleware which allows for rapid, high-volume virtual transaction processing. The objective is to handle two simultaneous requests like each had been delivered separately or terminated individually, however, in reality transaction submissions occur several times a second, and determine various other factors and circumstances. Basically, CICS technology offers services that expand or replace the roles of the software system. It is most commonly applied in financial services firms.

The term CICS means Customer Information Control Structure. It is an all-purpose transaction processing substructure for the z/OS operation system. CICS offers services for managing an application online, through request, concurrently as many other operators are submitting requests for running the same applications, through the same databases and programs.

CICS is effective in managing the distribution of resources, data integrity and prioritizing of implementation, with quick response. CICS approves users, apportions resources (actual storage and cycles), plus dispenses database requests from the application to proper database manager systems (like DB2). It can be said that CICS functions like, and does majority of the same roles as z/OS operation system (Lin and Huang, 2011).

3.2.1. Usability of CICS

Within the last few years, this technology has been useful in building customer transaction systems in the realm of large business mainframe computing. A considerable number of legacy system applications are still in operation today, COBOL, and CICS applications being among them. By employing the application program interface (API) offered by CICS, the programmer shall be able to write programs which interrelate with virtual operators and recite from or provide reports to clients and other records, such as orders, customer data, and inventory statistics) in a database (typically known as "data sets") utilizing CICS facilities instead of software access procedures directly.

Same as other transaction systems, CICS can guarantee that transactions are finalized and, if not, restart partly completed transactions such that the reliability of data files is maintained. Some businesses also use applications like Transaction Server to manage e-commerce transactions from Web users and direct these to a computer server which gains admittance to an existent CICS order, or inventory database (Lin and Huang, 2011).

3.2.2. Programming

Multi-user interactive-transaction software programs must be a re-entrant to support various concurrent transaction sequences. The modular structure of CICS re-entrant / recyclable control programs means that, through careful "pruning," different uses with many applications might be implemented on a processor with only 32K of exclusive magnetic core solid memory (as well as the operating system).

Some effort is needed by CICS application operators to ensure that their processes are as effective as possible. One common technique is to restrict the scope of particular programs to roughly 4,096 bytes, such that CICS may effortlessly reuse the memory expended by any program that's not presently applied for another different program, or remote application storage needs.

When digital memory was included to CICS, the 4K system became even more crucial in reducing paging and thrashing fruitless resource-contention overhead. Still, the proficiency of compiled top-level COBOL as well as PL/I language systems need to be improved. At the beginning, CICS application programs were inscribed in the assembler language, long after COBOL or PL/I support even became available. Later, when crucial path code was detected, a code snippet got shared around by programmers.

Each individual had to either lessen the amount of code bytes required, or by reducing the quantity of CPU cycles needed. The younger researchers learned from what their more-experienced advisors did. Ultimately, when nobody could do perform either of the processes mentioned above, the code was regarded as optimized, meanwhile they carried on to other different snippets (Segall et al, 2018).

Small businesses with just a few analysts began to discover CICS optimization and how it could streamline their operations. Since application programs could easily be distributed by several concurrent sequences, the use of fixed variables implanted within a database-or retrieval of operating system (OS) memory-was restricted through convention only.

Regrettably, most of the "policies" were often broken, particularly by COBOL computer operators who may not fully comprehend the workings of their projects or fail to apply the essential restrictive compile duration options. It resulted in the formation of "non-re-entrant" code which mostly was unreliable, causing artificial storage violations and complete CICS system crashes. Initially, the whole partition, or Multi-Virtual Storage (MVS) area, worked with similar memory protection keys such as the CICS kernel encryption (Segall et al, 2018).

Additionally, database corruption and CICS operation block corruption became a recurrent cause of system disruption. A program error in a particular application program may overwrite the memory, consisting of a code or data, covering one or all presently running application transactions.

Identifying the offending system code for complicated transient timing errors might be a rather tedious OS analyst issue. But despite these shortcomings there has been high demand for quality CICS programmers. In fact, CICS application transactions continue to be an essential for most public utility firms, large banks and even multibillion-dollar corporate institutions. Moreover, it is possible to offer a portion of advance application security by performing assessments under management of a monitoring system which also offers Test and Debug functions (Segall et al, 2018).

3.2.3. Structure

In the z/OS framework, a CICS installation consists of one or several regions (typically known as the "CICS Region," which spread across a few or multiple z/OS system images. Even though it processes shared transactions, each CICS area is typically initiated as a set processing batch location space with typical JCL statements: this is a job which runs indefinitely up to finish. Otherwise, each CICS region can also be launched as a beginner task. No matter whether it's a batch project or a started job, CICS regions have the ability to operate for days, weeks, and even months before closing down for maintenance.

Following restart, the parameter determines whether the start would be a "Cold" (no recovery) function, or "Warm"/"Emergency" (employing a warm closedown or relaunching from the log ensuing a crash). Cold starts of massive CICS regions with multiple resources might take a long period since all the descriptions are re-processed. Furthermore, installations are subdivided into several address spaces covering a wide range of reasons, like, function separation and application separation (Segall et al, 2018).

A normal installation comprises of various distinct applications which constitute a service. Every service typically has a variety of "Terminus Owning Region" (TORs) systems that redirect transactions to different "Application Owning Regions" or (AORs), even though other topologies still are possible. For instance, the AORs may not implement File I/O. Rather, there shall be a "File Ownership Region" (FOR) which executed the File I/O substituting AOR transactions. This ensures that VSAM files were only capable of supporting recoverable text access from a single address span at a time.

However, not all CICS programs use VSAM since the key data source (or traditionally other single address bars at a time database like CA Datacom) might use either Db2 or IMS/DB as the primary database or MQ as the queue manager. From all these examples, TORs can load-balance exchanges to groups of AORs that then openly use the collective databases/queues. CICS promotes XA dual-phase commitment between information stores and thus transactions spanning MQ, Db2, and VSAM/RLS for instance, are feasible with ACID properties.

Furthermore, CICS promotes distributed transactions through SNA LU6.2 modules between the address bars which may be operating on similar or different batches. This provides for ACID updates of different data stores by uniting distributed applications. In application, there are concerns with this in case a structure or communications failure happens since the operation disposition (commit or backout) might be in-doubt in case one of the interactive nodes hasn't recovered. Hence the application of these programs hasn't yet been widespread (Segall et al, 2018).

3.3. OPEN SOLUTIONS FOR LIFECYCLE COLLABORATION (OSLC)

OSLC describes a set of instructions that facilitate the incorporation of software upgrades and software products or services like Product Lifecycle Management or Application Lifecycle Management. The goal is making it simpler for software designers and tools operators to work together effortlessly. Basically, OSLC allows for development of corporate and technology ecosystems (Mehta, 2017).

In particular, OSLC Core Specification serves the role of a Hypermedia-API standard that's primarily adopted in application and structural engineering domains, however, with the potential of providing value to whichever domain with information integration challenges. Similarly, OSLC Core provisions improve on the W3C LDP functions, by defining the essential and shared technical aspects of OSLC domain conditions, and provides guidance on some common concerns for developing, updating, retrieving, or linking to lifespan resources.

OSLC domain-specific provisions outline the equivalent of RDF schemas needed to enable data interoperability. These typically consist of RDF languages and OSLC resource forms. The RDF vocabularies are applied to define standardized resource categories and properties. Likewise,

OSLC resource shapes are applied to define constraints like multiplicity limitations on properties of particular resource types (Mehta, 2017).

OSLC project is subdivided into different OASIS TC (Organization for Advancement of Systemic Information Standards Technological Committees), and previously described working groups as well as user groups. Every OASIS TC develops provisions in context of the specific aspect of the lifecycle. Case in point, there are some OASIS TCs for Conversion and Configuration Management, Mechanization, and Project Administration for Contracted Delivery or (Delivery Chain).

OSLC is an open-source platform in a sense that anyone can participate (example, in User Groups). In order to partake in the specification enhancing OASIS TCs, all players must sign the IPR guidelines to ensure irrevocability. These specifications are registered under 'Creative Commons' licensure, and may be freely applied by anyone (Mehta, 2017).

3.3.1. Role and Function

Open Services for Lifespan Collaboration (OSLC) can be defined as a group of specifications which are created to streamline tool integration along the software provision lifecycle. The technology was developed in reaction to some long-lasting impediments to effective applications for lifecycle items, OSLC promotes the development of large-scale and sustainable incorporations in a heterogeneous device environment.

Applying the model with linked information and WWW proprieties, OSLC specifications offer a standard technique for developing integrations autonomous of product APIs. Similarly, OSLC specifications minimize tool incompatibilities as well as free operators from being restricted to particular products or product editions (Mehta, 2017).

Integration-specific information store eliminates the need for map data forms amongst systems and eliminates obstacles between tools. This ensures that the user can easily access product information directly and efficiently. Ultimately, OSLC facilitates information access without complicated installations or configurations which other integrations typically require.

Tools, which use OSLC stipulations, can more effortlessly maintain tool incorporations from diverse vendors and improved share data among tools. For instance, a quality administration tool can solidly integrate with a change administration structure to log and trace software defects. Similarly, OSLC specifications are formed by workgroups within the OSLC community (Mehta, 2017).

3.3.2. Integration Basics

In case a product is facilitated as an Open Solution for Lifecycle Corporation (OSLC) provider or client, you can develop your own integration. Furthermore, the descriptions and resources which are described offer a good introduction to the application. Data about OSLC enablement additionally can be found on the OSLC website's Resources page.

Integrations, which are developed with OSLC, depend on OSLC Core requirement and domain specifications. The key specification defines basic integration procedures, use of RDF (Resource Definition Framework) and HTTP, while also identifying the common features which every OSLC solution supports. Domain provisions are personalized to a specific ALM area, like change management, requirements management, test supervision or architecture management (Segall et al, 2018).

Domain specifications also conform to the core specifications. For instance, the change control specification describes a broad set of formats, resources, and RESTful applications for use in modification management tools (consumers), plus by provider tools. Furthermore, specifications define a batch of computing services or formats useful for interacting with various lifecycle implements. These specifications don't seek to standardize the performance of an apparatus or cluster of tools. Before beginning any work with OSLC specifications, it is essential to get familiar with programs such as the Eclipse Lyo copyreader, and with various basic OSLC concepts.

The OSLC service providers offer implementation of OSLC solutions. A service provider gives consumers the necessary information for checking the links to resources and clear previews of the ultimate resource. An OSLC consumer, on the other hand, is a web system that uses resources, which a service provider offers (Segall et al, 2018).

Each object in the lifecycle gets represented by the HTTP resource, which has a URI on its name. Additionally, this object can be manipulated through HTTP methods, such as POST, GET or PUT. Each artefact or resource consists of an RDF representation which has a subject, predicate, and object. For instance, when linking up from a basic requirement to sample case, the RDF exemplification shows the prerequisite as its content matter, the kind of relationship or resource form as its predicate, and the test sample as its object.

There are various resources for creating integrations. Eclipse Lyo is a powerful computing tool for helping users to adopt OSLC stipulations and develop OSLC-compliant tools. It comprises an application development toolkit which is written in Java, a sample suite to help guarantee that your adaptation is OSLC-compliant. It contains a reference system with working samples, including a basic server which you can apply for testing (Mehta, 2017).

3.3.3. Post-Installation Tasks

Most OSLC-based integrations have common post-installation roles to establish strong communications between incorporated applications. Some of these include the following:

- *Server cross-communication:* Safe networking among servers for incorporated applications should be established. For some business computing products, the networking is based on server friending. Basically, a server-friend is one which permits communication with different friend servers in quite a safe way. You need to establish strong server communications from each software of your integrations. As an example, when one uses the HP ALM Rational Adapter to operate with other business applications, one should create server submissions for each application. As an operator, you need to approve every request individually from the primary server as well. Based on your security system, you may be required to develop OAuth consumer keys also.
- *Project associations:* After cross-server networking is established through requesting and approving safe access to application information stores, you can form project associations. The project space association permits users to develop links from artefacts, such as test cases, work objects, and requirements in a single project zone to artefacts present in another project space. In cases, where the projects are integrated, it means operators can use services such as change requests, requirements, and quality projects to system like the Rational ALM task which are being connected to. These facilities are defined by the link forms you choose while configuring projects. Data for supported link categories is also available in the Extension product function subjects in your Rational item help section.

3.4. DB2 DATABASE

Database applications are used by businesses to store and incorporate data compiled at various times. They allow for data changes and new applications to be implemented. DB2 is an advanced AI database, which is helpful for companies seeking to develop the necessary architecture for supporting their

AI implementation. Similarly, administration, assimilation, and business-intelligence play significant roles in the journey of a business implementing AI to streamline its operations.

This application is also developed to store, process, and retrieve information efficiently. The system is further enhanced with support of Product-Oriented functions and non-relational systems with XML. A catalogue or a database refers to a group of Tables, Buffer pools, Schemas, Logs, Storage structures, and Tablespaces working mutually to handle database processes efficiently (Lin and Huang, 2011).

3.4.1. Database Directory

Database directory refers to an organized depository of databases. Once you form a database, it is important that all the details concerning database are kept in a database catalogue, such as details of default storing devices, configuration archives, and provisional tables list among others.

Partitioned global directory may be developed in the instance file. This directory features all universal information allied to the database. Basically, this partition universal directory is called NODExxxx/SQLyyy, whereas xxxx is the information partition integer and yyy functions as the database token.

As for the partition-global catalogue, mostly a member-specific listing is created. The directory comprises of local database information, while the member-specific catalogue is called MEMBERxxxx whereby xxxx is considered a member number. Additionally, DB2 Enterprise Server Version environment operates as a single member, plus has just one user specific directory. The member specific directory is uniquely referenced as MEMBER0000 (Lin and Huang, 2011).

3.4.2. Computing Sequences

A sequence refers to a software system that produces integer numbers in form of an ascending or descending format and over a definite range in order to produce main key and coordinate various other keys within the table. The sequence is used for providing numeral integers say, for worker_id or transaction_id. Similarly, a sequence may support various data types such as BIGINT, INTEGER, DECIMAL, and SMALLINT.

Plus, a sequence may be shared among different applications. The structure is incremented or reduced irrespective of transactions, and a sequence is formed through the CREATE SEQUENCE configuration. There are two forms of sequences that can be used. The first one is NEXTVAL which delivers an incremented worth for sequence numbers, as well as PREVIOUS VALUE that returns a freshly generated value.

3.4.3. Ways that DB2 Database Can Benefit Businesses

Figure 3.2: Company staff accessing business data through their workstations.

Source: https://www.gettyimages.com/detail/photo/technician-with-laptop-checking-server-in-data-royalty-free-image/595460884.

The updated version of DB2 Database known as Db2 11.5 is developed for – and run by – AI. It allows for running queries considerably faster, supports prevalent data science languages as well as frameworks, while also making it easier to execute natural-language querying. All these factors, among others, constitute some of the key ways that Db2 11.5 can aid your business to go ahead of the market.

This technology ensures that business data is readily available, no matter the place where it resides. Furthermore, the typical SQL engine (CSE) present in Db2 11.5 offers improved access to information within various systemic offerings, so that users can offer more holistic insights. The CSE's in-built data federation permits users to access information from Db2 family renderings like Db2 Warehouse, Integrated Analytics System, Db2 Big SQL, including existing Pure Data systems for Analytics (Netezza). Because of these federation capabilities, there can be enhanced information access to Microsoft (MS) SQL Server, Oracle, and Teradata, including cloud sources such as Amazon Redshift and liberal-source solutions like Hive (Lin and Huang, 2011).

Furthermore, as a business application, Db2 is deployable almost anywhere. The number of deployment opportunities for Db2 is constantly growing. Db2 delivers the same expertise and functions across on-premises, cloud options, and hosted systems so that operators can leverage existing knowledge and rationalize transitions between the physical space and cloud. Besides, Db2 can be employed on a range of open cloud platforms such as IBM Cloud and Amazon Web Services for users to continue or initiate the multi-cloud plan.

System performance is similarly optimized. Employing Workload Management, Db2 11.5 mechanically manages the resources while scheduling the implementation for its workloads. It allows for fine-grain resource distribution, monitoring, and supervision of workloads depending on service groups, workload features, elapsed time, period of the day, and so much more. Consequently, users can concentrate on more vital roles than simply monitoring system performance (Lin and Huang, 2011).

Not only that, but the technology allows Queries to be processed much quicker.

The business queries run much faster compared to previous programs, since it monitors SQL activity over time and connects it with queries through applying machine learning (ML) algorithms. This permits models to be formed and restructured for particular SQL statements.

Additionally, DB2 databases support confidence-based querying which ensures data results are made more precise. Db2 11.5 further uses ML technology to assess SQL query results, as well as score them depending on their accuracy. Thereafter, it can apply those scores for ranking or reordering results, giving users higher amounts of confidence for the insights they'll use to propel their business.

With DBs, companies can also benefit from streamlined and easy to upgrade IT and computer operations. They can begin with the free version, move to Db2 Standard Edition, then moving over to Db2 Advanced Edition in case their business develops to require the necessary level of scalability. Besides, all three editions use the same program base, meaning it may not be easy to scale up or down (Lin and Huang, 2011).

3.4.4. Importance of Computing in Business

Almost any business uses computers for performing its functions. Right from creating reports to linking with clients, computers perform a lot in terms of ensuring efficiency for businesses to run. The machine has taken the business world a long way, back from the days of papers, pens, and folders kept in large storage compartments to digital storage options that are way more efficient.

Whether it is in production, marketing or the distribution process, computer applications help to fast-track business processes and operations for increased productivity. Technology is very important in automating functions, thereby reducing costs and increasing throughput. Moreover, it allows for faster communication with clients through the internet, online networking tools, and web phone system. Plus, important for fostering the management of both large and small organizations, including various fields responsible for managing resources and business prospects (Lin and Huang, 2011).

Enhancing communication: In matters of establishing strong contacts with clients, technology plays a key role in both creating and maintaining that contact. It allows corporate bodies to connect with clients through applications like email, IM, collaboration software, and Skype, including different other communication solutions which a company may wish to use.

Whenever a business is able to stay in touch with the clients, it becomes simpler for customers to make inquiries with the business, or request for more details about the services or products that the company offers. It also gets easier for the company to provide customer support solutions to its customers in a timely, proficient manner. The company shall also be in a position to keep its clients updated on any fresh developments regarding the business.

Communication is more than just the business' clients. A company must also communicate well with its personnel, and computing plays a role in that too. Instead of having time-wasting personal meetings with workers, managers can easily email their personnel or message them about any other suitable communication platform. Essentially, this saves time and expands the internal communication channels of the business (Mehta, 2017).

Marketing: Through modern technology, a company's department of IT developers are able to create professional websites equipped with attractive graphics and material with various forms of media, like images, text, and videos. Additionally, computer technology allows for search engine optimization or SEO, so that a website can appear more conspicuously in the results page, this then draws traffic, which, eventually, will allow the company to sell their items to website visitors.

With computer science, a company can develop and execute holistic marketing campaigns which span across different social media apps on the internet. A business can generate ads to be displayed on websites or social media systems, through special software, besides it can also purchase marketing solutions from other companies – all linked to the web (Mehta, 2017).

Accounting: Accounting is a function where accuracy is very important. While doing accounting, having only a pen and paper may not help since you're exposed to errors, but an accounting software may help avoid that from happening. An accounting software allows businesses to quickly and precisely obtain clear reports of the firm's financial status. All the operator must do is adding their financial details into the software, plus – with just some few clicks – the operator shall be able to understand everything concerning the financial status of their business' operations.

Similarly, computers are crucial for tasks like invoicing customers; managing details on debtors and creditors; planning payroll, calculating, and preparing tax forms, including various other functions. Through technology, accountants are now able to concentrate on the greater picture in terms of business financing, delegating the lower level work to the machines.

Storage: Companies have come quite a long way since the age of filing cabinets all thanks to computers. Even though a filing cabinet may occupy a huge space in the office, it stores just a small portion of information. Technology will occupy just a tiny fraction of the space; however, it can store a lot more information than filing cabinets. With processors and servers, businesses can store and categorize millions of files, allowing the company to access whichever files they want at any time.

Similarly, they allow businesses to store their data in various ways. They could store it in a central place, or have other workstations on the network gain access to stored data whenever a user needs to, or when the company has official permission to retrieve the data. Not just is virtual storage much larger compared to physical storage with regards to capacity, it's also way more efficient due to the amount of sorting which takes place, that's among the top benefits of technology. Digital storage is likewise more secure, since it's much harder to lose or breach files from an encrypted database (Mehta, 2017).

Preparing business documents: Most companies need to produce different documents during their day to day operations, which can either be in form of printed documents or spreadsheets. Technology provides word processors and database software to assist with this. Through these two kinds of software, a company can produce nearly everything, including memos, letters, tutorials, reports, and ads for their day to day operations.

Likewise, spreadsheet applications allow businesses to manage alphanumeric data and arrange it into graphs, tables, diagrams, and reports. Yet another type of software which many businesses use is the presentation software. Through it, a corporate agency can prepare slides for presentations, whether internal or external, useful for their customers. They can also make reports, letters, and memos through word processing applications, either for distribution to clients or just internal use. Generally, a computer has lots of productivity software which a business is able to use for making its functions simpler; this is software which allows the company to be quicker and more efficient in its functions.

Skills development: Technology can be applied to educate staff. A business might use a processor to educate employees on various matters such as the business policy, software use, and standard policies and safety. Instead of hiring tutors to train its employees, a company can allow employees to learn what they need personally, through learning at their unique pace through live Q&A forums and webinars. Through the web, a business' staff members can have access to vast information around the world. At the same time, the business won't have to develop all of its unique educational content. Technology also allows workers to learn in such a way that's enjoyable. Staffs can learn through different modern media, like text, videos, or even games, allowing them to fully understand the subject material.

Similarly, computer science can be applied for business research purposes. They allow companies to do various things, such as researching about their competition, or what the customers really want. Using modern data-mining procedures, a business may acquire insightful data about its clients as well as competition details from various places, such as forums, web engines, sector-specific websites as well as social networks (Mehta, 2017).

Other key roles of computing in business: When companies want to print their marketing or advertising material, oftentimes they use computer programs. Marketing and ads are the lifeline of any business, particularly for small businesses and home-based companies to survive. However, to create quality marketing and advertising content, they must use common computer applications like Adobe Photoshop, Corel Draw, MS Office and Adobe Illustrator among others, which are available on the computer.

Figure 3.3: The smartphone is increasingly being used to connect businesses and consumers.

Source: http://lcmsuccess.com/lcmultimate.php.

In the absence of technology, it would be tough to form such marketing content (photos, videos, slideshows, letterheads, business cards, and brochures) fast and accurately. Besides, using computer applications for purposes of creating online and offline promotion materials is also possible.

Furthermore, nowadays companies can hire workers through digital means. By using the internet, job applicants are able to send in their credentials to the company for review instantly, without having to visit the office physically to deliver their papers. Not only that, but they can actually use their Smartphones to apply for positions rather than a traditional computer.

Moreover, using technology to access to hire freelance staff online or remote workers from different geographical location is possible. Rather than hiring permanent employees, which can be costly especially for startups or short-term projects, a company can hire remote workers to complete certain projects on a fixed rate, this cuts down the rate of doing business both online and offline for businesses.

Nowadays, millions of people search the internet daily for business ideas, blogging tips, travel advice and so much more. This shows that technology and computer science in particular plays a significant role in our daily lives. Nearly every sector of the economy is connected to computing in one way or another, and therefore it is important for businesses to embrace this modern trend in order to remain profitable in the market and take advantage of the opportunities that technology provides (Mehta, 2017).

3.5. COMPUTER SCIENCE SKILLS RELEVANT TO THE MODERN BUSINESS WORLD

Figure 3.4: A helpdesk staff using technology to respond to the company's clients.

Source: https://weskussakekamer.co.za/small-business-owner-why-you-need-computer-skills/.

As an employee looking to enter the business world, there are certain computing skills you must have in order to increase your chances of success. This shouldn't be taken by surprise, particularly because computers have become an essential component of doing business in the current age. With smartphones and tablets further playing a major role in commercial activities since the 2000s.

Effective computer science education should prepare students to use technology effectively and resourcefully, no matter the sector where it is being applied. Here are some of the essential computing skills which are relevant to business:

3.5.1. Master Microsoft Office

There is no doubt that most people living today have used MS Suites, especially Word, Excel, and PowerPoint which are the most popular. The MS Office software is acknowledged as the standard tool across many industries. In case you have any kind of office job, then you're expected to be proficient in at least one or more MS programs. The application features a variety of unique software with special functions, which may further complement each other. Of all the accessible tools, the most popular are Word and Excel. The former is used for processing and developing of word documents, while Excel is useful for creating spreadsheets (Lin and Huang, 2011).

For Word, formatting is a crucial skill to learn, which involves modifying font design and size, putting bullet points and headings among other related formatting tasks. It's a necessary skill for anybody who handles computers. It's also crucial to learn how to create and use templates. Based on your role in the business, you might be handling custom report templates which are unique to your organization. Learning how to operate these templates or developing fresh ones is a valuable skill to acquire.

Similarly, having excellent MS Excel skills is indispensable. Excel formulas in particular serve a crucial role in nearly every task, project or business operation. They help users to compute the value of various cells and are applied in different ways based on what your objectives are. Comprehending the essentials of Excel formulas shall help you develop a better grasp on more complicated functions and gain greater respect from other colleagues (Lin and Huang, 2011).

Just as important is reporting. Formulating excel reports is quite a common activity in business establishments, since data is often professionally featured on spreadsheets. In fact, most employers require their employees to have some basic understanding on how to formulate an Excel report. You must also get familiar with pivot tables.

The pivot table allows users to reorganize data in a spreadsheet, so as to extract the information they need. This function is especially practical when working with large volumes of data, plus it is used widely across different sectors to prepare reports instantly.

3.5.2. Code Navigation

Among the most undervalued skills for computer programmers is code navigation, or finding quick ways around a project. Some computing novices become lost in codebases since they haven't trained in this skill sufficiently. It may seem like a rather small thing, however, being able to evaluate and understand what's happening with an existent code is a crucial aspect of programming.One simple code navigation is Back/Forward, which can be activated by pressing (ALT+← / →). It's by far the quickest way to navigate from a section of a file onto another. While there are people who say that CTRL+TAB does literally the same function, still the former is a more comprehensive feature as it preserves history in venues on the same folder. Besides the history is reserved even after applying this shortcut (you can navigate back/forth but not change the real history).

In addition, to navigate over to the subsequent error, you only require to press (F8). When doing refactoring, this function is among the best to use. Simply hit F8 and adjust every particular error until you completely run out, plus have completed refactoring. It would be just a breeze to rectify errors using this function. Similarly, you can steer rearward (to the preceding error) by pressing SHIFT + F8. However, one issue with this command is that there's no way to navigate through just the errors or simply the warnings (Lin and Huang, 2011).

3.5.3. Online Networking

It wasn't very long ago when the best means to connect with co-workers was through email. Currently, however, apps like Workplace and Slack from Facebook provide users the ability to direct messages to teams or individuals instantaneously.

The best part is that these processes are quite simple to learn — the activity is more like transferring a text message for communication with friends. Nevertheless, you must work on brushing up your communication skills so as to be more effective in online networking (Mehta, 2017).

There are various things that you must remember when using Workplace or Slack. First, they're professional tools, meaning some topics and language are prohibited to use. Furthermore, as a newbie, you may want to check the business culture before getting too active. If users don't post messages on the platform after work hours, for instance, take heed not to breach that unspoken rule.Same as with email, you can easily send a wrong text to the wrong individual. It's therefore recommended to be keen when sending messages through these systems. For example, if putting out a complaint about the manager, don't do this in a group forum where the manager is a member (Mehta, 2017).

3.5.4. Business Process Modeling

Business process modeling or BPM refers to the process of representing systems of an organization in business, such that the present process can be analyzed, enhanced, and computerized. BPM is usually done by business analysts that offer expertise in the entire modeling procedure.

The business goal is often to enhance process speed or minimize cycle time; including to improve quality; or minimize costs like labor, scrap, materials or capital expenses. In practice, the management choice to invest in corporate process modeling is frequently motivated by the requirement to document needs for information technology (IT) projects. Oftentimes, change management programs are required to put any advanced business systems into practice. Through improvements in software development (SD), the goal of BPM systems becoming completely executable is getting closer to reality.

In computing, a business model is defined as a structure for developing social, economic, and various other kinds of value. The word 'business model' is hence used for a wide variety of formal and informal definitions to represent crucial features of a business, such as purpose, strategies, offerings, organizational structures, infrastructure, operational processes, trading systems, and policies.

In its most plain sense, a digital business model refers to a group of related, organized activities or duties that produce a particular service or item (serving a definite goal) for a given customer or clienteles. Basically, there are 3 kinds of business processes.

The first one is management processing software which determines systemic operations, some common management systems include strategic management and corporate governance. There are also operational processes, constituting the main business and forming the core value stream. Some common operational processes include procuring, manufacturing, marketing, and sales. In addition, computers can be used for supporting processes which promote the core business processes like accounting, technical support, and recruitment (Segall et al, 2018).

A business process may further be decomposed into various sub-processes, each having its own unique attributes, while also contributing towards attaining the objective of the super-procedure. Through computer systems, an operator can analyze business processes which typically include mapping of procedures and sub-processes up to activity level. The corporate process model refers to a system where one or more corporate processes are managed by a computing system, further covering the ways that operations are performed to accomplish certain intended goals of a business. Such a model, however, continues being an abstraction and relies on the projected use of the structure. It can define the workflow or incorporation between corporate processes, plus it can be developed at multiple levels.

A workflow is defined as a portrayal of a set of operations, defined as the work of an individual, of a basic or complex structure, of a collection of persons, an arrangement of staff, or even of business equipment. Workflow can be defined as any conception of real work, subdivided into work split, workshare, and other forms of ordering. In terms of control, workflow might be seen as an actual work under a given business aspect (Segall et al, 2018).

Similarly, the artefact-centric corporate process model has grown to become a holistic system for modeling business systems, since it offers a highly flexible model for capturing operational specifications needed in business processing. It specifically focuses on defining business system data, commonly known as "artefacts." This is done by digitally characterizing corporate-relevant data systems, life-cycles, and related solutions. Similarly, the artefact-centric structural modeling system promotes the automation of commerce operations, while supporting workflow flexibility in terms of enactment and progression.

3.5.5. Software Development

Software drives the global business environment. Current work-life is inseparable from the internet, including computer and smartphones. Software represents the vital cog that makes all these machines to run.

There are 3 pillars to software development (SD) which include: human (user) side, business side, and technical side. These pillars are essential in achieving positive outcomes in business and they help in supporting any development team (Segall et al, 2018).

Complexity demands creativity: Working with SD can be considered a challenging task for both businesses and developmental teams. Projects are complicated and demanding. Similarly, software developers deal with complex business matters or issues which are complicated for the client.

Blending together business and operator needs should be the ultimate goal of any software expert. Making quality software needs great analytical skills from the application designer. They must lessen its complexity into comprehensible and programmable elements. Furthermore, creativity is needed to find the ideal approach to handle the technical complexities.

Humans are complicated beings, plus industry and the world which we live in also has a high range of complexity and diversity. Change is often defined as the modern constant. Individuals and organizations need to learn techniques for dealing with the above-mentioned pillars of SD. As the rate of change is heightening, the lifespan of firms is declining. Meaning humans, who essentially dislike change, need to learn how to adopt it so as to be successful.

3.6. SOFTWARE DEVELOPMENT ACTIVITIES

Figure 3.5: Business intelligence allows entrepreneurs to keep track of vital processes like sales digitally.

Source: https://www.chetu.com/blogs/technical-perspectives/sap-business-objects-and-intelligence-solutions.php.

3.6.1. Identifying the Need

The creativity sources for software items are abundant. These ideas may come from industry research comprising of demographics of prospective new customers, present customers, sales leads who rejected the item, other internal application development staff, or even innovative third parties.

Potential concepts for software items are typically first assessed by marketing staffs for economic viability, for fit with present channels distribution, likely effects on present product lines, requisite features, plus for fit with an organization's marketing goals (Preece, Sharp, and Rogers, 2015).In a marketing assessment stage, the price and time considerations become appraised. A decision is arrived at early during the initial phase on whether, depending on the more comprehensive information produced by the promotion or development group, the project ought to be pursued further. Scholars note that oftentimes students of marketing only learn marketing, but are seldom exposed to other disciplines like financing or engineering. Many people become specialists in only one field. To further complicate issues, very few people meet with interdisciplinary staff in the workforce, meaning there are very few roles to copy.

Similarly, software product formation is essential to the development process, and definitely needs understanding of several disciplines. Since SD can involve compromising or reaching beyond what's needed by the customer, a SD program may spread into less technical issues like human resources, intellectual property, risk management, budgeting, and crisis mitigation. These procedures may further cause the function of business development for overlapping with software formation (Lin and Huang, 2011).

Planning: Planning is essential for every computer science activity, especially those involving discovery of matters belonging to a particular project. One crucial task in developing a software product is removing the requirements or stipulation analysis. Clients normally have an abstract concept of what they require as an end outcome, but don't realize what software must do. Trained and experienced software experts recognize incomplete, vague, or even contradictory needs at this stage.

Frequently describing live code can help minimize the chances that the possible requirements are incorrect. Even though a lot of effort is needed in the requirements phase to ensure that the requirements are comprehensive and consistent, but rarely that's the situation; leaving the application design stage as the most prominent one in terms of reducing the effects of fresh or changing needs.

Sometimes, requirements volatility may be challenging since they affect future or ongoing development efforts. When the basic requirements are collected from the client, then an inquiry of the developmental scope must be determined and openly stated. It's often referred to as a scope report.

Designing: When the requirements have been established, next the software design may be formed in a software planning document. This entails a primary or top-level design of the central modules with a comprehensive picture of how different parts fit with each other.

Both the language, operation system, and hardware modules must be understood at this time. Thereafter, a detailed or model design is developed, possibly with prototyping being validation-of-concept or for firming up requirements.

Execution, testing, and documenting: Execution is the aspect of the process whereby software designers basically program the code to fit the project. Moreover, software testing forms an integral and significant part of SD procedure. This aspect of the process guarantees that defects are detected as soon as feasible.

In some procedures, generally referred to as test-based development, the tests might be developed just prior to implementation and act as a lead for the implementation's accuracy. Detailing the internal software design for future purposes, preservation, and enhancement is performed throughout the development stage.

This might also include scripting of an API, whether internal or external. The software designing process selected by the developing group shall describe how much internal recording (if any) is needed. Plan-based models normally produce more documentation compared to agile models.

Deployment and maintenance: Deployment begins directly following the code testing process, including approval for release, plus sold or otherwise circulated into a production setting. This might involve installation, personalization (like establishing parameters to the client's values), testing, as well as possibly a lengthy period of assessment.

Both software training and assistance are essential, since software is only effectual when it's used correctly. Additionally, maintaining, and enhancing applications to cope with freshly detected errors or requirements may take considerable time and effort, since missed requirements might force redesigning of the software. For some cases, maintenance is needed on a systematic arrangement to fix reported matters and ensure the software keeps running.

3.6.2. Importance of Maintaining Business Value

Everything a software designer does must contribute to its business value. In case you are a developer, you probably like the technical part, such as coming up with the most inventive and creative solution. Though focusing just on this feature, may develop a product not (wholly) covering business or user needs, or moving overboard on working hours and deadlines.Keep in mind, a business may only persist if it generates value. The word value doesn't just refer to a fully monetary value. Other factors like client value, mental capital, and worker satisfaction are equally business values (Mehta, 2017).

It's where the "human" side of the designer becomes of key significance. In daily operational exercise, the developer must define the corporate value so that the Product Owner can "sell" the product to the internal system. Designers often accept that the rate of a 200hr refactoring is evident. Practically, this isn't not always the case. Furthermore, the PO will have to answer queries like "how can the 200hrs be gained back?"

3.6.3. Reasons Why Soft Skills are Important?

While the tide looks like it is slowly changing, development of soft skills still doesn't get enough priority throughout one's education. A research by Harvard University, Stanford Research Center and Carnegie Foundation found out that 85% of job achievement comes from having great soft and people skills, whereas only 15% of job success originates from technical abilities and knowledge (often called the hard skills).

Furthermore, soft skills, such as verbal or non-verbal communication, compassion, and teamwork are vital in achieving business value. If lacking soft skills, developing software and communicating business values may not succeed. Furthermore, underestimation of these Soft Skill abilities, is the leading cause for most software programs to fail or budgeting getting out of control (Mehta, 2017).

SD teams should understand that, in contrast to well scripted and logic code, people tend to display occasionally illogical and irrational traits. Besides, there's no way that great UX product or a progressive API, will assist developers to cope with their lacking of soft skills.

3.7. PROJECT MANAGEMENT

Nowadays, project managers are increasingly moving their staffs and processes online in order to stay ahead of competition and provide at a faster delivery rate than previously.

Through online project management, networking software and cloud filing storage networks, work towards getting matters done competently and with greater results. These virtual project managers comprise the fresh faces that make up digital management, besides if you're seeking to delve into the field, then you must start preparing immediately.

3.7.1. What's Online Project Management?

It's a rationalized process of managing virtual projects from onset to completion, on budget and employing various useful resources. It entails planning, allotting, tracking, assessing, and measuring results — typically all done through project management application. The objective of each project is different, though the overarching goal is to nurture business and enjoy decent ROI from their project. Forms of projects may vary from events to online content projects. Moreover, digital projects are available in different forms, including websites, e-commerce, mobile apps and advertising among other factors (Mehta, 2017).

3.7.2. Duties of a Virtual Project Manager

The goal of a virtual project manager is ensuring that all the essential deliverables for the project are finished and delivered on time as well as on budget. Lately, project managers have assumed responsibility for ensuring that the project also conforms to business goals. Besides, for certain tasks, understanding the best ways to execute projects online is of utmost importance.

Essentially, digital project managers ensure that all aspects of the project proceed smoothly. This may include; clearing roadblocks, assigning duties and deadlines, and planning regular check-ins. The virtual project manager's job description may vary depending on the kind of project or the tool the firm uses to supervise those projects.

Some businesses may need you to already possess some experience about a certain tool, meanwhile others may train the appropriate candidate on the particular project (Mehta, 2017).

Typically, qualified candidates should have experience with matters such as planning, directing, and coordination of technology projects as well as teams.

The professional may further report to other higher offices within the business. A successful project manager should be capable of networking with other experts at the highest administrative levels within the clientele base. For fulfilling these roles, it's necessary for digital project executives to be updated on modern technology trends.

3.7.3. Basic Skills Required for Online Project Management

Figure 3.6: Technology provides modern tools for managing business projects more efficiently.

Source: https://bppbusiness.com/online-project-management-tool-a-brief-overview/.

Various digital project management skills can be acquired through simple work experience and partnership. Skills like planning, organization, resource management, time management, delegation of duties and project communication management may be cultivated in nearly any role. Nevertheless, there are certain online project management programs, publications, and certificates which you can acquire through the web for standing out against any competition.

The skill set of each digital project executive is unique and reliant on their personal experience and background. Ensure that you are continually learning ways of enhancing your project management abilities. Even so, some of the skills you may need in this profession include; problem solving, solid communication skills, strong organizational abilities and attention to detail among others (Mehta, 2017).

3.7.4. Digital Project Management Systems

Every project manager employs a unique virtual project management technique, depending on the organization, group, and the project. There are no two projects which can be the same, since they will likely need unique procedures or methodologies.

However, there are various options to choose from. Among the most common project management techniques fall into two groups which include waterfall or agile. The first consists of methodologies which are conventional project management approaches, such as building scopes, resources management and progressing in phases. These procedures are popular since they are direct and sequential. They work particularly well in construction tasks where one factor must be completed so that another thing may be launched (Mehta, 2017).

Agile applications provide a highly evolved methodology for project management, which is built on flexibility and collaboration. Even though waterfall follows a strict policy plan, the agile framework enables teams to react swiftly and efficiently. It further allows the customer or stakeholder to get involved at various stages and ensure that their expectations are met before going forward.

Additionally, there are various virtual project management tools that can be utilized. For instance, cloud-hosted project management and networking tools permit project managers to take advantage of the entire power of virtual project management. Acting as a primary source of truth, these systems show you precisely where the project status lies in real time.

These resources allow users to connect with team members, administrative stakeholders, collaborators, and others in real, using up-to-date information. It means you can minimize on status-update meetings, and save your team time for doing the implementation. Furthermore, it is important to keep all files, photos, and data in a cloud project management system or document storage tool such that people may download the documents they need require just when they require them. All information is placed in a centralized place. This enables the team to go forward without waiting for any response. It also keeps projects on track. Similarly, work feedback might be kept in one place, so that you can easily reference it when necessary. There are absolutely no arguments about who is accountable for what since all matters are visibly documented in a single place where everyone can access (Mehta, 2017).

In addition, if a key team player unexpectedly takes leave for some days, this can cause some significant delay in your program. Still, by using project management equipment together with Gantt charts, you can find a solution for such kinds of situations. Simply check your Gantt chart and determine if you can accept to wait so that your team member can return back. In case you want to wait, then just re-arrange the duties on your Gantt graph to showcase your new deliverable periods, and have the team understand that they must look at the updated schedule. If, however, you can't wait, then just reassign the work.

Since this project management technology allows the original assignee to track progress in the virtual project management instrument, it means the new assignee must have all the data they require to effortlessly pick up from where their colleague left off (Mehta, 2017).

Furthermore, when you arrange your projects and duties in a virtual project management instrument shared with your teammates, it means stakeholders can effortlessly determine where a particular work project lies. Everybody has access into who's given what role, when jobs are due, the stage that work is in, those bottlenecking progress, plus what's coming next. Basically, you're empowering team members on your project by providing them the knowledge which they require to be effective.

Digital project management can mean different things to people, depending on their type of business and particular project being undertaken. For some ventures, for instance, the cloud can be used for storage of files and documentations, while in others it can be applied for distant communications among stakeholders.

Generally, computer science and technology provide a faster, efficient, and convenient way of managing business transactions. Some common uses of computing in business include matters such as accounting systems, sale point systems and management information systems (MIS). No matter how large or small your company is, technology provides tangible benefits to help you generate the results which you want customers to experience, and increase profitability as well (Mehta, 2017).

CHAPTER

4

Where Computer Science and Linguistics Meet

CONTENTS

4.1. INTRODUCTION

Linguistics has a strong correlation with language thereby linguistics refers to the study of language. From the term linguistics, we get the term linguists which refers to the person who studies linguistics. There is a great need to study the language. This is because for one to be able to correctly and accurately use a language they have to have a great understanding of the given language. In the world today, there is a great appreciation for diversity. This also applies to language. There are various languages used among people in the world today for instance Latin, Belgium, and German among others. To come up with such languages, some aspects have to be considered. For instance, what syllables will be put together, the sound of the words and the pronunciation of the words among others (Vetulani, 2011).

It also involves sentence construction. The words have to be properly placed so that the sentence makes sense and the recipient of the message will be able to understand what is being said. This brings about the need for linguistics. It can research the various languages around and also assist in coming up with new languages. Linguistics is useful in countries in which the citizens speak different languages. The government will be able to choose the most appropriate language that can be used by all the citizens and also in official matters such as discussing bills in parliament.

The study of linguistics involves various phenomena. They include phonetics, syntax, grammar, morphology, and phonology among others (Vetulani, 2011). Phonetics refers to the study of sounds in speech. The sounds being studied may be in their physical aspects. For the sounds in a speech to be right, various things should come into place. For instance, the position of the mouth, teeth, and tongue may affect how a word sound. Linguistics involves studying the different kinds of sounds that have been produced and the identification of the different sounds that have been produced. As there are people with disabilities for them more so the deaf, phonetics is used in sign language when making the different shapes and movements and also the use of physical space.

Phonetics has brought about the term phonology. This refers to the use of phonetics in a given order so that the sounds and signs are arranged in a given system. It is more involved in ensuring that the terms used are constructive when used. This brings about the replacement of certain sounds in a statement so that there is a constructive meaning. It involves certain aspects such as rhythm, tone, and phrases. Phonologists study how the vowels and constants can be constructively used. They also study how the placement of the syllables can affect the pronunciation of different words (Vetulani, 2011).Morphology deals with the formation of words. For individual words to be formed, it requires the combination of small chunks of words that are meaningful. For instance, the word unite is made up of two parts that are (un) which refers to the reverse process of action and the second part is (tie) which refers to the closing of something, for instance, a shoelace among others. With the use of this phenomenon, complex words have been formed. This has been a useful resource more so for students who participate in spelling bees as they can accurately separate words to correctly spell big letter words. Syntax deals with the study of phrases, clauses, and sentence construction.

Linguists have to know grammar to join different verbs and suggest different phrases. They also use the knowledge so that they can create a set of rules which enable people to create sentences that are grammatically correct and easily understandable. The rule may involve the outline of the word in a sentence. For a person to correctly use a word in a sentence they have to have meaning. This brings about the term semantics which is the study of meaning. Different words have different meanings and some words have similar pronunciation but different meanings. Linguists, therefore, have to identify such words so that they can make a clear distinction between those words.

Discourse analysis focuses on the bigger chunks of language such as texts, conversations, stories, and speeches among others. The different types of these use language differently. For instance, there can even be differences in how a language is used based on various aspects such as the genre. Discourse analysis is used in making phrases such as once upon a time and at the beginning that have mostly been used in the storytelling sessions more so for children. Linguistics is a broad chapter that contains several branches. For instance, there is historical linguistics. This branch of linguistics deals with the study on the changes in language over some time (Vetulani, 2011).

As time goes by, new languages are being invented and changes are being made to the existing ones. Some of the changes may include the meaning of the word or even pronunciation. Linguists use the different aspects of linguistics such as grammar and syntax to identify the previously present languages. Sociolinguistics is another branch of linguistics. This branch involves the study of society and language. It deals with the study of how the different languages are used in different environments such as church and markets among others.

It investigates the variation in a particular language and how it correlates with social factors such as speaker age, ethnic identity, and location (Vetulani, 2011). Psycholinguistics deals with the formation of language in the brain. It mostly entails studying the brains' reactions to different stimuli. Applied linguistics deals with the application of linguistics in real-life situations. Stylistics deals with the study of literature and language. Comparative linguistics is the study of the different available languages and their respective linguistic systems. Computational linguistics. This branch deals with the application of computer science in linguistics. It also entails the use of computers in linguistics. This leads us to the topic of the application of computer science and technology in linguistics. There are several applications of computer science and technology in linguistics. They include the following:

4.2. USE OF TECHNOLOGY IN STORING OF LINGUISTICAL DATA

Linguists get to interact with voluminous amounts of data. Of course, this attributed to the fact that several languages are being used in the world today. The use of technologies has availed a variety of storage devices for linguists. In the current world, the different computing devices offer some kind of storage memory that linguists can use in storing information. There are basically two main types of storage. They include static and dynamic storage. Static storage is referred to as non-volatile storage while dynamic storage is volatile. There are a variety of storage technologies that linguists use in storing data. There are three main types of storage technologies that are used. They include magnetic storage, optical storage, and solid-state storage (Hausser, 2013).

4.2.1. Magnetic Storage

Magnetic storage is a storage technology that works by encoding data in various patterns. The patterns can either be of positive or negative magnetic polarity. The data is stored on some magnetic medium like organic metal. They include devices like floppy disks, tape recorder cassettes, and hard disks that use magnetic storage technology. For the hard disks, their insides are made up of round platters which are made of metal oxide material and they rotate around the spindle at a high speed. They also have a mechanical part that is an armature. Its head does the reading or writing of the patterns of magnetic polarities on the platters. The patterns are usually stored in the form of bits. They are stored by magnetizing the platters in positive and negative polarities. A hard disk storage device offers a variety of storage capacities. Linguists depending on the amount of data they handle are able to choose the appropriate hard disk to use (Hausser, 2013).

4.2.2. Optical Storage

Optical storage technology is known to be more advanced as it uses laser and optical reflection aspects so as to read or write data. There are two major elements needed so that optical storage works. They include:

- Optical media
- Optical drives.

Optical media are usually made of circular disks while optical drives contain laser beams that provide the lightening and photodiodes that generate the voltages patterns when the reflecting beam hits them. The disks can be divided into three categories that include the compact disks that are created to store some programs but they have low storage capacity and may not be as useful to the linguists.

The other type is the digital versatile disc that is mostly used in storing standard-definition movies. They usually present itself in the form of two layers that is DVD-DL which is a double layer. It offers a slightly larger storing capacity compared to the compact disk.

Finally, the Blue-Ray Disc is used in the storing of high definition movies. It offers the largest storing capacity compared to the digital versatile discs and the compact disks. Unlike the rest that use red-colored rays, it uses blue-colored rays.

The discs can be categories into two other groups. That is:

- Read-only memory
- Random access memory.

The read-only memory permanently stores data while the Random-access memory temporarily stores data.

Figure 4.1: An image of a compact disk which is an example of an optical storage.

Source:-https://all-free-download.com/free-vector/download/compact-disk-05_116527.html.

The optical drives can be further categorized: Read-only drives that do not allow the user to key in more data to the storage device. Write-only drives allow the user to key in more information but not read the data placed. The Read and write drives enable the user to read and also key in data to the storage device.

4.2.3. Solid State Storage

Solid-state storage is a storage technology that make use of non-volatile memory also referred to as flash memory to facilitate the retaining of data when power is off. This kind of technology does not have any moving parts. Though the solid-state storage technology is expensive it has plenty of advantages. It is lighter, faster, quieter, and efficient compared to other storage technologies. Examples of solid-state technology include the USB flash drive. It is mostly in the form of a stick and it is portable. The user plugs it in the USB ports on the computer. The flash memory cards are also an example of solid-state storage technology. It comes in various formats which include the Compact Flash, Secure Digital and Micro SD among others. The most commonly used solid-state storage device in portable devices is the Flash Hard Drives.

Figure 4.2: An image of a USB flash drive which is an example of a solid-state storage technology.

Source: http://www.photo-dictionary.com/phrase/5371/flash-drive.html.

All these storage technologies offer a wide range of technologies that linguists can use as they go on with their work (Hausser, 2013). Because they will need to refer to previously collected data, they will require a storage device that permanently stores data. Hence linguists will require a storage capacity that permanently stores data.

They also need storage technology that will retain knowledge when there is an unstable source of electricity. This prompts many of them to use the non-volatile type of storage technology.

The non-volatile storage technology stores data even when the power is cut off, unlike the volatile storage technology that loses all the presently entered data when the power supply is cut off.

For linguists, deal with large amounts of data. They work with different languages and have to record all the information concerning the studied language group. They, therefore, a storage device that will facilitate the storing of numerous amounts of data.

They look at all the crucial aspects of storage for them to be able to select the appropriate storage. This is one of the benefits of technology to linguistics as it enables the continuous storage of large amounts of collected data (Hausser, 2013).

4.3. USE OF TECHNOLOGY IN TEACHING LINGUISTICS

The recent advancements in technology have affected every aspect of human living. This includes the education process (Management Association and Information Resources, 2014). Technology has been used in various ways to make the learning process more so for linguistics to be more effective. This includes using it as a learning tool.

Figure 4.3: The use of technology in a linguistics class is an effective tool for the learning process.

Source: https://www.utoronto.ca/news/first-year-u-t-course-shines-light-language-based-discrimination.

The learner must be able to use technology as a major tool for their learning process because the current learning process advocates for a student-centered learning environment. Linguistics students need to acquire a large amount of knowledge and skills for them to get good and well-experienced linguists. They can also improve their linguistics skills through the use of technology.

One of the ways that technology has improved the learning of linguistics is by increasing learner cooperation. Cooperation is an important key in ensuring that the teaching and learning process is effective. Through the use of technology such as the internet, the teacher is able to learn new ways to improve student cooperation and integrate them into the classroom. This may be through the use of group discussions or engaging the students in projects that are based on linguistics. The use of technology has assisted in meeting the learners' needs during the learning process. Not all students are

the same. Some learn at a faster pace and others at a slower pace. This shows that learners have different learning needs. To accommodate all these, the teacher is able to use the internet as a learning resource in order to cater to all the students. For linguistics teachers, the use of technology such as the internet is a key resource in improving teacher preparation for the lesson (Management Association and Information Resources, 2014).

Teachers are able to acquire more knowledge on linguistics making them have more content that they can use in the classroom. If the teacher has more content, they will be more confident and will be able to effectively relay the knowledge they have to the students. This will make the learning of linguistics to be more effective as they will have the capability of using examples and illustrations and will have an upper hand when the students will have questions. The use of social technology has widened the opportunities for learning. Social sites enable students to connect with other students from distant schools. There they are able to interact and share more knowledge amongst each other.

For linguistics, it is more beneficial as they interact with students from different countries. This gives them a diverse learning channel as they get to interact with people from different languages. They can be able to confirm the ideologies and concepts of the given language. This makes it a primary source of information as it is first-hand information. The use of technology helps teachers of linguistics know how to practically use teaching skills in the classroom. This is through the use of virtual simulations of classroom situations. Through the use of this resource, the teacher is well equipped to handle various classroom situations. This ensures that in the long run, the learning process is effective (Management Association and Information Resources, 2014).

Linguistics deals with language and for the teacher to be able to correctly teach languages such as English, pronunciation is a key aspect to be sensitized. Search engines on the internet enable the teacher to know how to properly use various languages while in the classroom. The use of technology has also been used to improve the learning environment. For instance, it has led to the eradication of chalkboards and in place, digital whiteboards and smartboards are used. This has improved the learning environment and ensured that the learning process is effective. The learning environment entails the classroom setting. The classroom setting should be well laid out so that all the students will be able to hear and understand what the teacher is saying (Vetulani, 2011).

Figure 4.4: image of a digital white board.

Source: https://www.gettyimages.com/photos/interactive-whiteboard.

The integration of technology in the learning environment has brought about the embracing of the technology-enhanced teaching environment. This is an important learning setup for linguistics as it has proven to be more effective compared to lecture-based learning. Since linguistics has much content, the lecture would be long and the lecturers would do most of the talking. With the use of technology, all these changes as the learning process are made to be student-oriented. The use of technology also makes the teaching and learning process to be more interactive. The students get to participate in the education process.

Figure 4.5: The usage of multimedia texts has also been used in the classroom to assists learners to become familiar with vocabulary and language structures.

Source: https://www.cdsofficetech.com/classroom-technology-revolutionizes-education-schools-sustainable/.

The use of multimedia entails the use of print texts, film, and the internet among others to improve the learners' linguistic knowledge. The use of these tools of multimedia provides learners the opportunity to collect vast information as well as offering them several different materials for the analysis and interpretation of both language and contexts. The technology was integrated into the learning process due to the emphasis that by using computer technology, linguistics class will become an active and interactive place full of meaningful tasks where the learners are solely responsible for their learning. This independent use of technology provides learners self-direction (Management Association and Information Resources, 2014).

The use of technology in learning is beneficial as it increases learners' motivation. Technology such as the internet assists in doing so. The use of media such as film in teaching linguistics helps learners to realize the topic with enthusiasm and improve their knowledge. Learning is meaningfully when technology is used in the process of learning and teaching by using the computer and the internet. These are some of the ways in which technology has been applied in the teaching of linguistics. Among researchers, it has proven to be a very effective tool and method for use in the learning environment (Management Association and Information Resources, 2014).

4.4. USE OF COMPUTER SCIENCE AND TECHNOLOGY IN LINGUISTIC RESEARCH

Computer science and technology play a major role in terms of research in linguistics. As linguistics deals with the study of language, it is more of a learning process for linguists as they get to study and learn more about the different kinds of languages. Being a study, linguistics like in the learning process will revolve mostly around research. This implies that research is the basis for linguistics. Research is a broad field and entails several aspects. Technology and computer science has been used to facilitate this element of research. For instance, research entails several steps such as identifying the area of interest, literature review on the identified are of interest, coming up with research questions, identifying the type of research design to be used, identifying methods of data collection, carrying out data analysis, getting the findings and interpreting the collected data (Vetulani, 2011).

Linguists starting their careers may not have obtained much experience in carrying out linguistical research. Though they may be given some guidance on what to do, it may not be enough to enable them carry out a successful linguistical research. In computer science we get tools, such as the internet, developed from networking and collaborating with other disciplines. There are computer programs designed using the computer science knowledge. These programs are useful in equipping the young linguists with skills useful in conducting research. Hence, computer science facilitates the development of those skills through the use of virtual simulations of various research programs.

This enables the young linguists to gain hands-on experience in research. This is crucial because research skills are part of the basic tools that a good linguist should have. Computer and technology have not only been applied in teaching young linguists on how to conduct research, they are also considered as direct tools for research. As stated above, computer science has been integrated into various aspects of research. For research to be conducted, one has to have knowledge on the area of interest. Technology tools such as the internet have been useful in identification of the different areas under linguistics for instance the history of a certain language among others. After the identification of the area of interest there is the aspect of literature review (Vetulani, 2011).

For a linguist to be able to write a literature review on a given topic, they need to have in-depth knowledge on the given topic. Some of the books used in linguistics do not offer as much content that the linguist may require. The internet has been applied and used as a source of information. The internet provides a vast and a variety of knowledge. It enables linguists to compare information that they acquire in order to form a basis of what is correct and what information is biased. Computer science has been integrated into the process allowing the linguists to access other sources of information. They include e-books and also books that have been published online for the readers to access. Since publishing of books may be costly, some researchers opt to sell their content online. Later the linguist should be able to come up with research questions that will guide the direction of the research.

Here they may interact with other linguists personally or through social media platforms so as to get insight on what kinds of questions they should have and what to anticipate. Computer science and technology has mostly been applied in the process of data collection and recording. Technology provides a variety of ways in which data can be collected. For instance, a linguist can acquire information through a telephone interview or even use of electronic mails to send questionnaires to a variety of respondents. Telephone interview is beneficial if the respondent is far way (distance poses a barrier). Sending of electronic mails is useful when the respondents are several and live in different countries. This makes the work of the researcher much easier and it does not take up much of their time. In recording of collected data, technology provides a variety of options. This is because of the advancements in technology that have facilitated generation of multimedia tools. Tools such as cameras, tape recorders and writing pads on smartphones are just but some of the ways that linguists use in recording of collected data (Hausser, 2013).

After data collection and recording is done, data analysis is done. Computer science has been useful in the creation of computer programs that are used in data analysis. An example of such programs is the python which is a programming language (Hausser, 2013).

After all the data analysis is done, the linguist obtains the findings which is mostly a report obtained in the course of the research process. They them use the acquired information in making an interpretation of the information they obtained as a result of the study. They use the computer to record all the steps that were carried out during the research. In research, originality is key therefore after most of the research are carried out and a report turns out to have remarkable results, it is most likely that these research findings will have to be physically printed out and handed in. This requires use of technology tools such as printers in order to publish the research. Technology is useful for the linguists in gaining more information on a given language and also the rules that have been changed and made with reference to linguistics. By looking at this aspect it is very evident that computer science and technology has been greatly applied in linguistics (Management Association and Information Resources, 2014).

4.5. USE OF COMPUTER SCIENCE AND TECHNOLOGY IN FILLING

Filing is a key aspect in linguistics. It involves organizing of data and grouping them systematically for different purposes. It may involve putting similar data into one file or files depending on the amount of data. It is a key resource used in determining the smooth running of an institution as it deals with the access to information.

Traditionally, the sorting of linguistical data was hectic. Linguistics having much data within itself, will require a much more sufficient system to be used in the sorting of data. Initially, paperwork was much of the work that was done.

The different types of data were recorded in papers and later on sorted into different files. This would cause so much chaos in terms of retrieving of the required files when needed. It would take up much time. This made linguistics more tedious as they had to look through all the files present.

It was disadvantageous as it would take loads of space. For linguistical researchers, they had to set aside rooms for storage of the linguistical research data as well as all documents used in linguistics. This has been the major reason why technology has been greatly incorporated into linguistics. They require a filing system that will work efficiently for the entire institution. Computer science has been incorporated into linguistics in making programs that are used in filing of linguistical documents.

Computer science and technology has been incorporated into linguistics in the creation of a filing system. It is important in ensuring easy retrieval of data and information. The linguistics institution sets up a filing system that is suitable for them. It depends on the amount of data that they handle. This enables them to adjust the storage spaces to have a suitable storage capacity.

The use of technology and computer science in filing has brought about electronic filing. The use of electronic filing has been advantageous for linguistics. This includes improving the security of the information. Electronic filing makes use of tools such as computer. It works by making filing the documents in index forms. For computers, when files are to be stored they are given a unique identity. The identity depends on the properties of the document. If the documents are related, they are stored in folders. Folders are created form the registered files. The advantages of using computer technology is that the institution is able to manage how the linguists are able to access information (Management Association and Information Resources, 2014).

For linguists, security of the information is important more so when conducting research. The research should be unique for every individual. Use of computer science and technology makes this possible. Computer science has been useful in the invention of new security features. There are features such as password control and protection and safe file sharing features. The safe file sharing features ensures that the files are not sent to the wrong person. It is useful in instant file retrieval. This is one of the major reasons why technology and computer science where integrated into linguistics.

Different files are used for reference in the study of language. Computer science and technology have been merged to facilitate the instant retrieval of files. Computer science has been used in the making of the CMOS battery. The CMOS battery is in every computer. It is useful in the retrieval of files. As mentioned earlier, the files are electronically stored by being given a unique identity. The identity may include the name and the time the file was created. The CMOS battery locates the required file by mapping it using the date and the unique identity (Management Association and Information Resources, 2014). This makes the retrieval process much easier and it saves on time. It has also made the files created to be resistant to disaster. Initially, paperwork was the mode used for the filing of information. This made it to be vulnerable and prone to disasters such as fire. This was disadvantageous as crucial information would be lost and the linguists would have to start over again to recover the information. Computer science and technology offers a disaster resistant filing system. Computer science offers networking options that allows the user to back up information even to features such as the cloud which is virtually based. In case of a disaster, they are able to sync their information and retrieve any lost information. Most of the linguistic institutions have WIFI networks that facilitate the backing up of the filed information.

Figure 4.6: Cloud computing used in backing-up linguistic data.

Source: https://www.pinterest.co.uk/pin/505318020675743974/.

Computer science and technology by providing electric filing has enabled the linguistics institutions to save money. Compared to using paperwork, electronic filing systems are much cheaper. Paperwork involves purchasing of tools such as ink, printers, filing cabinet and paper among others. For electronic filing they are able to use computers that provide readily available filing systems. This will save them on money that they would have spent on traditional forms of filing information (Bodomo and Adams B, 2009).

The other advantage is that is saves on space. Unlike the traditional forms of filing information, the electronic filing system offer more space that can be used for other purposes. The traditional filing system was not key on space. Some of the files would fill up the rooms and would require some rooms to be set aside to cater for such.

The advantages of computer science and technology in filing is numerous. As it is beneficial for the filing system used by linguists, this has led to the use of computer and technology in linguistics. It makes the study of the various languages to be much easier. It enables the smooth running of the linguistics institutions.

4.6. USE OF COMPUTER SCIENCE AND TECHNOLOGY IN CREATING COMMUNICATION BETWEEN LINGUISTS

Communication is very important for linguists. They need to work together so that they can be able to develop various linguistical theories and share information that enable them to design those new theories. If the linguists are to collaborate, they need to know and interact with each other. Distance poses a challenge to the linguists as they are located in different parts of the world. This makes it hard for them to interact face-to-face which is an effective way of interacting and sharing of knowledge (Bodomo and Adams B, 2009).

As collaboration becomes more dependent on communication between the linguists, there is need for them to have communication tools. Initially, communication was based on traditional means. They used letters and mails in order to communicate with each other. This type of communication would take time for the other to get feedback from other linguists. The interactive process therefore was not efficient. This would make the process of coming up with theories a much slower process. It also posed a challenge when giving linguists information on forums for linguists.

One of the ways in which computer science and technology have been applied in linguistics in the communication factor. The advancements made in technology has been useful in improving the communication process. This has led the world being referred to as a global market. Communication has been made a very simple and accessible component in life. Computer science and technology has widened the number of devices that can be used in communication. Some of the devices that have been introduced include the smartphones, telephones, and faxes among others (Bodomo and Adams B, 2009). The use of these devices enables linguists to easily communicate between each other. One of the ways in which linguists get to share knowledge and interact with each other. It is one of the most popular ways of communication among people today. Computer science has also been extensively used in the creation of social media platforms. One of the core principles of computer science is networking. Knowledge on this has been used by computer scientists in the creation of social media platforms.

Some of the social media platforms include Facebook, Twitter, Instagram, and Telegram. Particularly, Telegram has been popular amongst linguists as it provides a variety of interactive resources for them. It also enables the creation of interactive group forums to facilitate a conversation amongst a larger group of people. It is efficient because linguists from different parts of the world can get to interact using this platform so long as they have internet access.On the other hand, researchers tend to favor face-to-face conversations. This is why they tend to have interactive forums where they physically interact with one another. For linguists, this is the same case. They have forums, seminars, and interactive sessions where linguists get to interact with each other. For some of the linguists they are not able to attend such meetings. The use of communication media such as teleconferencing enables them to attend such meetings. This is one of the benefits of using technology and computer science in communication. Teleconferencing makes use of both computer science and technology. Technology tools such as smartphones and recorders are used.

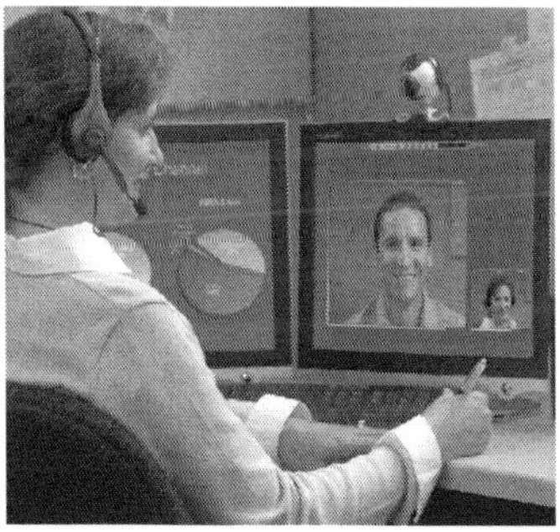

Figure 4.7: Computer science is used in facilitating teleconferencing through the use of networking which creates a link between the computers and also creates a network to facilitate the communication.

Source:-https://encyclopedia2.thefreedictionary.com/Video+teleconference.

The use of computer science and technology in facilitating communication between linguists is beneficial in so many ways. For one it facilitates accessibility of the linguists. Accessibility in the aspect of instant communication. The advancements in technology has been vast in that the information to be shared can be transmitted at an instant. Rather than using letters that would take a longer time, tools such as the electronic mail enable the instant transmitting of information.

Apart from the electronic mails, tools such as instant messaging also makes this possible. It also facilitates accessibility as it reduces the barrier of distance in communication.

Linguists hold seminars to enable them to discuss on the various theories that have been innovated.

They also discuss on changes that need to be made into different languages as well as the rules in linguistics. While in this seminars, they need to speak to large audience and not every individual is able to be audible enough. Technology has been used in the provision of tools such as microphones and speakers. Computer science has also been used in the creation of these instruments. Though they are not directly a tool in communication, they are very key tools in ensuring effective communication.

These instruments ensure that everyone will get to hear what is being discussed. It also avails tools such as translators that are used during the meetings. This is used in translating the languages so that the linguists can understand it in their own languages (Bodomo and Adams B, 2009).

Compared to using the traditional forms of communication, the use of technology and computer science in communication is much cheaper. If one uses the traditional forms of communication such as letters is much more expensive. As there are mailing costs, buying ink and paper among others. The latest technology only requires an individual to have a smartphone and internet connection.

These days even those phones that support internet connection will be able to facilitate communication.

This makes the use of such technology to be much cheaper mode of communication.

The use of technology and computer science in facilitating communication between linguists has enabled remarkable progress it be made in the world of linguistics (Bodomo and Adams B, 2009).

4.7. USE OF COMPUTER SCIENCE AND TECHNOLOGY IN MANAGEMENT OF LINGUISTICAL INSTITUTIONS

There is a lot of work that goes into the management of the linguistics institution. Good management is very crucial for these institutions to be able to run for many years. For linguistics, this is a very important because there are several aspects of linguistics that require much funding. For instance, things such as research require much funding and the institution has to have a good management to be able cater for such research. Traditionally the management systems were not as advanced as today. The institution finances were documented in papers, there were files containing the list of the workers in the institutions and records of the linguists in the institution (Vetulani, 2011).

This system was not efficient as it allowed mismanagement of the institutions to take place. It also took more time and it would pose a challenge in creating the strategic plan for the institution. The incorporation of computer science and technology in the management of the institutions has made it much efficient for the running of the institution. Technology has been used in making the management much easier and beneficial for the running of the institution. It basically makes technology work for the institution.

The management plans include budgeting and management of staff. Technology has been used in management by utilizing network systems. For instance, technology has been used in monitoring the attendance of workers that offer services to the institution. In other wards it is part of employee management. Computer science and technology has been used in providing tools such as CCTV cameras that are useful in monitoring of the employees. Not only is it beneficial for employee management but also for ensuring security in the institution (Vetulani, 2011).

Computer science and technology is useful in keeping of records of equipment that are preset in the institution. For instance, such institutions have furniture and computers. There are computer programs designed by use of knowledge on computer science to enable them to keep records of the instruments present in the institution. It makes it more efficient and time saving. This will help the institution in knowing how much money they should put into purchasing of such equipment. Computer programs such as excel can be used in making records of the employees and equipment available in the company.

They make use of tools such as computers in the making and keeping records of the financial status of the company. This is a useful tool for the management of the institution as it enables them to make plans for the institution. For linguists most of the funds needs to go into research. They are able to use the records to plan on how they can use their resources so that much of the company funds go into facilitating research. It has also provided ways in which the company management can get possible solutions to some of the problems that they encounter (Hausser, 2013).

They are able to use search engines such as yahoo to get feedback on how to tackle some of the problems that they have.

For linguists there is a lot of work to do and for some of them more so for those in management. It is beneficial for them to use computer science and technology as it provides for them tools such as virtual assistants. The virtual assistant reminds them of the various activities that should be undertaken. This will be beneficial for them as they can organize themselves properly and manage their time.

There are several advantages of using technology and computer science in the management of the linguistically institution. It enables the institutions to manage the data that they have. The use of technology enables them to compress the data that is within the institution. The data that was present in the institution is placed into hard drives for backup for the data. This will help them save on space as well as save on time. They are able to restrict the number of personnel who can access the information (Hausser, 2013).

It is also useful for the management to be able to create the strategic plan of the institution. This is because the management can access the records of the company be it financial or other records needed. This enables them to use this information in making future plans for the institution. It has enabled the efficient running of the institution. This is in terms of filing of documents, storage, and access of information. The use of internet back up will enable retrieval of information so that the

This makes the entire process less tiring and stressful. The other benefit is that brings about productivity as much work can be covered within a short period of time. The use of CCTV can facilitate monitoring of the workers. Improves the security status of the institution. As these institutions have libraries there needs to be a system to facilitate the good maintenance of books. Computer science and technology has been used in the automation of the libraries to enable easy access of the book. It enables the management to be able to identify the books present in the library (Hausser, 2013).

They are then able to identify the books that are needed to be bought. They are also able to pay for subscriptions of the e-resources such as e-books so that the linguists can get access to such resources. The need for a good management system is important for such institutions. This has led to the integration of technology and computer science in the management of such institutions. This will boost the working of such institutions. This is one of the ways in which computer science and technology has been applied in linguistics.

4.8. USE OF COMPUTER SCIENCE AND TECHNOLOGY IN CONDUCTING SURVEYS

Surveys are one of the crucial elements of linguistics. It is one of the ways in which linguists are able to gain information on the languages under study. From the results they get from the surveys they make an analysis and later on make a report on the findings and interpretation of the collected information. Conducting surveys is a good method of data collection as it is a way in which the linguists can get first-hand information concerning the language or topic under study. Some of the surveys conducted in the line of linguists include dialect survey. Dialect is a term that refers to language. There are different types of dialect. For instance, there is local dialect which refers to people conversing in their native languages.

These are some of the languages that are being investigated. It is very important to research these languages as majority of them are becoming extinct. This will create a challenge for the linguists as they need to get hold of individuals with knowledge of this languages to be able to know the origin of such languages. This makes linguistics a tool for the preservation of such languages. Technology and computer science are great facilitators of these surveys (Bodomo and Adams B, 2009).

They have been used more so in conducting the surveys in a large-scale audience as several people will be able to access the surveys. Technology provides tools such as computers that can be used to facilitate the survey. The computer will require internet access so that the public can access the survey. Basically, the dialect survey is used in gaining information on phonetic of the language. The survey is done in the manner that the linguist selects the words that would be used during the survey. The computers are then used in the production of punched cards which will contain the words picked by the linguists.

The punched cards are then presented to the selected audience. They will then be required to sort the cards in an order depending on the criteria given to them by the linguist conducting the survey. If the linguists want to access people that are far away, the knowledge of computer science is used in the creation of applications that will provide the same features as the physical survey. This way people in different areas of the world will be able to access the survey. Once the survey is complete, the next process is to sort the information obtained. They use computer programs to summarize the information obtained. The computers are programmed so that they can sort the information. The programs are set according to the set theories and statistics that are set by the linguists. With such information, the linguists are able to make rules concerning the given language. They can also learn more about the language in question (Bodomo and Adams B, 2009).

4.9. USE OF COMPUTER SCIENCE AND TECHNOLOGY IN TESTING OF LINGUISTIC STATEMENTS

A lot of work goes into ensuring that the linguistical statements used in conversations are correct for use. The work includes the testing of such statements to ensure there is good use of grammar, punctuation, and pronunciation. The testing of statements involves comparing it to the data present in the linguistical records. The testing also includes testing of descriptions of a person or place. Usually when giving a description, there are rules that guide the making a description. Testing is done to ensure that the guidelines are fully met for the description to make grammatical sense.

The process of testing if done manually, it may be a long and tiring process. This is because it entails comparing the description to the numerous data that is present within the linguistical institution. This created the need of applying computer science and technology into the process of testing the linguistic statements to make it a much easier and smooth process. It will also save on time. The application of technology and computer science in the testing process involves the use computer programs and applications that have been generated through the use of knowledge on computer science. The applications and programs are fitted with linguistical elements such as syntax and thesaurus. This will enable them to identify any short comings in the statements (Hausser, 2013).

The computer applications are linked to some of the historical statements as well as linguistical description methods. The programs are fitted with comparison tools and more of the elements of linguistics. This will enable the application or program to make a comparison to the statement that is to be tested. The computers used are programmed to automatically run for a diagnostic on the statement or description being tested. There are various ways in which the statements can be tested. One of the ways is by analysis. Analysis involves looking at every detail in the statement.

The order of the words, punctuation, and grammar are some of the things looked at when testing the statement through the method of analysis. This method is more beneficial as it enables easy identification of the problem in the statement and if the programs used in testing is more advanced it will be able to highlight some of the changes that can be made to improve the statement or description. The other method of testing a statement or description is through use of synthesis. This method involves synthesizing every portion of the statement on a basic level. It involves looking at the basic things such as the verbs used in the statement or description (Hausser, 2013).

The use of computer science and technology in testing statements and descriptions is very beneficial for linguists. They can run several words in the computer and get the feedback within a short period of time.

4.10. USE OF COMPUTER SCIENCE AND TECHNOLOGY IN USE OF SIGN LANGUAGE

Linguistics is a study of language. Sign language is also a part of linguistics as it is a language used to facilitate communication between the special groups of information. Initially, not much research was done in sign language. This is because before there was no emphasis on equality for the physically disabled people in the community. In the recent days, there is so much emphasis on equality creating the need for sign language to facilitate communication to the deaf. This is as a result of the creation of sign language TV channels as well as the great need for sign language interpretation (Hausser, 2013).

There is a growing market for sign language interpreters. Not only for work purposes but communication among people to pass information. Sign language is very important as it facilitates the learning of the children or individuals living with disabilities so that they too can be learned like other people. Computer science and technology has been useful in creating tools to aid communication for the people with disabilities. This tool include hearing aids among others but hearing aids may not be useful for people who are completely deaf (Hausser, 2013).

This is why there is more emphasis in researching on sign language. It involves comparison of the previously used sign language with the currently developed sign language. Computer science and technology has been useful in conducting research on sign language. They provide tools such as the internet where linguists are able to get vast information on sign language. It also avails for them tools that include e-books where they can get more information on sign language. This has been useful in developing the language and teaching various individuals on using sign language.

4.11. USE OF COMPUTER SCIENCE AND TECHNOLOGY IN IMPROVING THE ENGLISH LANGUAGE

The English language is a common language used by a majority of people from all walks of life. It is used to facilitate official and every-day communication. In some countries, English is the official language. In that case, the language should have undergone a purification process to ensure that it is optimal for the local context, such as discussing bills in parliament. In other countries English is taught in schools and examined similar to other subjects, such as physics or math.

With the English language being incorporated in computer science and technology, it has led to improvements being made to it. For instance, computer science has various principles and among them being programing. English has been incorporated into programming so that the user is able to operate the computer because it is programmed to use English as the preset language. This enables the user to easily interact with the computer as they understand the given instructions they need to have.

Technology has incorporated the use of English as majority of the internet sites have English as a preset language. Also, a variety of technological tools have manuals. Almost all the manuals have their instructions in English. The improvement in English as a language is as a result of the advancements being made in the technological world. As technology advances, there is also an advancement in English brought about by improved technology.

This is in the aspect that advancements in technology bring about more search engines and more technological tools. When put together with computer science then the quality of programs being developed is increased. We all get the concept that some of the programs are useful in carrying out research as well as in testing some of the linguistical theories that have been developed. If the quality of the programs are improved then the quality of research will also improve meaning that better results will be obtained. The better results are used in coming up with rules and theories that will govern the use of English as a language. This may affect the pronunciation of certain words and generation of statements that are very accurate. The statement may include clauses among others (Hausser, 2013).

4.12. USE OF COMPUTER SCIENCE AND TECHNOLOGY IN DATA ANALYSIS AND EXPLOITATION

Data analysis is a part of research. Research is also incorporated in to and is a big part of linguistics. Data analysis is part of the steps that is done when carrying out research. Usually, after data collection and recording is done, data analysis is done. This is the process involves analyzing of data that is collected. If the data analysis process was to be done manually then a lot of time would be taken up and it would have been frustrating in the long run. Computer science has been useful in the creation of computer programs that are used in data analysis. An example of such programs is the python which is a programming language.

It has also been useful in data exploitation. Data exploitation is where the data obtained can be analyzed to give more information other than what was being aimed at. For instance, if there was a study on the phonetics of a given language the data obtained can be exploited to that the linguists get to obtain other information such as the syntax and the phonetics of the given language.

In conclusion, there are several applications of computer science and technology in linguistics and this is because of the variety of benefits that it offers to linguists. The benefits include helping them save on time as they use computers for various purposes which is much more efficient. It helps them save on money, it reduces the work load, it helps in the management of the linguistic institutions and also facilitates research among others. This is the reason for their successful integration in the line of linguistics (Hausser, 2013).

CHAPTER

5

How Has Astronomical Field Benefited from Computer Science and Technology?

CONTENTS

5.1. INTRODUCTION

Astronomy as a science branch mainly deals with objects that are celestial, the space and the physical universe as a whole. Astronomy is a natural science that mainly looks into the celestial objects and the phenomena that revolve around this phenomenon. Heavenly objects also known as the heavenly objects are the natural objects which are not in the earth's atmosphere but they are found outside it. Therefore, astronomy involves the study of these objects.

Figure 5.1: Astronomy involves studying of stars and other celestial objects.

Source: https://www.ducksters.com/science/astronomy.php.

This remains where celestial objects are studied in-depth to determine how they evolve through the years their physical components, that is, what components form them, their chemistry and how they move. Astronomy is among the oldest sciences. People who study astronomy are referred to as astronomers.

Astronomers in the early civilization did methodical observations as they studied the sky at night and the artifacts, they found that were astronomical. These objects were found having fallen from the past and they did their research and came up with the results.

For astronomers to study the celestial objects they required special objects to enable them to carry out their research. These objects include the telescope which is necessary to study the stars it was therefore important for the telescope to be invented first before the coming up of astronomy as a science in the modern world.

Astronomy in the past was made up of diverse disciplines. These disciplines include astronomy, heavenly steering, observational stargazing, the production of almanacs and even astrology.

Expert astronomy is the same as the astrophysics. Astrophysics is among the many branches of astronomy that work with stars when they are in their physical nature of these.

In the early years of the 20th century, astronomers discovered that astronomy needs to be split into two groups. It was then split into the groups which included: Observational astronomy and theoretical astronomy.

The observational astronomy involves astronomy using optical things and objects, for example, optical mirrors, the optical mirrors and a solid-state detector that mainly looks at the light from close to infrared to near-ultraviolet wavelengths.

Theoretical astronomy is the using of the investigative representations of physics and chemistry to describe astronomical objects and astronomical phenomena. It is oriented towards the coming up of models of a computer or analytical models to describe astronomical objects and phenomena.

The dualistic arenas work together with the theoretical astronomy in an attempt to show how the results of the theoretical astronomy are determined and found.

Astronomers who are amateurs that are a person who is incompetent or inept at a particular activity have been of great help in discovering astronomical discoveries since astronomy is one of the few sciences that an opinion of anyone counts such that the amateurs are also allowed to make discoveries. It has led to a positive impact since these amateurs have also contributed to discovering astronomy. In astronomy, they study celestial objects such as the star and the most studied star is the sun. It is not considered a variable star, but it does change in periods in the activity known as the sunspot cycle. For astronomers to understand the universe and bring others into this understanding they have to study and understand the stars and stellar evolution first.

The astrophysics of stars is easily determined by astronomers undergoing physical thought and anticipated understanding and from computer reproductions of the interior.

In the astronomical field, computer science is widely applied to enable research and to understand the findings. Computer science is the study of the computer and other related technology revolving around the computer. For one to understand astronomy they have to first understand computer science. In most ways, computer science is applied in astronomy by using computer science techniques. For example, computer science helps astronomers to explore the universe using the deep learning technique as explained below.

5.2. COMPUTER SCIENCE HELPING ASTRONOMERS TO EXPLORE THE UNIVERSE

Figure 5.2: An astronomer studying the stars using a telescope.

Source: https://www.rmg. co.uk/discover/explore/how-become-astronomer.

Computer science as seen earlier is the study of the computer and related technologies. Astronomers use skills acquired by computer scientists to explore the universe in the following ways:

In astronomy, the identification of things which are not recognizable is required. Computer science has brought about the development of Google which uses a thing called deep learning such that one can search for anything via the google and obtain any sort of information. Through Google, one can search for any information and acquire various skills and information that they were not aware of. Astronomers may identify a certain celestial object that they are not aware of but probably some other celestial objects that resemble or are close to resemblance with that celestial objects have been identified before. Astronomers, therefore, can easily google and they obtain information about these objects that enable them to know or identify the name of the celestial objects, its characteristics or even its impact. They can know if it is harmful or not. This is advantageous because it saves astronomers time, they would have used to go searching in books to find information about this object. This form of learning involves a computer being trained to identify or classify particular objects in images (Seidelmann and Kovalevsky, 2012). Astronomers use telescopes that covers one million of the southern sky and takes very many pictures. Astronomers are capable of identifying the objects in the pictures using deep learning by using computers easily. The pictures taken by the telescope are very complex and detailed such that they do not lack anything about what they want to find but they are able to acquire all the information they require, but using the computers the astronomers can deluge the data easily and quicker hence the astronomers can get information about the objects or identify the objects very fast.

According to an astrophysicist located in Illinois called Brian stated that astronomy is the next frontier to take on.A group of astrophysicists with Brian Nord included the search for gravitational lenses that show that there is the presence of massive objects skewing light rays. These scientists most times come across many images eye to eye one at a time which they may not easily identify. The invention of the computer and the computer science skills that have led to the invention of deep learning has enabled the astronomers to identify the objects that are in these images. This technology is easily at their disposal and has been of great help to them (Seidelmann and Kovalevsky, 2012).By the help of the cosmic magnifying glass, astronomers can easily see and identify distant galaxies which could not be possible without the cosmic magnifying glass because they look like magnified arcs.

Very many lenses have been identified and found by scientists that confirm Albert Einstein theory of the general relativity in the year 1930s.

Figure 5.3: Since deep learning was invented it's the expectation of scientist. By the use of the computer deep learning scientists can easily identify this objects and lenses have aided the astronomers in their search.

Source: https://tecnologiaparalaindustria.com/ebook-tecnologias-para-una-trazabilidad-en-tiempo-real-para-el-sector-alimentacion-de-forma-automatizada-e-inteligente-2/.

It is very difficult to find gravitational lenses but by the help of deep learning it creates a way to create a model of a complicated system. Nord said that deep learning is a way for us to create prototypical of a complex system (Seidelmann and Kovalevsky, 2012).Astronomers use statistical machine learning (ML) techniques which stands for automatic schemes with encrusted bulges connected in a web so that they can make complex classifications. When astronomers discover celestial objects, they need to classify them into various classes so that they can ease understanding. They classify them according to their similarities and the use the statistical ML techniques to enable them achieve this. Statistical ML techniques is described like the neurons of the human mind.With the facemask acknowledgment software, the image of a person is first fed into the system, and the system first detects how the person looks like that is their edges, lines, and curves.

In-between sheets are then combined to high level features, like the person's eyes or their mouth, and eventually a face. It notices how the person looks by capturing the facial description of the person. The same concept is applied when it comes to gravitational lenses because for gravitational lenses, the software that is installed in the computer will recognize a big galaxy surrounded by the arcs that indicate lensed background objects.

The art of algorithms currently can correctly know and identify the lenses in a few percentages of the time when they mistake a particularly messy image for the real thing.Colin Jacobs with the help of Karl Glaze Brook of Swinburne University of Technology in Melbourne, Australia stated that if it works but is 97% accurate, you could be vastly swamped by false positives. This proved a problem that needed a solution. Therefore, Nord and Jacobs and their other colleagues worked tirelessly to discover and find solutions to address this issue. They designed such that the algorithm to be strict ensuring it finds the crops cream that is the cream of the crop. Also, they tried to avoid being harsh in their search criteria because they knew it would mean they later weed out by handsome images that happen to look a little bit like lenses.In the past years, astronomers have been working to apply deep learning in not only few areas but they also try to apply it in other areas especially for deciphering images in other many ways. They have used computer techniques to distinguish between the various distant galaxies and the different stars in the Milky Way. They also use the knowledge of computer science to estimate the distance to far way objects and to put the structures of galaxies which can take on a variety of spiral and elliptical shapes (Seidelmann and Kovalevsky, 2012).

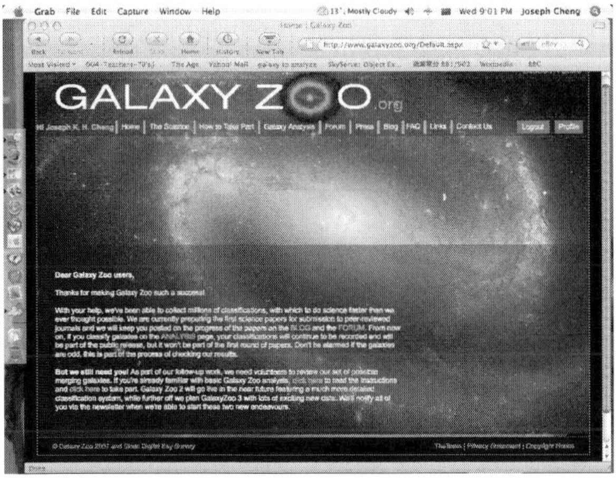

Figure 5.4: Some astronomers have come up with a project called galaxy zoo that they have used computer science to recruit people around the world to help them to sort and classify the images they obtain.

Source: https://sites.google.com/site/jkhcastronomy/Home/galaxy-zoo-project---my-other-information.

5.3. COMPUTER SCIENCE REVOLUTION IN ASTRONOMY

Computer science has revolved over the years and in most ways under the aspect of astronomy. As we have seen earlier, astronomy is the stars' study and other celestial objects. Sun is also studied and the galaxies. Computer science revolves with time such that new technologies are invented to a better technology. Revolution is the coming up of new technologies and improving the already available technology to better versions that are more useful.

The computer technologies have been greatly used in the central to advances in astronomy and astrophysics for the past 40 years and will be used even more importantly in analyzing more important role in analyzing more complex phenomena in the decade.

In early 1950s, the cycles of John von Neumann's new Maniac computer was devoted to the first stellar evolution codes. The Maniac 1 computer stands for mathematical analyzer numerical integrator and computer model 1. It was an early computer that was built and developed by Nicholas metropolis and the Los Alamos scientific laboratory. Its architecture was designed on the von Neuman architecture and it was developed by a scientist called John Von Neumann. Like all the computers that were invented in that era it was one of the kind of machines that was not used to exchange programs with other computers since it lacked ability to do so. It could also not exchange programs with other several machines based on the IAS. Nicholas metropolis selected the name MANIAC in a bid and hope of stopping the rash of silly acronyms for machines names. John Von Neumann had also selected a name for it. It was as heavy as 1000 pounds Its first task involved it to perform a more precise and extensive calculation for the thermonuclear process. In the year 1953, the maniac was able to obtain the first equation of state calculated by modified Monte Carlo interrogation over configuration space (Way et al, 2012).

The mathematical analyzer numerical integrator and computer model 1 was successfully set to start operations in the month of March in the year 1952 and it was shut down in the year of 1958 in the month of July. It is noted, however, that it was transferred to the University of New Mexico in a very critical and bad condition and they restored it back to its full operation. Dale sparks was the one who restored it back to its full operation. It was then featured in at least two UNM maniac programming dissertations from the year 1963. It remained in this operation until it gave up and retired in the year of 1965 and was successfully succeeded by the maniac 11. Maniac three which was a third version was built at the institute of computer research at the University of Chicago in the year of 1964.

Computer science affects astronomy during the evolution because as new technologies are invented then the astronomy process changes and becomes more complex. In the year 1953 the maniac was able to obtain the first equation of state calculated by modified Monte Carlo interrogation over configuration space. As early as the 1959s John von Neuman invention that is the maniac computer was dedicated to the progression codes. It was an among the first computers to be invented and that was constructed and developed by Nicholas metropolis. The name John VonNeuman is among the greatest names in the history of computing. John was a half cast of both American and Hungarian. He joined an institute of learning called Princeton institute that taught him his advanced levels learning in his early years between the year 1993 and 1994. He had a read passion to become a great man like Albert Einstein and his main area of qualifications was mathematics and this enabled him to be able to operate well in the computing field. When it was wartime and countries were fighting, John was employed in an institute called in Los Almost on mathematics and shockwaves that explode for a specific type of weapon. He also worked in the IBM. John worked tirelessly basing his discoveries on mathematics and tabulating them as he was a mathematics genius. He was involved in his job and did not take anything lightly and this led to his growth. Nearing end of the war, John wrote down a report on the architecture of such a Machine that could work out very complicated mathematical sums and calculations. A man named Alan Turing assisted him with most part of his worksite is therefore evident that the skills obtained from the study of computer science are highly applicable in astronomy. The Fanatic computer brought rice to key subjects like astronomy since it pioneered new inventions in this field. It also enabled new discoveries of celestial objects that were not present in the past and therefore it proved advantageous. In the year of 1960s the more innovative processers permitted the first thorough and complex representations of the supernova blasts. Supernova explosions are stellar explosions of cosmic proportions in the literal meaning.

These are among the most dangerous and advanced happenings that took part in the world. One supernova explosion produces a lot of vigor. This energy is so much that it can destroy the whole universe and everything that is in it therefore it is a universal disaster and a worldwide one too that affects the whole world. It enables mankind to be able to survive in the planet earth. This is as studied by astronomers by the knowledge in computer science. Scientists today are giving out information that they can has enabled to touch the heart of the heartless. At work in hand together with people from universities specifically ones in Germany, Arnett developed a great invention that was able to hinder the falling of the universe. It is important also to note that the astronomers discovered that Astronomers in the early civilization did methodical observations as they studied the sky at night and the artefacts, they found that were astronomical. These objects were found having fallen from the past and they did their research and came up with the results. For astronomers to study the celestial objects they required special objects to enable them to carry out their research. These objects include the telescope which is necessary to study the stars it was therefore important for the telescope to be invented first before astronomy was able to develop into modern science. We also discovered that astronomy exists in two forms that is; Professional astronomy is now considered to be the same as astrophysics. Astrophysics is the branch of astronomy concerned with the physical nature of stars and other celestial bodies, and the application of the laws and theories of physics to the interpretation of astronomical observations.

5.4. ASTRONOMERS ARE ABLE TO ACQUIRE SKILLS THAT CAN ASSIST THEM IN THEIR WORK

Students who learn computer science acquire skills that are important to them in the future. When astronomers study computer science they too can acquire this skill. The skills include

5.4.1. Analytical Skills

This is skills that one can look into a problem and find the most suitable solution for it. It is, therefore, the problem-solving skill. Analytical skills are very vital especially in interviewing an individual. This is because managers want people who are equipped with analytical skills such that they can identify a problem look critically into it, come with a suitable solution and communicate it effectively. Analytical skills exist in various forms but there are 5 major types which include:

Communication: It is the ability to pass information effectively without any miscommunication, misinterpretations or misconceptions. When an individual analysis a problem he needs to deliver it appropriately to the others in the organization. It can either be in written or oral. If one lacks the skill of communication it may make information to be distorted in the organization such that the problem may fail to be solved in the appropriate way hence lack of communication skill is a major vice. Communication skills are shown through; How one reports a piece of information, written work of the individual, his oral communication, his presentation, problem sensitivity and active listening.

Creativity: It takes two paths; noticing a problem that others may not notice and solving or finding a suitable solution to these problems. Creativity in an organization applies majorly in budgeting where one should be very careful to notice if a calculation problem arises and be able to solve it. It may also apply in brainstorming, collaboration, optimization, predictive modeling, problem-solving, restructuring, strategic planning, and integration. An individual with this skill hence notices problems before they bring destruction to the companies' profits and hence these problems are solved early enough.

Critical thinking: One should have the ability to evaluate information and decide based on their findings so that they can be termed as having the skill of critical thinking. It involves thinking deeply to find as much information as one can get that is related to what one initially had then put them together for evaluation. Critical thinking is what helps one make decisions that help solve a problem in the company. It is shown by diagnosis, dissecting, evaluating, record keeping, data interpretation, judgment, prioritization, judgment, troubleshooting, and attention to details. It's a skill acquired by very few individuals since people often look at the upper meaning instead of digging into it.

Data analysis: This is the ability to analyses and understands a certain amount of information or data. It includes; business analysis, SWOT analysis, cost analysis, credit analysis, critical analysis, descriptive analysis, financial analysis and policy analysis.

Research: This is digging into information to get more information or hints to collect more data. It includes; Insertion, merits, data collection, data entry, taking inventory and checking for accuracy. Computer skills enable one to have analytical skills since it involves identifying problems and coming up with solutions to address these problems.

5.4.2. Problem-Solving Skills

Problem-solving is the ability of an individual to find a solution to a problem at hand. When a problem arises in an organization, an individual with problem-solving skills looks into the problem to find the cause then comes up with ways to solve the problem. There are five major steps for problem-solving. They include; analyses the cause to the risen problem, generate a set of alternative interventions to achieve your goal, evaluate the best solutions, implement a plan, assess effectiveness. These steps are discussed below for better understanding.

Analyze the cause of the risen problem: This step involves an individual looking deeper to find the cause of the problem. For one to solve a problem there is a need for them to understand what caused the problem from the first place. The problem can be found by gathering and evaluating data, putting aside possible contributing circumstances, and pointing out what needs to be addressed. The skills required for problem-analysis include; active listening, data gathering, data analysis, fact-finding, historical analysis, cause analysis, process analysis and needs identification.

Generating interventions to achieve an end goal: This is the coming up of possible solutions to certain problems. It may be found by one person or by brainstorming of many people. More than one person should be involved in finding possible solutions so that in case the master plan fails other options may be used. The required skills to generate interventions include;

brainstorming which is discussing with several people such that each person gives their views to solve the problem, creative thinking, prediction where one foresees the possible outcome, forecasting, project design, and project planning. When possible, solutions are invented then they are evaluated.

Evaluating the best solutions: This step may involve the major decision-makers in the company. From the possible solutions that were found, the major decision makers select the best solution that will not only be the most effective but will be cost-effective and will not promote losses. The step can also be done by selected trusted teams or team leads. The required skills include; analysis, discussion, corroboration, teamwork, test development, mediation, and prioritizing.

Implementing a plan: This involves applying the solution found so that the problem can be solved. The skills required include; project management, project implementation, collaboration, time management and benchmark development. This step, therefore, involves solving the problem at hand.

Assessing the effectiveness of the intervention: This step involves checking to see if the problem has been solved and how quickly it is working. If the problem has not been solved, then alternative methods are used for solving the problem. The skills involved include; communication, data analysis, surveys, customer feedback, follow through and troubleshooting. One can improve their problem-solving skills by; acquiring more technical knowledge on the field, setting out an opportunity to solve the problem, do practice problems and observing how others solve their problems. Computer science involves solving very complex and complicated problems systematically and logically. It is mainly applicable to finding solutions during projects that computer science students undertake.

5.4.3. Creativity

This is the ability to invent a new concept. Most employees want employers who can develop a new idea. Creativity involves thinking deeply to come up with something new and different. It involves coming up with new ways to carry out tasks, solve problems and meet challenges. Critical thinking skills include analysis, open-mindedness, problem-solving, organization, and communication. Analysis involves thinking about what you want to design and examine the information. Open-mindedness refers to being open to new ideas. People should not be limited to what they know. Instead, they should be ready to receive new information. They should eliminate bias and assumptions that they may have and look at the concept from another, unseen perspective. Problem-solving refers to being creative enough to see a problem and design a better solution. Problem-solving will help the employers to hire a qualified individual who can be relied on to solve various kinds of technical and non-technical problems. Any organization needs to be organized such that its employees can arrange and present their ideas logically.

This will help other people to see their vision and point out any obvious flaws. Communication refers to being able to express one's ideas and suggestions, both in oral and written forms. Examples of creative thinking include artistic creativity, problem-solving creativity, and creativity in STEM. Artistic creativity is impulsive one and tends to respond to or act on certain current incentives. It may involve designing the company's logo, proposing a new look for a cloth line, devising an engaging lesson plan, designing the packaging of a product or writing an advertising copy. T

herefore, artistic creativity involves being creative in the art section. Problem-solving Creativity is the coming up with creative ways to solve a new problem. when one has problem-solving creativity, they can come up with new ways to solve problems such that these ideas had not been invented before. it may involve brainstorming and coming up with new ideas. STEM simply stands for science technology engineering and mathematics. Creativity in the side of STEM involves inventing, designing or coming up with projects that lie in the sector of math's science technology or engineering.

This field requires a very creative mind so that the projects created can be working. It needs one to think outside the box on how they will eliminate factors that may lead the project to fail. In computer science, students work on various projects that need a lot of creativity to solve them so that they may eliminate problems, use their knowledge in STEM and be open-minded.

5.4.4. Critical Thinking Skills

Critical thinking refers to ability to analyze information and make correct judgement. It includes considering and evaluating facts, data, and observable phenomena in order to draw corresponding conclusions.

A person with critical thinking skills can be easily trusted to make the companies decide on their own and these decisions are relevant and effective. Critical thinking skills involve five major steps which include; Analysis, communication, open-mindedness, problem-solving, and creativity. These are the top critical thinking skills which are discussed more below.

Analysis: It is the capability to examine a set of data, information or a text. A person with analytical skills can look deeply into a piece of information, know what it means by interpreting it then bring it out by explaining to others. The analysis involves asking yourself questions that enable you to dig deep into the information. it requires one to ask themselves several questions related to the topic. It also involves analyzing the data that one has, researching, and interpreting. One needs to do more research to find more data then interpret their findings to know if it relates to what they are analyzing.*Communication*: As discussed earlier, communication is the ability to share one's information with other people in a way that they will bring a clear understanding to them. Communication assists people to work as a team to come up with solutions. It involves active listening where one listens attentively so that they may not miss any piece of information, assessing the information to check its accuracy and importance, Explaining the information, presentation, teamwork, interpersonal, verbal communication and non-verbal communication. Communication skills not only enable the passing of information but it also promotes teamwork and togetherness in an organization.

Creativity: Creativity involves coming up with new ideas and it, therefore, involves critical thinking where one needs to think deeply so that they can come up with the new idea. It involves flexibility, conceptualization, curiosity, imagination, drawing connections, predicting, synthesizing, and vision.

Open-mindness: This is putting aside what we know or think to be open to new ideas without bias. For an individual to be open-minded, he needs to think critically about the new idea to check and confirm if it is relevant or not. It is having a third eye to new opinions and options to make conclusions.

Problem-solving: In problem-solving, one has to think critically to find out the real cause of the problem. It involves paying attention to every detail, clarifying, making a suitable decision, evaluating, and identifying patterns. In problem-solving, a problem arises, the most suitable way of solving the problem should be applied to ensure that it is solved faster, therefore, an individual should think very critically if the method he wants to use is the most suitable to use.

Computer science requires critical thinking skills because in the coming up with projects the individual needs to think deeply so that they can come up with the right approach.

5.4.5. Resilience

It is the process of being able to readjust to changes. If a problem or stress comes up, an individual with resilience skills can adapt well and bounce back very quickly. Most organizations face problems frequently from time to time and only a person with resilience skills can adapt to changes that these problems may bring. An example is in case of the death of a workmate, the employees should be able to overcome this challenge and start working without the presence of the employee. It also applies if an individual loses his loved one or the company faces losses. A resilient person has the following characteristics; he easily adapts to a new environment. In case one is required to work somewhere else or is given a transfer, the person should adjust very fast and fit into the new environment to prevent wasting time while adjusting. The person can cope with difficulty and challenges. This individual must be always ready for anything that comes along the way. He should not depend on things to work in his favor all the time but must have the understanding that things can change at any one time. A person with resilience must have the skill that enables him to handle stress effectively and positively. Most people when they face stress, they often experience a break down since they do not know how to handle it. Others go to the extent of having depression but when one can handle stress effectively, they know how to put everything behind them and move forward positively. They should be persistent that is they should always advocate in making things change for the betterment of the organization. In case of a problem, a persistent individual always tries to make issues work out and bring back the organization to stability. They should also understand that not everything they have control of. The individual knows that some things are beyond their understanding for example death and they cannot change them. If they get this understanding then they will be able to cope with any changes on their way. How a person adjusts to a situation is very different from another person because different people react differently to different situations. It should, therefore, be noticed that it's a person own initiative to achieve resilience. The main factors that contribute to resilience include a good support system, always maintaining a positive relationship, having a good self-image and having a very positive attitude towards situations. One can develop resilience by having a plan that includes; recognizing one's signs of stress, building physical hardiness, calming one's body and mind, identifying one's strength, increasing on one's positive emotions daily by being happy more, engaging in meaningful activities, removing unhelpful thinking and creating a caring environment. Computer science instils resilience because some units like programming are quite challenging and require one to be ready to fail several before they pass. It is Therefore noted that Computer science is a major subject to build the essential skills that employers require. Therefore, when astronomers acquire this skill, they can be able to improve their work output by a greater percentage.

5.5. COMPUTING SUPREMACY HIERARCHY

In the next decade, great computing power will be provided by a hierarchical network of more powerful machines to an individual researcher. Starting in the 1980s, many scientists were given ultimate rule by personal computers (PCs) and workstations; supercomputers also became readily available. In the next decade, these trends will secure and become more strongly engrossed (Way et al, 2012).

On every astronomer's desk new processor technology will be put by very affordable and powerful computers.

The machines that are close to being as powerful as today's supercomputers, will make possible for the process of acquiring large datasets.

Automated systems enable scientific partnership teamwork and collaboration. These machines, with their huge memories that can store a lot of information.

The huge memories are the storage space is large enough to store a lot of information.

Fast processing means that a lot of information can be processed fast enough hence there is no wastage of time. Input and output rates mean that it has the capability to put information quickly and to retrieve the information quickly enough too as an output to the user.

Computing power hierarchy is useful in astronomy since it enables programming of astronomy and assists the processes of astronomy to take place.

It is widely used to describe and help in processes of astronomy and the study of stars and other celestial objects as it connects the technologies used in computer science that enable the astronauts to identify the celestial objects and the stars hence it should be easily understood (Way et al, 2012).

5.6. COMPUTER SCIENCE HELPS IN THE MANUFACTURE OF ASTRONOMICAL TOOLS

The tools used to study the celestial objects and stars require the knowledge of the computer science to form them. Long ago people studied the stars by gazing upon the heavens with their naked eyes. This method was not adequate enough because it did not help them to learn the stars in depth and also the distance was quite far. In the early 17th century a scientist called Galileo invented a great and ever progressing telescope that was a major improvement in the study of stars. These objects that are invented to enable the study of the galaxies and stars include:

5.6.1. Optical Telescopes

It was invented by galilee Galileo. The inventions that were done before enabled him to acquire skills to invent the optical telescopes the invention of the telescope has revolved gradually over the years and have been made more technological such that the astronauts do not use their hands to view but can view through the computers. In this way, computer science skills have been implemented so as to develop these tools and also so as to enable the study and interpretation of the tools.

5.6.2. Radio Telescopes

Optical telescopes collect visible light and bring it to a focus then they amplify it and make it available for analysis by various instruments. Radio telescopes also collect weak radio light waves, bring it to a focus, amplify it and make it available for analysis. The study of computer science aid in the making of the radio telescopes and they also help the astronomers to know how to read the signals that have been passed to them through the telescope. It is therefore necessary that astronomers should study computer science so that they can apply the skills in their work.

5.6.3. Spectroscopes

Spectroscopy involves looking into unlikeness in wavelengths of light. These waves of light are studied by the use of the spectroscopes. Computer science knowledge is applied in the making of the stethoscopes as it requires technology for its manufacture.

5.6.4. Star Charts

Star charts are also called the star map. The use of computer science knowledge to form the telescopes has aided in the coming up of the star charts that use is widely used in astronomy.

5.7. THE ADVANTAGES OF COMPUTER SCIENCE INTEGRATION IN ASTRONOMY

The purpose of computer science in astronomy is to provide that kind of atmosphere through which astronomers are able to work in because when astronomists acquire the knowledge of computer science they acquire skills of application and the right attitude that makes them useful citizens in the society. Computer science instils skills in a person example analytical skill, critical thinking skills, and resilience skills. It can also help them to understand comprehend global functions of computer science and act locally to meet their needs. The main reasons for teaching computer science in schools include;

It enables diverse thinking in astronomers and enables them to solve any computer-related problem. As discussed, earlier computer science gives the astronomers the skill of thinking critically and problem-solving skills. There is an astronomer's studies computer science in high school they will be at a position be able to solve problems when they arise. They will also be able to think critically and come up with new things (Way et al, 2012).

Astronomers also develop the right kind of attitude to develop and acquire the knowledge and skills that are required in the current technological world. Astronomers who learn computer science can acquire skills that are required to operate any technological or electrical appliance. Due to the technology revolution, these astronomers will acquire jobs from any field.

Astronomers are also trained to develop scientifically to appreciate the technological advances and adapt in their lives. Astronomers who learn computer science appreciate when new technology is introduced or when the existing technology is improved. Since they have the required skills they can easily adapt to this change as they can fit in and use the new technology of any kind or version. This is due to their understanding that they gained earlier and also the skills such as analytical skills that enable them to analyze the new technology, evaluate it and figure out how it works (Way et al, 2012).The astronomers are also trained to make meaningful contributions to make the world and society proud of. Many computer astronomers have developed new technologies, software, and hardware that not only speed up work but also enable communication and transfer of information. For instance, mobile phones that are being invented daily and new versions being made daily have been manufactured by astronomers who know computer science. These technologies are of great importance to society and the nation at large. This makes the society and nation to become very proud of the astronomers who invented the new technologies.

Using the computer and related technologies require teamwork. Teamwork is the ability of people to work together regardless of their background to achieve a certain goal. Astronomers need to be trained to work as a team. Computer science promotes teamwork since the astronomers are grouped into small groups that will work together when doing their projects. When they work as a group, they can share the knowledge to come up with a comprehensive and perfect project. Since two heads are better than one when people work as a group, they can accomplish so much than when one works alone. Teamwork also helps build harmony therefore people interrelate together appropriately and they can stay together in peace.

When astronomers learn computer science at higher educational levels, teachers can identify their mistakes from the mistakes they do when writing their report when delivering their report or even from their project itself, therefore, teachers can help astronomers to correct their mistakes early enough and avoid them from making the same mistakes in future. Also, the teachers can identify astronomers' talents for example if the astronomers are talented in coding therefore, they can build and help the astronomers to grow their talent by guiding them through the process. This talent can come to develop into the astronomers' future career or employment (Way et al, 2012).

Just like any other core subject computer science enables the students who want to become astronomers to listen attentively and come up with solutions or gain the required information. This is enabled in class when other astronomers are presenting their projects the other children sit silently and listen attentively to what is being communicated. IT also benefits the astronomers by enabling them to be open-minded since they are open to other people's ideas and from that they can gain new information, new ideas or even discover where they make have made a mess in their project so that they can correct on it early enough.

Higher secondary schools are a bridge between school and society. Ones one is done with their higher secondary school they are fully integrated as members of the society. For those who decide to stop their education when they complete their higher secondary school, computer science can help them gain employment but for those who decide to continue with their education, it helps them seek higher education and continue with their studies. Computer science teachers, therefore, give their astronomers the necessary information and skills that enable them to fit into the world. The current world terms these skills as very important and requires all astronomers to acquire them (Way et al, 2012).

Astronomers gain decision-making skills hence they grow into complete personalities who are mature in words, actions, and deeds. When astronomers study computer science they can make decisions on their own and these decisions are logical. Astronomers gain decision making by solving problems writing algorithms, coding, and decoding which are basic computer science skills that they gain during their daily lessons. It is therefore important that astronomers who are in high school to learn computer science to prepare them for their future careers.

Astronomers need to be proficient and professional in learning computer science. They must be trained to acquire the principles of electronic devices and get the diversity of operations. Most astronomers who do not have the opportunity to study computer science in schools should find their way into it. Some vocational training facilities, for example, offer computer science and these astronomers should ensure they enrol in them because it is for their benefit. This will help them to be overcomers of any competition they may get from those with computer science skills hence they can be equal (Way et al, 2012).

5.8. FUTURE IMPROVEMENT IN THE FIELD OF ASTRONOMY AND COMPUTER SCIENCE

In the next few years, the field of astronomy will have grown by a great extent since new technologies will have been introduced.

Our current world with the discovery of the galaxies the planets and colliding stars. Interest has grown in scientists and astronomers that they want to know more about the planets and how they move therefore they gain interest to develop more technological tools. In the world we are living in, a lot of interest has been developed in the area of astronomy and may students be undertaking astronomy as a course. Different countries have developed interest in the field of astronomy and they have invested their money to this field so that they can learn and acquire knowledge about the planets, the galaxies and the stars at large.The following are some of the ways the technology is being improved in the field of astronomy.

5.8.1. James Webb Space Telescope (JWST)

This is a telescope that looks into the dusty regions of the galaxy and it looks into where the stars originated from, the system of the planets and it can spotlight from the first stars and the galaxies. The James Webb Space Telescope (JWST) can cover a distance of six and a half million and can carry a collection of infrared cameras and other tools that are used in the astronomical process. It is placed about one and a half million kilometers away from the earth where there is a balance between the earth's gravities and the Sun's gravity. JWST helps the astronomers to have a better understanding of the universe unlike in the past. JWST is mainly a success due to NASA and The European Space Agency working together with the Canadian Space Agency (Seidelmann and Kovalevsky, 2012).

5.8.2. Extremely Large Telescope (ELT)

Positioned on top of a mountain in Chile, the ELT will peer out into space allowing us to image planets outside of our solar system to see if they could potentially host life. It will be the world's largest optical/infrared telescope with a main mirror measuring 39.3 meters across. The UK along with the 15 other member states of the European Southern Observatory (ESO) have supported the construction of the ELT, with the first of approximately 800 mirrors being cast this year, 2018. The ELT will be more powerful than any other telescope in existence, gathering 100,000,000 times lighter than the human eye. For astronomers, physicists, and stargazers everywhere, developing a telescope of this size with these capabilities is a major priority because it will enable new types of science, including studying the atmospheres of planets orbiting stars other than the sun.

5.8.3. Square Kilometer Array (SKA)

The Square Kilometer Array (SKA) is a lot of radio telescopes antennae assembled or put together. It does not work as one single machine but as a combination of many antennae of the radio telescopes. These antennae are distributed over a large area that works like one single antenna. The two many antennae that comprise of the SKA are in the area of Australia and South Africa and it covers a wide area over 1km square. When compared with other telescopes, SKA is faster in surveying that gives out over ten times the data traffic of the global internet. When the SKA is given support by the global associations, it can give answers to many commonly asked questions that revolve is astronomy and astrophysics. Some of these questions include the work of the dark energy and dark matter in the world and universe and SKA can give answers to this (Seidelmann and Kovalevsky, 2012).

5.8.4. GAIA

How one knows about the planet is highly dependent on indirect measurement and estimation and many assumptions in our current world today. Taking, for example, how would people wonder and ask themselves questions if the map of how the whole galaxy looked Like was found. The need for this has led to the development go GAIA which is being developed so that the largest 3D map of the galaxy can be made together with the milky way. This telescope is put closely to about one and a half million closes to the earth and its work is to map the places, speed, and the properties of as many stars more than a billion of them. The stars are observed one by one for about seventy times in a period of five years. Apart from this GAIA can also spot many other astronomical objects like the asteroids and the comets that help the asteroids to discover more about the planets. In the year 2016, in the month of September, the first data from GAIA was read and the results had more than one billion objects. Following this announcement was the announcement that was read in the year 2018n and the number of objects read had increased by half a million (Seidelmann and Kovalevsky, 2012).

5.8.5. The Laser Interferometer Gravitational-Wave Observatory (LIGO)

The Laser Interferometer Gravitational-Wave Observatory (LIGO is an improved version of the telescope that bears very little resemblance with the telescope. The telescope mainly focuses on observing the light but the Laser Interferometer Gravitational Wave Observatory mainly focuses on calculating the ripples in time and space which go by the name gravitational waves. Gravitational waves are formed by occurrences that are great enough to have an impact on the material of space and the amount of time.

The LIGO is mainly grouped into two groups of separated detectors in different states in the united states of America that are separated widely. It consists of perpendicular arms and each of this arm consists of about a size of 4km. There are lasers that move up and down these arms and their duty is to calculate the size of the tiniest change in their length that shows that a gravitational wave has been experienced or has moved. In India the Laser Interferometer Gravitational Wave Observatory is developing with a 3rd detector site in this country. The LIGO is accompanied by the Virgo detector that is situated in the country of Italy and the GEO 600 instrument that is situated in Germany. The LIGO still undergoes several improves and upgrades that are being supported by more than 92 institutions that are working together. The LIGO and the Virgo work together and a certain organization called the KAGRA is planning to join and collaborate with them. KAGRA is a Japanese detector. This joint operation gives way for concurrent observation of the gravitational waves that are given out by similar occurrence giving way for finding out the origin of the signals and all other nature aspects. The LIGO in cooperation with other telescopes can describe the universe in many ways. With the improvement and advancement of technology it has brought about improvements in the sectors of astronomy. Telescopes have been improved and the UK has been on the forefront in these advancements. These improvements in the telescopes has been of great benefit as it has brought about more study of the stars and the celestial objects and it has improved astronomy as a field. The improvements are still ongoing and new and improved technology is still being introduced (Seidelmann and Kovalevsky, 2012).

CHAPTER

6

Computer Science and Robotic Technology

CONTENTS

6.1. INTRODUCTION

Robotics is a field in Computer Science and Engineering concerned with creating, designing, and operating robots using Artificial Intelligence (AI). Robots are computer systems programmed using software. These software systems are used to control the behavior of robots, such as their sensory feedback and information processing while carrying out different activities. The person creating a robot has to have theoretical knowledge on how to design and develop. Robotics does overlap with other fields such as electronics, mechatronics, nanotechnology, and bioengineering (Dominik and Jacek, 2014).

Electronics knowledge is required in robotics. Robots are electronic devices, which require low voltage current for them to run efficiently and for longer hours using less power. Important design aspects to consider include robot's speed, accuracy and precision of the feedback delivered by robots, robot's flexibility. All these decisions can be made only after one has mastered computer science and electronics.

Mechatronics field is closely related to Robotics in the sense that mechatronics deals with the systems in which inputs must be provided by an external factor whereas Robotics deals with systems which acquire inputs by their own. A Mechatronic expert must be pretty much qualified in manufacture of a robots' mechanical parts; knowledgeable in its electrical aspect and programming aspect too.

Nanotechnology knowledge is used to create and design nanobots (devices which range 0.1 to 10 micrometers and constructed of nanoscale or molecular components) which allow interaction with nanoscale objects. Such robots are used in areas such as the atomic force microscope instrument configured to perform Nano manipulation (Dominik and Jacek, 2014).

Bioengineering field is used to provide Robotics experts with the knowledge of how to incorporate automation processes in medical activities such as medical trainings, prosthetics, and assisting the aging population and persons with disabilities.

The functional unit of Robotics consists of:

- Its body structure which in most robots consists of a metal-based physical body that provides protection to the internal mechanisms within the robot;
- Body shape which is based on the robots intended use but for most robots their shape does resemble humans in appearance

to help in its acceptance in certain replicative behaviors usually performed by people;

- Muscle system which are made up of different mechanisms such as gears, thrusters among others;
- Sensory system which can either be simple or complex depending on the function of the robot;
- Power source which ensures the robot operates efficiently; and
- Finally, the brain system which is closely related to and works hand in hand with the sensory system enabling the robot to interact with objects surrounding it.

Study of robotics in computer science is being advance because;

- Designing, building, and Programming of robots is totally cool motivating students to explore more on Robotics;
- A program designed to control the functioning of a robot does at least have a dynamic physical presence to fully interact with the physical world;
- Robotics does provide an ideal way to learn about reliability, error detection and error recovery for components fail and sensors are objects to error hence giving students a chance to find a solution for these errors;
- With Robotics, Computer Scientists have a good environment to work on Control; and
- Study of Robotics brings together different disciplines which does encourage perfection of the end product produced.

Different programs have been used to equip learners with Robotics knowledge in the field of computer science.

Physics concepts being one of the programs used, has great impact to Robotics for its various concepts are being used in perfection of robots. The Solar Energy concept can be used to power robots, cool down various machinery parts of a robot which heat up during its operations, and help in assembling of a robot.

The use of solar energy in robotics does contribute to the preservation of the environment for it is a clean source of power which does not pollute the environment in any way and it is cheap to harness. Kinetic energy theory in physics can be used to create movement, get rid of excess potential energy making movement easier (Gallier, 2011).

Graphics programming has been of great help to the creation of robots. It does help in planning out the entire structure and operations of a robot. Graphical programming tools enable robotics experts to employ block diagrams, virtual instruments and connectors; it can also be used to monitor and control automated processes in a robot by dragging a layout of symbols representing robot design and motions onto a storyboard that stores the sequence of motions needed to perform a task.

Linear algebra such as 3D mathematics, dot products, cross products, matrix manipulations, 3D transformations, matrix inversions, and transpositions are of great importance to Robotics for they help in manipulation of various variables which must be estimated before manufacturing a robot.

Discrete Mathematics is required to create software's which control robots. The famous binary computer mathematics used to store files in software's is purely Discrete Mathematics. The assigning of activities to a robot does require Discrete Mathematics for combinatorial optimization is employed. The wiring of the entire robot does also use discrete mathematics concepts for it to function effectively. Robots arms which is a type of linkage is also part of Discrete Mathematics (Gallier, 2011).

Visual processing programs are used to help a robot to interact with the world. Robots use systems which perceive to act and acts to perceive while performing various operations assigned to them. Robotic vision aids in object detection, estimation of moved distance by counting any type of moving, application of security and surveillance, defense applications, navigation by mobile robots and autonomous vehicles and computer-human interaction.

6.2. TYPES OF ROBOTS DESIGNED AND MANUFACTURED TO PERFORM VARIOUS TASK

The Aerospace robots: The Aerospace robots have been designed to specialize in flying activities. The Roven surveillance drone has been greatly used in aerial surveillance for various reasons such as; search for missing objects, aerial inspection of a field, and in filming industry to help in production of films. Space robots have also been invented such as the Mars Rovers which are being used for the exploration of planet mars among other robots used to explore various parts of space.

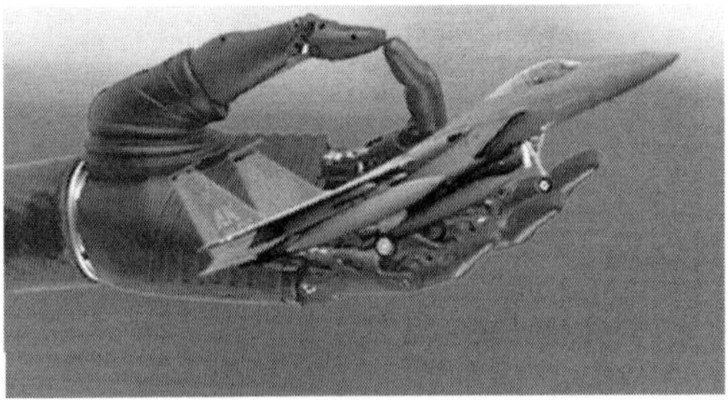

Figure 6.1: Aerospace robot.

Source: https://www.mtwmag.com/robotic-accuracy-improves-aerospace-manufacturing/.

Consumer robots: Consumer robots are a trend in the market for they are capable of operating autonomously in homes and offices fueling more visions of having robots living alongside humans. They are a combination of simulation, reinforcement, and collaborative learning which enables them to perform various tasks assigned to them. They are and will be of great help to humans for they make work easier, can be used for fun activities limiting cost incurred in entertainment activities among other benefits. The Artificial Intelligent powered robot assistant, Robot dog Aibo, Roomba vacuum are examples of consumer robots in the market (Pires, 2007).

Figure 6.2: Consumable robot.

Source: https://www.artstation.com/artwork/yeaRJ.

Disaster response robots: Disaster response robots are being modified day in day out to save the human race from deadly rescue missions. They can be used to defuse setup bomb attacks, find survivors in unstable ruins, and explore mines and shipwrecks saving miners from the risk of having to face the dangers of breathing deadly gases in mines and collapsing of the mine sites. After an earthquake and tsunami attack struck Japan in the year 2011, Packbots, disaster response robots, were sued to inspect damage at the Fukushima Daichi nuclear power station.

Figure 6.3: Disaster response robot.

Source: https://www.roboticsresear.ch/articles/14982/the-centauro-a-new-disaster-response-robot.

Education robot: The famous STEM program (Science, Technology, Engineering, and Mathematics) is of great importance to the education sector. It provides learners with hands on information on how to make advancement to the society by addressing the major issues affecting our society by use of Robotic knowledge. Learners do have hands-on programmable sets from Lego, 3D printers with lesson plans and many other STEM programs (Pires, 2007).

Figure 6.4: Education robot.

Source: https://digitallearning.eletsonline.com/2019/09/robots-become-teachers-in-a-school-in-bengaluru/.

Entertainment robot: Robots are being designed to serve in the Entertainment industry. Robotic Engineers are trying their best to help humans curb on the cost incurred from entertainment purposes by creating robots with can evoke emotional responses and make humans laugh or feel surprised or in owe of the robots' unique movements and activities which to humans are rare.

Figure 6.5: Entertainment robot.

Source: https://csjbot.en.made-in-china.com/product/SCVnqOZxGkWF/China-Bumblebee-Entertainment-Robot-Attracting-Popularity-with-Dancing-Singing-Storying.html.

Robotic exoskeletons: Robotic exoskeletons are designed and created for use in physical rehabilitation for the physically disabled people, enabling a paralyzed patient to walk again and endure the weight of bulky loads without the help of others. This will be a great boost to the society for the physically disabled will not be dependent on anyone increasing labor force in the work places hence boosting the economy.

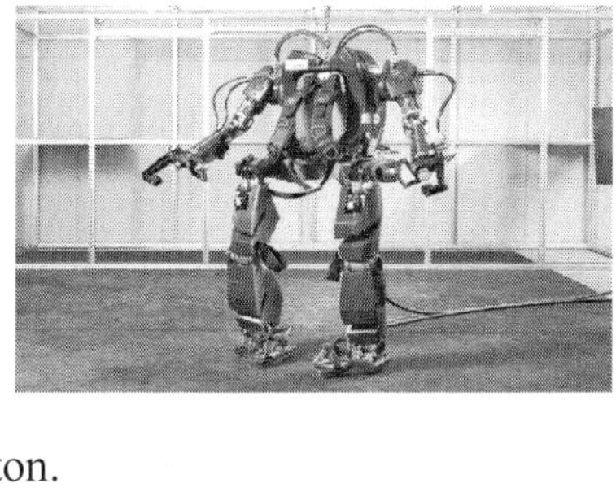

Figure 6.6 : Exoskeleton.

Source: https://newatlas.com/hyundai-robotic-exoskeleton/43331/.

Humanoids robots: Humanoids robots which are designed to look like humans are of great help to humans for they help in various activities which are performed by humans.

Figure 6.7 : Humanoid.

Source: https://www.forbes.com/sites/zarastone/2018/02/27/ten-incredibly-lifelike-humanoid-robots-to-get-on-your-radar/#4182581934d2.

Industrial robot: The industry sector is greatly making use of robots for control processes. Robots are being used in industries to perform repetitive task which are tedious to humans increasing the accuracy of the products produced, help in manufacturing of poisonous chemicals and automation of production activities in the industry.

Figure 6.8: Industrial robot.

Source: https://www.designworldonline.com/sales-of-industrial-robots-grow-7–2-in-first-half-of-2019/.

Medical robot: The medical sector is really trying its best to introduce robots into its activities for automation purposes. The IBM question-answering Supercomputer is really spreading in the many healthcare applications used to aid in collection of patient information and for improvements of the services being offered to patients based on their frequent suggestion for perfection of the applications (Zhang, Dan, Wei, and Bin, 2018).

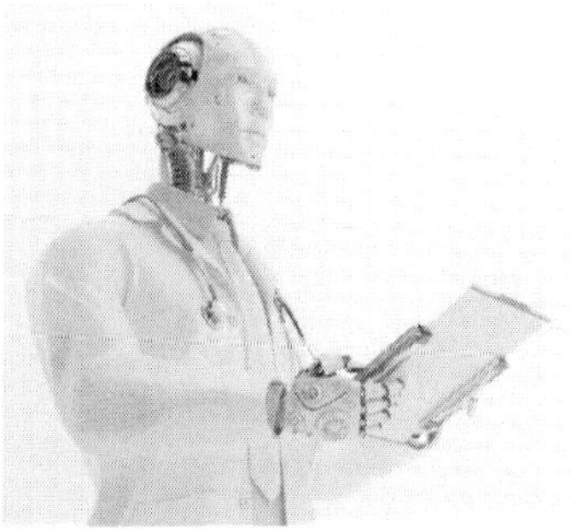

Figure 6.9: Medical robot.

Source: https://trotons.com/robotics-and-medical-science-the-incredible-machines-that-have-made-treatment-simple/.

Military robot: Robots are being used by the military to improve security features in different countries. Surveillance robots are being used to ensure that data is only accessible to the authorized users. Drones are being used to initialize attacks on terrorists. Ground systems, such as Endeavor Robotics are being set up for protection purposes. Scout improvised explosive devices, such as the Packbots, are being used to setup explosive attacks by the military to avoid the danger of massive deaths.

Figure 6.10: Military robot.

Source: https://www.razorrobotics.com/military-robots/.

Research robot: Robotics is as a result of research in the different University and corporate research laboratories. The laboratories have then decided to make use of the same robots to ease their research work by designing robots to be used for collection of information, carrying out experimental activities among others.

Figure 6.11: Research robot.

Source: https://greenbookblog.org/2013/02/01/research-robots-more-than-meets-the-eye/.

Autonomous robot: The transport sector is really advancing with the inventions of robotics. Self-driven cars are being manufactured and sold in the market, flying cars, autonomous vehicles build on DARPA's autonomous competitions reducing loss of lives through road accidents due to reckless driving. The aviation sector is also being advanced with introduction of the autopilot system, advancement of security features in case of a plane crash among others (Zhang, Dan, Wei, and Bin, 2018).

Figure 6.12 : Autonomous robot.

Source: https://www.robotshop.com/community/blog/show/would-you-be-transported-by-a-robot.

Telepresence robot: Telepresence robotic technology which allows one to be present at a place without actually going there is spreading especially among Corporations. Corporate members are using this technology to conduct their meetings and inspections of their industry activities at the comfort of their homes by logging onto a robot avatar via the internet and controlling the robot by driving it around their desired locations seeing what it sees (Zhang, Dan, Wei, and Bin, 2018).

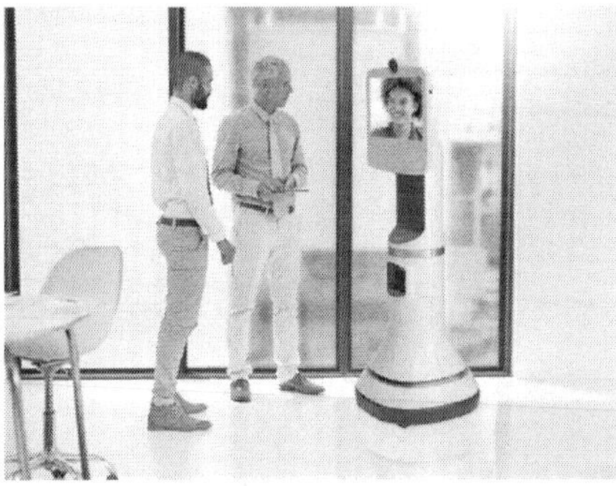

Figure 6.13: Telepresence robot.

Source: https://www.networkworld.com/article/3261970/a-new-telepresence-robot-takes-the-stage.html.

Underwater robot: Robots such as the Aquanaut are being used for deep-sea submersibles saving humans the dangers faced during deep-sea explorations.

Figure 6.14: Underwater robot.

Source: https://newatlas.com/underwater-mine-exploring-robot/60475/.

AI which is a computer program that is capable of creating a machine having its own intelligence and behavior is one of the main reasons for existence of robots. AI gives a robot the ability to learn humans through ML. Depending on the tasks assigned to a robot during its manufacture, different type AI is used (Schwartz and Yap, 2016).

The weak AI is used to enable a robot to have the simulation of human thought and reaction character. It allows a robot to respond to commands assigned to it despite the fact that the robot itself does not seem to understand the commands. This is possible because the robots have been programmed with already predefined commands and the possible responses. A suitable example of a robot produced through Weak AI is famous Siri and Alexa found mostly in Apple products.

Strong AI is used to create robots which perform their task on their own without any supervision. The robots are programmed to do their task correctly. This AI is widely used nowadays as many things are being automated to perform tasks on their own such as the self-driven cars among others.

Specialized AI is used to create robots which perform only a specific specialized task. Industrial robots are mainly in this category for specialization is required to improve the quality of products produced without having to face the threat of inaccuracy in measurements or any other form of inaccuracy performed by humans for specialized task are tedious because they are repetitive (Schwartz and Yap, 2016).

6.3. EXPERTS THAT AID IN DEVELOPMENT OF THE BEST ROBOTS

Robotics Engineer: This is one of the experts required for the perfection of robots. He or she is responsible for creating and designing robots and robotic system by designing the machines and processes necessary to assemble the robots. Once the creation of the robot is done with, a robotics engineer role switches from that of designing to that of being a technical support person who will be responsible for the analyzing and evaluating the robotics device to see which ways it can be improved.

A Robotic Technician: He does perform task closely related to that of a robotic Engineer, but the main difference is that a robotic technician will be more focused on testing and repairing robotics systems while helping robotics Engineers create and design them. In addition to testing roles, a robotic technician will interact more frequently with the customers to ensure that the robots are functioning properly, serving as a liaison between the customers and robotic engineers (Schwartz and Yap, 2016).

Sales Engineers: They are responsible for the selling of robotic devices. Apart from mastering selling skills, they need to be knowledgeable about how the robotic device works, and be able to make some adjustments to meet their customers' expectations of their merchandise.

A Software Developer: This is responsible for developing the software system of a robot. The software system is a vital component to robots for it is simply the brain of a robot. The Software developer ensures that the system has all commands and responses to be carried out as safely and precisely as possible once a robot is instructed either verbally or by typing to perform a certain task.

Many believe that introduction of robotics in labor market is leading to more and more job loss, but the truth is, robotics is creating more and more jobs. A robot is a machine which faces the threat of crashing, hence a Robotic Operator is required to oversee the functioning of a robot, and be able to fix it with immediate effect in cases of break downs (Schwartz and Yap, 2016).

Robotics field does include accounting, thus an expert with a strong background in robot technology, sales, accounting, and customer services, a Robotics Account Manager is required. His roles will be to connect with customers and make sales to them within the robotics industry.

6.4. HUMAN COMPUTER INTERACTIONS (HCI) IN ROBOTICS

Nowadays, the topic of HCI is becoming quite popular for the purposes of research, especially in robotics where it promises to fill up the gap between robots and humans. Today, robotics, and technology play a substantial role in learning by utilizing e-schooling surroundings and varying computer-based educational and confirmative instruments. The inclusion of systems like Information Communication Technology (ICT) steers sectors like industry and education towards an age of electronic as well as supportive technology.

6.4.1. Models of HCI

The primary function of HCI is promoting collaboration between people and machine. Typically, humans interact with one another through speech. They equally back their expressions with gestures like emotions, body movement, and various expressage. The non-cognitive attributes of computer technology on users should be looked at carefully, since humans typically have a strong mental attitude towards responding on computers in similar manner as they respond to the real world.

6.4.2. From HCI to Human Robotic Social Interaction

It's believed that the human robotic fundamental interaction, together with human-computer fundamental interaction will benefit from one another's progress. In fact, even robots involved in human robotic interactions are typically structured to be computerized and self-governing, something that differs from computers. To develop Humanoid robots is presently one of the leading topics that every key technological company such as Apple, Google, and MS is seeking to figure out. Through creating successful robots, HCI is helping to play a crucial role in machine and human connectedness (Dominik and Jacek, 2014).

In order to go unchallenged in human settings, it's vital that robots should adopt cultural traits through responsive facial expressions, plus respect social conventions that could easily be adapted to them through means of HCI. Various studies have been done involving different emotional facial expressions, such as Avatars which comprise of virtual human-like form, typically imposed by Informal Virtual Agents and communicated alongside humans and other agents via a multimodal communicative trait, for instance, Sophia, and Greta, which are two of the most popular AI robots.

Among the benefits of HCI innovations is that when the machine has been programmed to do certain tasks, it can do the same work of Human beings though more precisely and very quick as that of people. No matter what transpires to them or the situation being faced, they can still remain focused on their learned basics (Dominik and Jacek, 2014).

6.4.3. Affect in Human-Robotic Interaction

Preliminary studies in human-robotic interaction (HRI) show that most people seem to "personify" computers. Personal pronouns like "him/her" and "you" are nowadays used to refer to robotic computers, plus they can be very emotionally involving when people use them, even for basic strategic computer games. These emotive reactions are mostly related performance, displaying the separation between normative, logical interaction with the workstation and the particular socioemotional reactions of the operator. In regards to these findings, researchers came up with the popular media equation theory that suggests, since human-machine interactions are integrally natural and social, most of the rules which apply to person-person interaction may also be adopted to human-machine processes.

Based on ideas from the media equation model, it's been demonstrated that humans often endeavor to interact with workstations like they were autonomous social actors-a concept also known as computers as sociological actors (CASA). This theory suggests firstly that people use the same set of procedures and heuristics when networking with computer, same as they do in situations where they're interacting with people, plus secondly that being "illogical" sometimes, human actors aren't mindful of their actions toward computers. Borrowing from principles of social psychology as well as empirical tests, various studies have offered support for the concepts behind CASA (Dominik and Jacek, 2014).

In classroom samples, for instance, various stereotypes that were anticipated to apply just to humans were equally used in connections with computers. For one particular study, for instance, contributors showed stereotypic gender traits when interrelating with a computer having a female, male, or impersonal voice.

In another research, players were shown recordings of people of either similar or different culture from their own. For one case, they were revealed to that they were interrelating with a human, while in another case they believed they were communicating with a go-between software agent. For both cases, participants displayed stereotypic in-group inclinations. It has been concluded from research like these that people react instinctively to social cues, regardless of whether or not these cues come from machines.

The CASA theory maintains that individuals will seek to interact with processors like they were human, despite computers not resembling people at all. Researchers add that the propensity of human users to display human-like behavior towards a machine grows when the amount of human-likeness is increased (Dominik and Jacek, 2014).

The notion that human-resemblance in machines improves the human propensity to constructively interrelate with it has likewise been put forth in other multiple studies in human-robot interaction around the world. For instance, in a 2001 research by Nourbakhsh, Simmons, and Bruce, it was found that people are more inclined to interrelate with a robot that has human-like attributes, such as when it has a moveable screen or moves its head.

Some factors that contribute towards the human affinity to personalize robots are autonomous movement, and facial features.

Human-likeness, nevertheless, has its limits, like is demonstrated in some findings.

One such study is known as the uncanny valley theory, which was originally brought forward by Japanese roboticist and inventor Masahiro Mori.

It states that people normally react constructively to an improvement in the human-resemblance of robots, however, if there's any negligible deviance from this perfect human-resemblance, they often tend to react unfavorably. Empirical studies in more recent times have examined the uncanny valley model from various research perspectives, for instance, developmentally or through using eye-tracking, including functional brain imaging technology (Dominik and Jacek, 2014).

So far, nevertheless, little evidence on people actually reacting emotionally towards robots is accessible. Studies exploring the emotional responses of people when damaging a robot or observing a robot getting harmed, showed that the inclination of individuals to "harm" robots is higher in comparison to their disposition to harm an individual in the standard Milgram experiment, plus that nearly all participants were willing to damage the robot that they perhaps wouldn't have been in case it was an "actual" living being.

At first sight, these findings may seem to contradict the notion of human-resemblance in HRIs.

Though at the same light, nearly all healthy participants showcased the same undesirable feelings, the same ethical concerns, plus the same arousal and distress which they would have encountered if asked to injure or terminate a living-being, even if the "injured" robot is only a robot having a functional, non-emotive embodiment.

Researchers argue that this emotive-behavioral dissociation is because of the understanding that no real damage is being done since the robot isn't a living being, plus that this self-justification counteracts the emotional reaction. It's also been shown that most individuals do attribute emotional conditions to robots and regulate their behavior comparatively. These results are in conformity with the supposition that, there's a disconnection between logical behavior on one hand, as well as socioemotional response on the other (Dominik and Jacek, 2014).

6.4.4. Significance of Human Robot Interactions

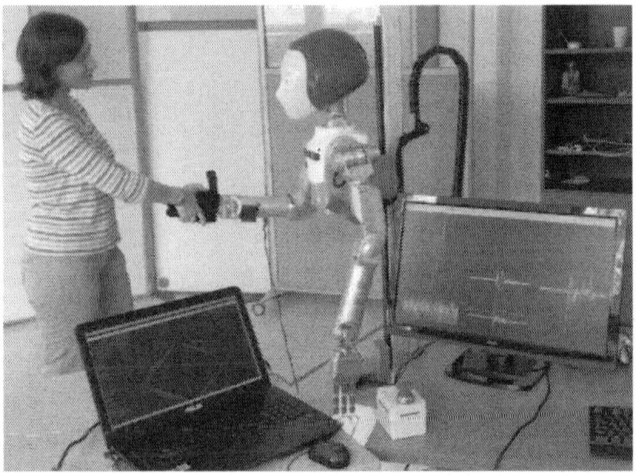

Figure 6.15: Robotics is a field of HCI that is more practical and hands-on.

Source: https://techxplore.com/news/2017–09-handshake-team-focused-human-robot-interactions.html.

Human-Robot Interaction or simply HRI is a branch of human computer interactions that's devoted to understanding, planning, and assessing robotic structures for usage by or with people. Interaction, by description, requires adequate connection between robots and people. Communication between an individual and a robot might take various forms, however, these forms are mostly determined by whether the person and robot are in near proximity to one another or not. Therefore, communication, and, hence, interaction can be divided into various general categories (Morley and Parker, 2016).

HRI is a new study field concerned with robot steering and manipulation. It has been established through collaborations between scientists in the sectors of robotics and psychology. Experts of HRI are examining interactions and discussions between robots and people on the context of both robotics and psychological studies. The robots, particularly humanoids, developed through robotics researchers may be applied as testbeds for validating theories in psychology, plus the verified hypotheses might be used for upgrading the robots.

Scientists have developed some humanlike robots, known as androids. They can study fundamental matters in HRI through using the androids or simpler robots. One of the fundamental questions that experts ask is the best way to characterize human presence through using androids and robots. The other is what robotic conversation is. Another key question concerning the very human-like robot concerns how the robot may represent human presence. Basically, there should be certain minimum conditions that should be established for depicting human-presence by a robot (Morley and Parker, 2016).Understanding human–robot interaction without solid speech recognition systems is considered difficult. Nonetheless, by utilizing robotics as well as media technologies, researchers can develop robotic systems which can have live discussions with humans without use of speech recognition. There's need for development of various practical uses of interactive robots and the creation of a society, whereby interactive and communicative robotic systems offer various services to individuals.

Remote interaction are also possible in robotics. In this situation, the people and the robot aren't co-located but instead divided spatially or even partially. For instance, during NASA's voyages to outer space normally Mars Rovers are detached from the earth both in terms of space and time. But despite of this distance the robots can still be controlled from earth in real-time. In terms of Proximate Interactions, both the people and robots are co-situated (for instance, service robots could be in the same vicinity as humans.

Within these broad categories, it's necessary to distinguish between systems that require mobility, manual operation, or social interaction. Distant interaction with portable robots often is known as teleoperation or directional control, besides remote interaction with manual manipulators is often known as tele-manipulation. Proximate collaboration with mobile robots might take the role of a robot associate, and proximate interaction might comprise of physical interaction (Morley and Parker, 2016).

As for social interaction it includes social, cognitive, and emotive elements of interaction. In this model, the individuals and robots interrelate as either companions or peers. Notably, social interactions with robotic systems seem to be proximate instead of remote. Because the capacity of work in most social interactions is huge, most researchers present only a brief survey of their findings whereas a more comprehensive survey of this particular subject is typically kept for future work.

Various key changes in HRI-related areas with the objective of identifying crucial technological and research developments have been made. As a result, we can expect that HRI will grow as a discipline on its own. After surveying various key factors in the development of HRI, researchers have defined the HRI issue with a focus on those elements of interaction which an inventor can shape.

We also need to define the application domains that drive modern HRI. A majority of these issues are quite challenging and have significant societal implications. The application areas can be grouped into two main categories, which are remote and proximate connections. These areas detect important, impactful, or thought-provoking tasks within these two groups. Researchers have also gone ahead to describe various solution concepts as well as barrier problems which cross application domains, including interaction types. Including identifying related programs from other fields concerning human and machine interactions (Morley and Parker, 2016).

Generally, human-robot interaction or HRI examines human activities and environments to evaluate the practicality of robotics for human use. At the same time, the technology helps develop novel theories, procedures, and mechanisms which allow robots to network with individuals in effective, constructive, and ethical ways. Additionally, some studies focused on individual and societal effects of interactions between people and robots.

Modern investigations of human-based activities, environments, and interfaces with robots use detailed, advanced empirical-research techniques, as well as qualitative, quantitative, and multipronged approaches. Similarly, explorations of novel robotic concepts, human-robot interface paradigms, and design systems for applications utilize a research-by-design method. Some example frameworks for applications are social and physical support in domestic, labor, and clinical settings (for instance, education, manufacturing, and therapy), project-critical environments (e.g., search, and rescue, space exploration), and public spaces (e.g., transportation, museums, and retail settings) (Dominik and Jacek, 2014).

Technical improvements in HRI comprise of novel algorithms, structures, architectures, and platforms which allow for new kinds of human-robot interface and methods and settings for coding and prototyping robot structures. Finally, theoretical tasks in HRI apply grounded, meta-analytic, and case-study systems to develop models, frameworks, and models of human-robot interaction.Going forward, it is important to foster the development of highly inter-disciplinary HRI study communities and promote problem-driven work which incorporates design, methodical, and behavioral perspectives. There is also need for submissions which present robust, rigorous research in various sectors of HRI which make empirical, developmental, technical, or hypothetical contributions. Stakeholders must also seek to expedite the interpretation of research into practical projects through open-access publications which clearly identify the effects of the study for practice.

While HCI is a useful technology, stakeholders must realize that it's also important to develop human-friendly machines which add value to people in their workplace and other fields, but without jeopardizing human contributions where it's needed. There should be close interaction between computers and individuals who are skilled in operating them (Dominik and Jacek, 2014).

CHAPTER

7

Applications of Computer Science and Technology in Agriculture

CONTENTS

7.1. INTRODUCTION

Computers and applications that are associated with them helped change most of the traditional methods of doing things, including in agriculture. These days it is possible to collect milk using computers, estimate seeds, or predict the weather in an automated way. Computers have helped in the revolutionizing of farming practices. It is important for us to understand the ways in which this has been achieved.

Advancements in technology have led to many major changes in animal and farming husbandry. This, in turn, led to increased production. Computers have been integrated into the agricultural sector to replace human effort and intervene in the traditional farming machineries.

In addition to this, computers have also helped improve the support functions in agriculture, including the manner in which machinery and fertilizers are delivered. All of these activities have been automated successfully. Despite the fact that computers have changed a lot, introduction of internet has made it even better and has helped in doubling the pace at which these changes are occurring.

Figure 7.1: There is a great revolution that is about to occur in the agricultural sector. Information that is in a digital form on weather, soil conditions and crop health is already being utilized by modern farmers for the optimization of their harvest yields.

Source: https://www.research. bayer.com/en/digital-farming.aspx.

These days, talking about agriculture does not have to refer solely to the production of crops and livestock farming. There are many ecological issues impacting our environment. It is important for the growers to think about the impact on the environment due to the changes in climate.

Some of the general uses of computers in agriculture are:

- Computer software that predicts weather and crop quantity.
- Computer software that keeps track of costs spent on producing, transporting, and processing the agricultural produce. The software helps make estimations and calculations of profits and losses.
- Farmers are able to communicate with each other due to the help of the internet. This allows for farmers to have communication with experts in agriculture. This promotes exchanging of knowledge and helps the growers to increase their production rates and profit.
- Software technology has led to the evolution of farming practices. Therefore, farmers require less effort which in turn leads to a higher output.
- Automated procedures lead to a reduction in human effort and increase in the rate and quality of production.

7.2. MONITORING THE WEATHER

Weather is a major factor impacting everyone profoundly. Everyone is always hoping for a warm and sunny day so that no one is running in the rain and a muddy environment. There are also times we normally hope for a slightly rainy day so as to water some plants or even just play in the rain.

In the agricultural sector weather has a direct effect on the production in the farm. It has an effect on the growth of crops, their yield, the occurrence of pests, the amount of irrigation and fertilization that is needed, and all the activities that are performed in the farm during the season for growing. Farming outside in the open is highly dependent on the weather and any changes in the weather, considering its moody conditions, will have a direct effect in the crops that are being grown. This is all in consideration of the fact that climate change is having a huge effect on the weather patterns and this is out of the control of human beings (Li, 2008).

7.2.1. Farmers vs the Weather Which Cannot Be Predicted

It is impossible for a farmer to fight the weather. This being said, it is important to acknowledge the fact that the farmer can adopt the situation that is presented to him/her and use the extra management practices that are can be used to control this matter by reducing the loss of crops. It is therefore important for farmers to have the accurate information to do with the weather, so as to plan their farm activities without encountering adverse weather.

Figure 7.2: Above is an image of a weather instrument that has combined an anemometer for measuring the speed of the wind, a wind vane that shows the direction in which the wind is moving, and a rain bucket which helps in measuring the amount of rainfall.

Source: https://store.nerokas.co.ke/index.php?route=product/product&product_id=1349.

Awareness of the weather conditions in real time, such as the dew and air temperatures, humidity, and precipitation, goes a long way towards protecting the plants and ensuring a high crop yield. If the farmers do not do this, they have a higher chance of encountering floods, hails, drought or frost, which can lead to higher production costs. The only way farmers can be sure they have crop production that is profitable is through accurate weather forecasts. These can be found on most devices including smartphones, computers, radios, and even TVs. This is very important especially for the farmers that depend greatly of the state of the weather (Li and Zhao, 2019).

7.2.2. Monitoring the Weather Will Determine the Success of the Farmer

Different crops have different requirements and weather conditions are one of them. Some cops prefer high temperatures while others prefer low temperatures. Disease and pests' occurrences can be predicted using a combination of the temperatures and humidity. This information gives farmers the opportunity to decide when they will seed or harvest the crop to avoid the negative effects of weather.

Crop yields are determined by weather conditions. Weather monitoring includes weather observation to have the current information for growing crops (Li and Zhao, 2019).There are a set of instruments responsible for providing important information on the soil conditions. Technology has made it possible for us to collect consistent and automatic information. These sensors can be connected underneath the soil to collect and track the important weather and soil information. Information is the sent to computers or mobile devices and can be accessed anytime. Some of the aspects that these sensors measure include:

- The amount of rainfall – They can measure the amount of rain that has fallen in a certain time frame.
- Temperatures – They are able to ensure the tracking of changes in the temperature over different time frames: a day, a month, etc.
- The speed and direction of wind – This allows the farmers to make predictions on any storms that are coming up in a more accurate manner.
- Air pressure – This also helps with making predictions of upcoming thunderstorms in the areas that are surrounding.
- Humidity – This helps with managing the wanter usage.

All these parameters can be utilized for certain operations on the field, such as setting a schedule for irrigation, alarm models for pests, and even determining the correct time to fertilize and protect the crops. It is important to know the weather data so as to manage a farm successfully. In addition to this, it helps in promoting sustainable farming, which in turn protects the environment.

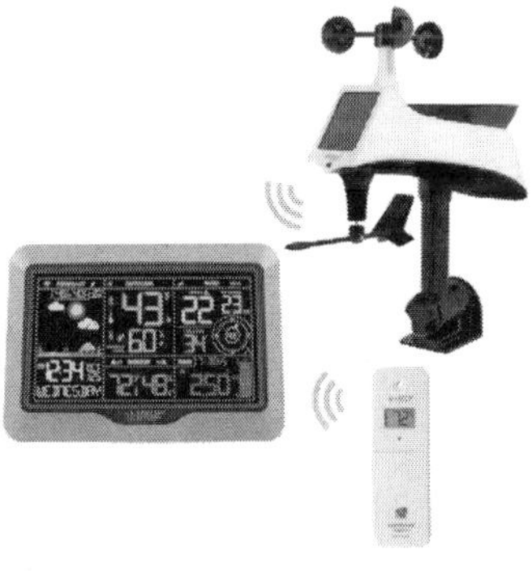

Figure 7.3: Above is an example of a computerized weather station. It is kind of similar to that in Figure 7.2, however, this is electrically run.

Source: http://e993.com/forex/Pro-Weather-Station/.

Farmers are able to utilize systems that provide precise measurements of the environmental conditions. These are called weather stations. There are many different types that are available and in accordance to the quantity of parameters that need to be measured, the precision of the work and the range of the work as well.

Farming is very important today, considering the fact that it gives us food, which is a basic necessity for everyone. Climate change makes it hard for this food production to be consistent. As a result, it is still necessary for farming to continue being more productive and sustainable due to the growing population. This means that having accurate ways to monitor the weather conditions is very important if we want to increase profit and productivity level.

In this new data-driven agronomy industry, it is important to set up accurate weather monitors in the fields. This will also help to optimize labor costs and usage of water.

Computerized weather monitors record specific weather data. These computerized monitors allow the farmer to:

- Make configurations on their number of samples each day;
- Track measurements that are historical over a certain date range that has been set;
- Be able to see where the sensors in the field are located;
- Visualize smart dashboards that have metrics which are monitored;
- Use sensor fleet management tools that are better;
- Setting of data that is open or data options that are secure;
- Have availability of data that is sourced from the community so as to make comparisons.

This information does not only make it possible for the farmer to gain access to the accurate data from the field sensors, but some are also created in a manner that allows the farmer to gain information on the weather from other sources.

This includes weather stations and rain gauges that are remote. This gives the farmers a higher opportunity for the tracking of weather patterns in their surroundings.

Some are also developed to allow the farmers to monitor other lands that have crops similar to the one's they are going so as to see how they are growing with the weather conditions.

Figure 7.4: There are phone applications that farmers are able to use to see predictions on the weather so as to ensure proper management of their farms.

Source: https://www.popularmechanics.com/technology/apps/gmp25804798/best-weather-apps/.

7.2.3. Benefits of Having Weather Monitoring Equipment

By using these applications that help farmers in monitoring the weather, they have a higher advantage than just knowing the basic weather conditions that are mentioned. They also allow the growers to have more information on the different analytics of data that are provided by the meteorological department. The applications can also allow the growers to maintain a way of monitoring the risk of pests and diseases (Ahuja, Ma, and Howell, 2016).

These applications also help in ensuring that farming is much more precise. The collection of data using the sensors in the field makes the information much more accurate.

This helps in allowing the farmers to make better plans of how to use water, plant, and maintain the plants in an accurate manner and therefore allowing them to use fewer resources. This saves time, money, and labor costs.

The computers also help in providing better information on the weather. Using this technology allows the farmers to make better predictions on their crops due to accurate information on the amount of rainfall, temperature, humidity, etc. They also get to better preparations for intense weather conditions. All these benefits help in increasing the quality and quantity of crop production (Ahuja, Ma, and Howell, 2016).

Some of the other benefits include:

- Saving costs – sustainable farming promotes reduced costs on water, nutrients, labor, and nutrients for the plants.
- Saving the resources of water – being able to gain access to information on the exact amount if rainfall for each plant can lead to the optimizations of watering, and therefore the crops cannot be overwatered. This can help in making sure the crops remain healthy.
- Saving if time and increasing organization – viewing the levels of water and the condition if the weather in a remote manner helps in saving the time which it would take the farmer to go to the field physically. In addition to this, knowledge on the patterns of the weather helps them to make better plans on the activities that need to be carried out before the heavy rains start to pour.
- Makes it easy in making decisions – having precise data can ensure accurate irrigation, use of pesticides and herbicides, seeding, and labor. Being able to track the patterns of weather that are historical can allow the farmers to make better predictions on times for spraying. It also helps in the better anticipation on risks of disease.
- Reducing human error due to efficient crop monitoring – computers have promoted automatic monitoring which makes the information accurate with shorter time periods and less labor.

7.3. RECORD KEEPING

Computers have played an important role in recording of data in the agricultural sector.

These records are kept by the farmers to as to help them in keeping track of important data such as the records of the budget, health of animals and crops, forms for tracking, inventories of equipment used, and even maps of the land. Computer technology can be utilized by both crop and livestock farmers for the tracking of the status and health of the crops and the livestock (Li, 2008).

Figure 7.5: Keeping records is important in ensuring a business that is sustainable and effective. It also helps in making predictions about the future dos and don'ts.

Source: http://shivjot1997.blogspot.com/2016/06/blog-post_24.html.

These records may have information on the age of the crops and livestock, the health, the level of production, the development cycle, etc. There are different applications, programs, and softwares that help in the organization and keeping of records of this data for the farmers. This makes it easier for them to keep track of the produce and ensure that it is a sustainable business.

There are many different reasons why financial information is reported for many different reasons. For a farm to be sustainable and effective, they all require to have effective and efficient farm records in place, so as to allow the farmers to make decisions that are more informed when it comes to the profits of the farms (Li, 2008).

There are many institutions that expect for farmers to keep records in everything they own as well as any loans that have not yet been paid. These institutions can also be forced to ask for the records of the farm production, estimates of the sales that are expected, and even the budget for the next year. There are also many different regulations on chemicals that have been set up, and farmers are expected to record each time they use pesticides and herbicides. This is because of the many concerns that have come to our attention due to the manner in which these chemicals affect the environment. Farmers are also expected to report all their cash sales, depreciation, expenses, and participation to the Internal Revenue Service.

Most of the times, these records are mostly only required by the Internal Revenue Service for filing. Despite the fact that records on tax are important, there is a need for additional information so as to make informed decisions when it comes to managerial issues. Farms that do not have effective record keeping tend to make less profits. Farms need to have effective record keeping so as to run sustainably.

Records are kept by farmers not only for the farm, but also many other reasons. Firstly, due to requirements from certain institutions. Some of the bodies in the government require records on the farm's financial and production records, and these have to be up to date. Secondly, due to environmental regulations. Farmers need to keep records on the amount of irrigation water they use, the waste from their livestock, and all the chemicals they use.

Figure 7.6: Keeping effective records requires for training of your employees. This will help in avoiding errors which could have been made while using paperwork.

Source: https://cropwatch.unl.edu/tags/farm-record-keeping.

Some of the advantages of record keeping include:

- They help in reducing the financial exposure and risks in the business incase of a recall.
- They allow for the reduction of loss, theft, and shrinkage through better management of inventories in the farm.
- It also helps in reducing the costs that are used to train workers through processes that are guided.
- It maximizes the efficiency of labor through labor planning and farm tasks that are better.
- Helps in the reduction of any chance if a budget shock due to having budget information in real time.

- It also helps in increasing the profits and yields due to the utilization of farming practices that are better.
- It allows the farms to maintain adherence to the international farming standards such as GlobalGAP.
- It helps in the reduction of the response time from the management to any problems that arise in the process of farming, due to the availability of real time information on issues to do with the farm.
- It also helps in reducing the costs for farm compliance by eliminating paperwork and promoting reporting that is automated.
- Making of quick audits.
- The farm traceability will be increased due to better inventory keeping.
- It promotes better practices which help in increasing the level of productivity and enforcing farming processes and practices that are sustainable.
- The farm-wide risk is lowered due to effective and efficient systems that are used for traceability.
- It helps in increasing the profits due to faster management responses through alerts from emails, monitoring using mobile phones, better reporting, and better observation systems.
- Better management of cash flow, giving the farmers better means for the assessment of the farm progress through analyzing the site, produce, farm or the farming area.
- Creation of newer opportunities and the evolution of the management style of the farms.
- Reduction of costs spent on labor and materials due to being able to accurately monitor the management of the inventory and employee labor.
- It also allows the farmers to pass their audits due to the effective traceability systems.
- Agronomists tend to support the farm better by giving permission to the farmers to monitor the activities of the farm in a remote manner.
- Improvement of communication between the teams in the farm using task management tools that are accurate, printing tasks, and systems that can provide them with alerts.

- Enhancement of cash flow and profitability due to the utilization of easy methods to plan resources and activities in the farm.
- It helps in the reduction of administration costs that results due to efficient systems for traceability.
- Lower the levels of inaccuracies and waste during the process of harvesting using systems that are based on mobile phones and bar codes.

For record keeping, the farms can use either computers or hand methods. Not all systems that keep records are able to perform all the aspects that are mentioned above. It is important for the farmers to choose a system that will cater for their needs.

There are comparisons that can be made between the hand and computer system. In the recent years, most farms are using computers and computer systems. There are still many farms that use the hand recording system. It is important for farmers to carefully consider the two systems before they pick one main one.

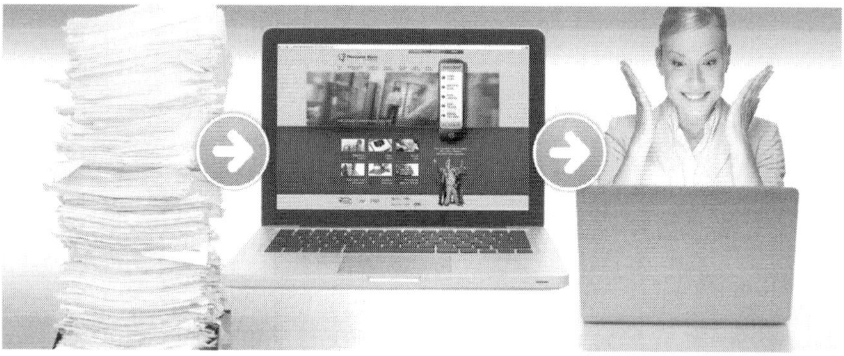

Figure 7.7: Computers have helped in reducing the amount of paperwork that most people gad to deal with. This has helped in increasing the accuracy of the record-keeping that is done.

Source: http://www.taco.ca/en/resources-electronic-records-retention.php.

- Some of the characteristics of the hand system include:
- Lower costs;
- Easier for implementation;
- It consumes a lot of time;
- It is easier to make errors; and

- It takes too much time and effort.

Some of the characteristics of the computer system include:

- It is much more expensive to maintain;
- Faster to deal with;
- Much more accurate;
- Helps in making analysis;
- It is much more expensive to train the workers.

7.4. COMPUTERIZED FARM VEHICLES

Autonomous farm vehicles are those that do not have drivers. They help in delivering high torque at speeds that are slow so as to perform tilling on the land, as well as other agricultural tasks. They are developed in a manner that allows them to run without a human being present on the tractor. They have a program that allows them to make observations of where they stand, make decisions on their speed, and even make sure not to come into contact with any objects, humans or animals in the field that is being tilled.There are some of these tractors that are fully autonomous, while others need to be supervised. This idea was developed a while back, around the 1940s, and it has developed greatly due to the development of technology. Considering the fact that they do not have drivers, they are installed with GPS and other technologies that are wireless that help them in farming the land without needing a driver. All they need is someone to supervise them at a control station, so as to ensure proper monitoring of progress.

Figure 7.8: Agricultural robots have proven to be very efficient. All the need is someone to supervise. Thus helps in reducing human labor.

Source: https://www.growingproduce.com/vegetables/agricultural-robots-no-longer-science-fiction/?amp.

These tractors were developed so as to increase the level of autonomy in agriculture. In addition to automated farm vehicles, there are also many other things that have been automated in agriculture, including automatic milking. This technology is hard to develop. So as to ensure that the technology is successful, there are certain deterministic tasks that the tractor needs to follow.

They also need to have a behavior that is reactive, so as to be able to react to any situation that may occur and also responses that are reflexive so that they can make decisions without hesitating or consuming too much time to decide.

The tractors need to be able to make perform actions that are similar to a human being when it comes to observation of spatial skills and even when it comes to their reaction speed (Jeong et al, 2013).

These tractors have been found to cause a slight controversy when it comes to how safe they are and their acceptance by the public.

There are some people who get nervous when they hear that the tractor does not have a driver. There is a lot of time and programming that is put in to the creation of these tractors so as to ensure they are safe at all times, even if they fail.

They all however, have motion detectors that allow them to stop in case they come across an object in their path.

These tractors use highly advanced sensors and systems that would also be found in self driving cars. In the United States, they have systems that allow them to steer themselves in harsh conditions that may have poor visibility. This is considered an advantage. Farmers are able to enjoy the benefits that come with this technology due to the advanced structures they possess. These tractors can also be made in a way that allows them to act as mobile hotspots, so at to aid in the collection of information from the sensors that may be found all over the land.

This will help in providing accurate agricultural applications due to the swift delivery if information.

These equipments may take over our farms in the future, however, there is also a need to consider all the disadvantages that they may possess before we fully adopt them into our agricultural sector.

Figure 7.9: Planting in a prescriptive manner allows the farmers to gain knowledge on the conditions of the soil and water.

Source: https://www.wsj.com/amp/articles/no-headline-available-1393372266.

Many argue that it is not possible to fully replace a human being with a computer. It is possible to rethink on the manner in which crop production is carried out, so as to make them more effective. There are some other people who argue that it would be better to have many small machines instead on one huge one. These small machines are allegedly easier to maintain, and they may not cause as much damage as the larger ones.

7.5. AUTOMATED MILKING

In addition to automated tractors, milking has also been computerized. It involves milking of dairy animals, mostly dairy cattle. These systems are able to milk cows without the labor of a human being. This technology was introduced in the late 1800s. They were introduced in the market later on. This technology is referred to as an agricultural robot considering the fact that they offer complete automation. Most of these systems utilize computers and farm management software (Li, 2008).

The process of milking involves a couple of tasks that have been set up to extract milk from a dairy animal. There are certain sub-tasks that can be mentioned in how the process is broken down. These include: being able to collect the animals before that are taken to be milked, showing the animals the route to the parlor, inspecting the animals, washing the cow's tits, giving the back of the udder a massage so as to ensure that any milk that is held back is relieved, extracting the milk, removing the equipment being used to milk, leaving the animals back.

Figure 7.10: Automated milking has helped in increasing the yield of milk for farmers, as well as has reduced the levels of human labor.

Source: https://www.gea.com/en/productgroups/milking-systems/automatic-milking-systems/index.jsp.

The lactation period is normally approximately 300 days and being able to maintain the yield of milk during this period is important, and it needs for one to be consistent with the intervals in which the animals are milked. This is normally twice a day and with adequate time spaces between one milking and another. This however, can have a few disadvantages. Despite the health of the farmer, he/she will need to avail themselves for work every day, twice a day. This is a major restriction when it comes to one's personal life. This is the case especially if the family cannot afford to hire more workers, as it is economically strenuous. Small scale dairy farmers have a hard time dealing with this issue. There are however, some techniques that have been investigated so as to lower these constraints, such as voluntary milking and once a day milking.

Voluntary milking involves giving the cow the opportunity to choose its own time and intervals for milking, instead of having to be milked as a group. This means that the automatic milking system needs to be fully automated, because the cow can choose any time within the 24hr time frame (Li, 2008).

The unit that is used to milk the cow has a machine, a position sensor for the teats, an arm that is robotic and automatically applies and removes the teat-cup, and a gate system that is used in ensuring the cow traffic is controlled.

7.5.1. Advantages

- Reduces the labor costs – They free the farmer from the process of milking and the rigid schedule associated with the milking process. The only labor that is needed is for the supervision and feeding of the animals.
- Ensures the milk is consistent – every cow should be subject to a consistent milking process. This process also does not undergo any influence from different people milking the cow. They reduce any threat of injury by ensuring that the four cups that are used for milking are individually removed. This means that there is no empty cup that will remain attached while the rest are still finishing off. There are even some developments that can change the rate if pulsation and vacuum level depending on the flow of milk from each teat.
- The frequency of milking is increased – it is possible for the frequency of milking to go up to 3 times a day, but mostly the average frequency is 2.5 times a day. This helps in lowering the stress that may be placed on the udder and ensuring the cow is increasingly comfortable. The yield of milk per cow can increase with an increase in frequency.

Figure 7.11: Above is a representation of the four automated hands that are used to milk the cow. Each is independent.

Source: https://www.youtube.com/watch?v=3PXcF8XnY5w.

- An environment that has less stress – There are people who have come up with a perception that cows have less stress when they have proper schedules.

- Better management of the herds – using computers has allowed the farmers to have much better collection of data. This allows the farmer to have better management due to being able to analyze any sequences amongst the herd, such as the feed that promotes milk production. It is also possible to use the computers to examine the histories of the cows, and they can even be set up to alert the farmers of any unusual vitals that may be a sign of an illness. This information is very important for the farmers in improving the quality of milk production, however, the ability to utilize this information is highly dependent on the skills of the farmer or how accurate the computer is.

7.5.2. Disadvantages

- Quite expensive to start – these systems are quite costly. One is approximately $190,524 per milking unit. The construction costs, how much the labor and the amount one has invested is what allow one to determine on whether it is economically advantageous to buy an automatic milking system instead of a parlor. It is also important to consider the availability of labor in addition to the cost of labor. These systems are much more beneficial to small scale farmers, and larger farms can use the parlors.
- The cost of electricity is increased – This is because the robots are run by electricity, but one can outweigh this using the reduction in the input if labor.
- They are quite complex to use – technological advancements always come with complexity. This is not an exception. The fact that they are complicated to use means that one has to pay more for maintenance services as well as the costs for operating the machinery. In case the whole system fails, the farmer will have to rely on the service provider to respond to this problem, thus more costs. Thus the system needs to be highly maintained because the cows are offered the choice of milking voluntarily, considering the fact that all the cows have to use that single system.
- It is had to use in pasture systems – This system mainly works best in the zero grazing system, where the animal is kept inside during the period she is lactating. This means that the land is at a premium. Cows prefer not to go to the unit to be milked if the distance is too long to walk.

- The quality of the milk is lower – the total number of bacteria and white blood cells that is found in a sample of milk is measured using the plate loop count and the somatic cell count. If the somatic cell count is high, that means that the health of the udder has reduced due to fighting of the infection by the immune system of the cow and therefore the quality of milk is reduced. Cows that are using these systems tend to have higher levels of somatic cell count than those that are milked traditionally. If the milk has a high plate loop count, the cow has a bacterial infection, normally due to a low level of sanitation, and this also lowers the quality of milk.
- Some cows may get stressed – cows are normally social. Some cows are normally dominant, forcing others to have to go for milking later in the night.
- The farmer and the herd do not get enough contact – it is important for the farmer to be knowledgeable on the state if the herd. In the traditional method, the farmers always observe the condition of the cows before they milk them and those that are not well can be noted for later treatment. In automatic milking, the farmer does not get to observe the cows due to less contact, and a cow that is ill may continue to suffer for a longer time period. This can affect the quality and quantity of milk and the cow could even die. These systems have sensors that can be used to sense any alterations in the cow's milk that could be caused by an illness. This as well as frequent inspections should be carried out by the farmer. This, however, brings us back to the time constraints. The automatic systems that are used these days try to fix this issue by collecting useful data such as the conductivity of milk, the temperature of the milk, the color of the milk, the weight of the cow, the time the cow spent ruminating, the speed of milking, the time it took to milk the cow, etc.

7.6. HAVING FORUMS ON THE INTERNET, ONLINE KNOWLEDGE BASES, SOCIAL NETWORKING, AND SOCIAL MEDIA

All industries in the world have been helped a great deal by the internet and the communication technologies that are related to it. This includes e-commerce, mobile computing, etc. Agriculture is one of these industries.

The internet has helped many different farmers connect with experts in the agricultural field, all over the world.

There are many different sites for social networking as well as forums where farmers are able to communicate with other farmers and certain experts in the field thus promoting the sharing of knowledge among them. To add onto this, there are various repositories for learning that help in providing information on many different things to do with agriculture. These sites have a couple of advantages:

- They help in reducing the divide between the rural areas and digital areas;
- They help in the influencing of public policies;
- They also help in fostering partnerships; and
- They bring together stakeholders from different parts of the agricultural sector.

Figure 7.12: Social networks the most popular way of communicating in this day and time. Majority of the population is found on these platforms.

Source: https://kampp. org/2019/10/30/social-media-management/.

This all makes it easier for a farmer to reach out to an entrepreneur who deals with agricultural products so as to communicate on different business proposals. Knowledge on certain information such as information on pests, information about the weather in real-time, the speed of the wind, the prices of grains and livestock, etc. globally, can be found right on the internet.

Communication within agriculture has really improved over the years. The internet has really helped us gain a lot of information on anything we want to know. In addition to the other aspects that one mentioned above, businesses to do with agriculture can also use social media as a form of communication. It will help in making the level of communication better, efficient, and effective (Li, 2008).

Due to the development of technology, the level of production in the sector has grown extensively. Using social media to communicate these developments in technology can be very beneficial to both the farmers and even the population at large. This however, can be a bit difficult considering the fact that there are many organizations that are fighting against the environmental values of the industries as well as the chemicals that are being used to treat crops and animals.

It is however, easier to change the perspective of the public using social media and other new methods of communication. Social media can be used to educate them and also enable them to form a better opinion on the production of food and other forms of agriculture. The diversity of agriculture is growing rapidly, and people who work in the farms are reducing. Most of the people these days live in the cities and do not exactly understand how agriculture works. Due to the great diversity of the population, it's important for agriculturalists to find ways to communicate and educate the population on agricultural matters. It is not exactly possible to have face-to-face conversations with the population due to the numbers that one has to deal with. Social media however, has proven to be one of the best ways to communicate and educated population on these matters. Due to the Internet as well as other forms of technology such as the mobile phone, tablets, etc., it is possible to pass on information from one end of the earth to the other (Li and Zhao, 2019).

Is farmers and agricultural do not take advantage of social media platforms to educate, communicate, and promote their jobs and livelihoods to the rest of the population, it will be hard for them to properly communicate why the public's opinion should be for agriculture and not against agriculture. As of today, there are many farmers who are now computer literate and have adopted technology so as to have better communication with their customers.

It is also much easier for agricultural experts who are having problems with implementation of new technology into the businesses to find organizations that can assist them and also provide the training that is needed for the farmers and businesses that are owned by the community due to the internet (Li and Zhao, 2019).

Figure 7.13: Internet forums are important in this sector. Above are the steps one should follow when passing on information.

Source: https://forumbee. com/article/y7h1xv/what-type-of-online-forum-is-right-for-my-community-.

One of the greatest advantages of integrating social media into agricultural businesses, is that the farmer gets to communicate with his/her customers as well as other experts in the agricultural sector, in a manner that will ensure that the relationship is developing. This is mostly because social media provides instant access and that is very important for the implementation of dialogue, management, and education of the end-user. It also allows for agricultural experts to have networking that is quick and responsive.

Farmers have the opportunity to create their own pages on social media so as to advertise their product using Twitter, Facebook, Instagram, or even YouTube. This will help them in the utilization of the format that uses storytelling in promoting what they are talking about to a large audience especially when utilizing a platform such as Facebook which contains more than 1.3 billion users. It also allows them to talk about the things that they would like to change in the agricultural sector as well as any new technology that has just developed, so as to gain the interest of the end-user (Li and Zhao, 2019).

These days it is very hard to find people buying newspapers. Newspapers have been found to be used mostly by the older generation, as the younger generation uses social media. It is evident that the population mostly consists of the younger generation. Using social media allows the farmers to talk to a large part of the population. Farmers can also look for youth workers to help them in social media advertising.

Most of the current news is also found on social media. Agricultural businesses will be able to see any new advancements that have occurred, on social media, seeing as this is the first place they will be posted. In fact, agricultural businesses that use social media will tend to have a competitive edge due to the advantage of seeing this information first. Social media has led to interaction of different people globally due to display of curiosity.

There are certain activists that are against agriculture and often use social media to talk about their opinions. There is a lot of negative talk that has been directed towards the agricultural industry especially on social media. This is quite unfortunate considering the fact that most of the people in the agricultural industry are not tech savvy. This means that any information that is put on the social media whether true or not will end up spreading to many different people. This can be disadvantageous if the information is not true and yet there are no agricultural experts on social media to talk about it. This gives the public an opinion that they should not have (Li, 2008).

Figure 7.14: Agriculturalists need to consider using social networks to create online communities that can help in keeping the population aware and well educated on matters to do with agriculture.

Source: https://techmag.xyz/creating-online-forums/.

There are many animal rights activists who have used social media to talk about how certain animals are mistreated before they reach the market. There are some organizations that do not practice ethical practices while supplying meat. As a result, the public is less inclined to buy any meat from any organization. This will end up being disadvantageous to farmers who actually follow all the ethical practices. This is why it is important for farmers to engage on social media so that they can see all these things that have been talked about and be able to shed light on the facts of these matters.

Agricultural businesses not using social media platforms may be at a great risk of losing their profits due to stereotypes and criticism. It is therefore important for them to take charge and use social media to communicate with the end-users so that it is not bad for business. Likewise, it is important for them to add value to the brand of their business and also change how the audience behaves (Li, 2008).

7.7. E-AGRICULTURE

This deals with ensuring that agricultural and rural development is enhanced through better processes in communication and information. It mostly deals with being able to conceptualize, design, develop, evaluate, and apply methods that are innovative in utilizing technologies in information and communication in the areas that are rural mainly to promote agriculture.

Information and communication technology in agriculture deals with mobile, applications, networks, devices, etc. Some of these technologies were created in the era of the Internet and others were created before the Internet existed, such as televisions, telephones, satellites, and radios. Some of the major components of electronic agriculture involves the methodologies, norms, the tools, the standards of the provision, as well as being able to develop both institutional and individual capacities and being able to support policies (Kaushik et al, 2019).

Interventions that involve electronic agriculture have undergone development and testing all over the world so as to promote the improvement on the livelihood of farmers through increasing the level of productivity as well as profits, and also by lowering the level of risk.

Some of the systems that are used in e-agriculture include:

- Wireless technology – there are very many applications for wireless technology in agriculture. This means that there is no need to install coaxial cables.
- The Global Positioning System (GPS) – this is very helpful when it comes to survey the land, Geo-fencing, and making maps. Over the years, GPSs have had their prices dropped and therefor multiple people them. Those who are using GPSs are able to get digitized maps that are highly accurate without having to use a

professional to achieve this. It is possible to tag certain animals with devices that will be able to send an alert to the farmers mobile phone anytime they cross a geo-fence. This helps in preventing certain animals from moving into farmland and leading to the destruction of food crops and therefore preventing losses. This technology can allow animals to move around freely however, the farmer gets an alert anytime it is near his or her farm.

Figure 7.15: Computers have made our lives easier. Above is a man using his mobile phone to watch over his cattle. This helps in saving time and money.

Source: https://www.euractiv.com/section/agriculture-food/news/e-agriculture-could-save-eu-farmers-time-and-money/.

- Geographic information systems – these are used greatly in this sector especially for precision farming. A digital map is created of the land and geodetic data that is pertinent undergoes combination with different statistical data so as to make it easier to analyze the soil. Geographic information systems help the farmers to make decisions such as where the plants should be planted, what crops they should plant, etc. while just utilizing data that is historical and samples.
- Systems that are automated – as discussed above, there are milking systems that are computerized and controlled in a manner that does not require human labor. These devices are called agricultural robots, because they are fully automated in the process of milking. This means that the farmer is not involved in the process of milking the cow, allowing for the farmer to have much more time in supervising and feeding the herd. Farmers are

also able to cause improvement of the management of the cows by using the information that has been collected by the computer. So as to obtain maximum yield of milk, farmers are able to use this information by making analysis on the different feeds that the animals are taking and how these are affecting the yield of the milk. This allows them to adjust the quantities to their preference. This technology also allows for the farmer to track each and every cow individually, because all the data is available in an individual level. This makes it possible for the farmer to know when one of the cows is unwell or has an unusual change in the milk.

- Mobile phones – Mobile phones are becoming very popular in the agricultural sector. The penetration of mobile phones has helped in enhancing the advantageous impact, that is multi-dimensional, on reducing poverty in a sustainable manner and also being able to accept that the main challenge in promoting the optimization of the agricultural potential, is accessibility. These days there are many people in the rural areas that have smart phones and this has been greatly beneficial. However, most of these places do not have Internet which still makes it a disadvantage considering the fact that it is easier to use social media to pass information. There are however, applications that can be I stalled in the phones that help in educating people on agricultural aspects.

7.8. E-COMMERCE

This refers to electronic-commerce which deals with being able to buy and sell services, goods, or products on the Internet. In this specific aspect there is also consideration of how money, funds, and data is transacted.

There are four different ways in which these transactions can be done: customer to business, business to business, business to customer, and customer to customer.

These transactions are commercial and they all happen over the Internet. There are many stores online that provide these services. Some of the common ones we know our Amazon, eBay, etc.

Figure 7.16: There are many applications that people use for buying and selling goods and services. It is important for farmers to develop theirs so as to promote their businesses.

Source: https://www.business2community.com/ecommerce/4-major-ways-e-commerce-benefitting-iot-01957768.

When it comes to the agricultural sector, using electronic commerce is very important due to the fact that it has become one of the most used methods of making transactions when it comes to buying, selling, and providing goods and services.

Most of the electronic-commerce we use these days normally use the World Wide Web for a minimum of one section of the lifecycle of the transaction, however, it can also use a different type of technology such as an email. E-commerce has three main sectors: the electronic market, auctions that are found online, and being able to retail online. In the global economy as of now, electronic commerce is becoming one of the fastest growing industries. It develops by around 24% each year (Kaushik et al, 2019).

There are four different models of electronic-commerce. These models are based on the people or the parties that are a part of the transactions that are being made. They include:

- Consumer to consumer – This means that two consumers are directly talking to each other. There is no one else involved other than the two, and this helps in the promoting of the selling of personal goods in a direct manner to a party that is interested.

Most of the goods that are transacted from consumer to consumer electronics such as cars, motorbikes.

- Business to business – this refers to two different companies doing business with each other. The end-user is not included in this model. This means that the transactions that have been done online only involve those who are manufacturing their produce, retailers, wholesalers, etc
- Consumer to business – this involves having the end-user refer the company to a certain service or product.
- Business to consumer – this involves the selling of goods or services in the direct manner to the end-user.

There are websites that are found online that can be used by the end-users to check for the products that they would like to buy. These products normally have comments at the bottom that give advice on whether other users have found the product useful or worth it. If they find it worth it, they are able to directly place their order on this site that is in question in these products as shipped to them directly.

Farmers are able to use these platforms to sell their products online. They are also able to create sites that can be accessed so as to show the prices of the goods and services that the end-user or the audience get to choose from depending on their preference. The farmers are provided with a global reach. This is because anyone can access the Internet to utilize the site. That means that the geographical obstalce is eliminated.

In addition to being able to sell your products online, the farmers are also able to have video calls or audio calls with the end-user. As a result, they obtain reviews on how the transaction process went along. This is referred to as the virtual world which cannot be affected by the location at all but it can be affected by the lack of the internet connection. Additionally, electronic-commerce helps reduce the costs of transactions. It eliminates fixed costs associated with maintaining certain aspects of their goods. This gives the industry an opportunity to become more profitable (Kaushik et al, 2019).

Shopping online or being able to sell goods and services online cuts down on delivery time and reduces work for both consumers and producers. The customers are also able to address the complaints quickly and efficiently.

Figure 7.17: Computers have made it possible for us to shop for the smallest things online, even vegetables. This is a very convenient manner of shopping, and it is becoming a lucrative business idea.

Source: https://www.newyorkecommerceforum.com/2019/01/11/e-commerce-and-agriculture/amp/.

Using electronic-commerce has also proven to be one of the most convenient ways of shopping. It is possible for the consumer to order products from the farmers at any time of the day because the websites are up and running 24/7. This is different when you compared to a normal shop considering the fact that the shop has restricted working hours (Li, 2008).

In addition, the electronic commerce allows the consumer to directly communicate with the producer without any intermediaries. This promotes fast communication and transaction. It also provides a personal touch.

Despite all these advances that have been mentioned before, there are also several disadvantages. The costs to set up the commerce portal can be high. Software and a hardware needs to be set up and employees need to be trained to use the software system. The system requires to be constantly maintained and the upkeep for the system is expensive.

Despite the fact that it may look like there are no risks that are associated with the electronic commerce, there is actually a major risk of failure. There are many industries that have ended up with this result of failure.

In addition to this, it is possible for electronic-commerce to feel like it is not personal. This means that it does not have the characteristics of an interpersonal relationship such as facial expressions, tonal differences, etc. which might be very important for some people. Security problems is another issue that needs concerns. There have been very many breaches in security when it comes to online shopping. This involves the stealing of customer information, theft of credit cards, theft of identity, lack of delivery, loss of money, issues with the shipping, mixing up of products, etc.

In addition to promoting good business, the farmers get to also improve their digital skills. It is well known that they are not the best in technology. Using these methods can allow them to learn more about technology and therefore adopt it in more than one way (Li, 2008).

Electronic commerce will help in the creating in mew job opportunities, due to the need for services that are related to information. It however, also causes others to lose their jobs. This is possible because those who will be working with the information may be more suitable and better trained to do the job, in comparison to those who were using the conventional methods. Electronic Commerce required highly skilled workers so as to have effective management of large amounts of data, demands from the customers, as well as the processes for production.

CHAPTER

8

How Computer Science and Technology Changed the Sport Sector

CONTENTS

8.1. INTRODUCTION

Computer science is the study of computer and the related technologies. Sports are activities mainly physical and mental activities that aim at keeping an individual both physically and mentally fit. Computer science has been incorporated in the sports sector as an interdisplinary discipline which main focus is putting the theoretic and the applied feature involved in the sport science and informatics sectors. Sport science is also known as sports and excursive science or sports medicine which involves studying how a person's body that has undergone exercise works healthily and the results of sports and physical manual activity brings about the correct health and the person's performance is boosted both cellularly and in the whole body. By studying sport science, it involves, exercising the physical body that is the areas of physiology. It assists the growth of the children and people and prevents illnesses and weakness of the body. Sports is an important field which is taken as such hence various ways to improve this sector have been invented and that is how technology and computer science found its way into sports.

Sport science has allowed the use of computer science by allowing the use computer based and mathematical techniques in the sector that they have a belief that it will improve the sport sector. The major cause for computer science to become an important part for sport science is that sport science requires the use of data contained in the computers, they also use the computers to design models and sport science requires the use of various tools that are present in computer science. This therefore has enabled individuals in the sport sector to have the urge to include computer science in their field.

8.2. USE OF COMPUTER SCIENCE AND TECHNOLOGY IN ASSISTING REFEREES

The different sports have their own referees. Depending on the type on the type of sport, the number of referees will vary. Usually it involves a main coach and the other referees assist the main coach so as to ensure that a match is fairly played. Referee play a variety of roles in the world of professional sports.

It mostly includes facilitating a match, identifying the time breaks within a match, and deciding whether a goal was scored or not among others. They are there to ensure that there is no foul play in the match when it comes to the players.

They also decide which player has made foul play in accordance to the rules and the punishment to be given. This is mostly seen in professional football where players who touch the ball with their hands or those who hit others are identified by the referee and they are given a sort of punishment for their action. This is most at times in form of a red or yellow card. It is the duty of the referee to know how many times the player has had foul play. In football, if the player makes on foul move, they are given a yellow card but if they make several others then they are given a red card.

The work of referees is so engaging. They are required to see and know everything going on in the field. This at times poses a challenge as some of the sports field are fairly large and it may be difficult to see everything. This among other aspects has brought about the use of computer science and technology in the field of sports (Dabnichki, 2008). There are several applications of the two and mostly in the aspect of assisting the referees with their work. Some of the ways are discussed below.

8.2.1. Helping Referees in Decision Making

The referee plays a major role of decision making. This is in terms of deciding whether there was a goal made. This poses a challenge for the referees if the field was large. They apply the use of technology and computer science in making decisions. For instance, in football, there are referees on the field and also some in a secluded area. In this room, there are several computers that employ the principal of networking in order to share information from other computers. There are cameras on the field that record the different angles and areas of the field while the match progresses.

The referees use this technology in that if there is a conflict concerning whether a goal was scored or not, they replay the footage of the match to enable them make a sound decision. This is referees to as video assistant referees. The videos help the referee to decide on various elements of the game including whether foul play was made or not (Dabnichki, 2008). They only have to replay the footage from the game. The video assistant is used in all the games apart from some, where by the referees are denied access to such footage.

Another way that technology and computer science has assisted referees in making decisions is by the use of the goal line technology (Dabnichki, 2008). This technology works mostly for football. The mechanism works in this manner. The knowledge of computer science has been combined with that of technology to produce motion sensors. These sensors are fitted within the goal line. Their duty is to track the position of the ball with reference to the goal line. This technology has been very useful in helping the referees make a correct decision and in case there is an opposition to the decision, they can always use the technology to provide proof. This technology makes good use of the magnetic field-base technology.

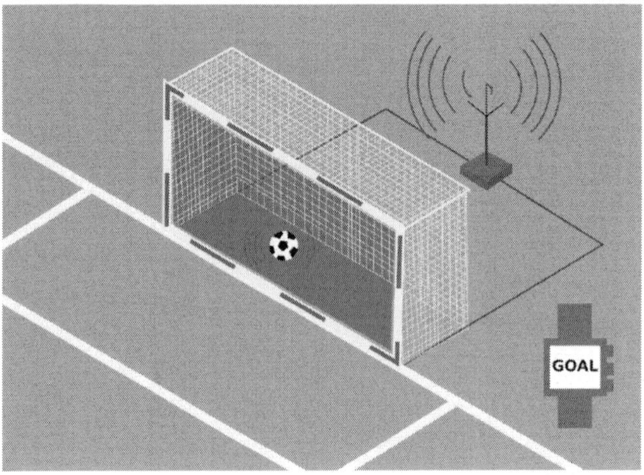

Figure 8.1: Showing goal line technology.

Source: https://en.wikipedia.org/wiki/Goal-line_technology.

This system is similarly applied to other sports but in different ways. For instance, cricket uses the Hawk-Eye technology. This technology makes use of a visual tracking software. This system is similar to the video assistant as it makes use of the videos made from the game. Computer science is used in programming the computers so that they automatically back-up the videos to the server for reference. The Hawk-Eye technology makes use of the smart replay technology. This technology as stated before records all the feeds and makes it available for the referees (Dabnichki, 2008).

The advantage of the Hawk-Eye technology is that it is able to make a prediction of the path the ball will take. The only short coming in using the technology is that the prediction may not be entirely true. There are scenarios that have not been included and adjusted in the system but generally the system assists the referees in making correct decisions. This technology is also used in tennis. For sports such as rugby, the referees make use of the Television Match Official which is a system that makes use of the video referee which will be discussed later on. This system is useful as it enables the referees in making consistent and accurate decisions.

Figure 8.2: *Showing the Hawk-Eye technology.*

Source: https://www.techentice.com/application-of-hawk-eye-technology-in-sports/.

They are able to make several identifications with the use of this technology. For instance, they are able to check for acts of foul play, the player contacts as well as the grounding of the ball. In rugby, the referee is the only person who can use the Television Match Official in the process of decision making. The system also makes use of the Hawk-Eye technology. In order to help the referees, they make use of the video assistant referee. The video assistant referee is usually an application that facilitates common ground in sports (Baca, 2014).

Referees on the field are not able to see much as the match progresses. There are various ways the video assistant referees assist the referees. For instance, the referee can call on the assistance of the VAR to identify whether there was a set-back when making the goal. In making penalty decisions, the referee under the guidance of the VAR is able to identify whether they should or should not award a penalty. This helps them make the right choice when they want to send off a player from the field. It reduces cases of mistaken identity so that only the player at fault is sent off the field.

The video referee works this way. When the referee needs guidance on something, they ask the video assistant referee who then gives the referee a recommendation on what action to take.

8.2.2. Facilitating Communication

For the referees, communication is a very important aspect more so if the game they are facilitating is done on a big field. If this is the case like in football, there are several referees; some on the ground and others in the media room watching the recorded part of the game. For the match to be successfully facilitated, there is need for communication between all the referees in which in most cases the referee on the ground is the one who mostly receives communication from the other. Communication is applied in the video referee assistant.Computer science and technology has been used in facilitating the communication through the use of a special type of headsets that contain both the mouth and the ear piece (Baca, 2014). The headset is wired on the referee and through the principle of networking in computer science, the headsets on all the referees are linked to each other. This will enable the main referee as well as his assistants on the ground to receive communication from the one in the media room. Such tools enable the referees to ask for assistance and get information on thing such as substitutions as well as identification of foul play.

Figure 8.3: Showing a headset used in communication between referees.

Source: https://www.amazon.com/V4-Football-Wireless-Headsets-Communication/dp/B07Q74FGXN.

8.2.3. Facilitating Referee Training

One of the ways to make referee's work much easier is by equipping them with the latest knowledge and rules. Computer science and technology have come in handy in this task. They both provide the referee with tools such as the internet where they can access more information. They can also access e-books on refereeing and gain more insight. It is more beneficial for the referees that are undergoing training as they can be able to access the records of previous games. By watching such games, they are able to know what is expected of them.

They are also able to gain more experience through the use of computer programs that facilitate virtual simulation. With the use of these programs, they are able to know how to apply the skills that they have. The virtual simulation entails them facilitating a match according to the sport they are specialized in. computer science and technology has greatly assisted referees through the development of social media platforms. In such platforms the referees are able to share knowledge amongst each other. This way, they are able to learn more on refereeing (Baca, 2014).

8.3. THE HAWK-EYE TECHNOLOGY

The Hawk-Eye technology is a sports technology which is invented that it keeps trace of the ball and how it moves in the field as the players are playing. Hawk-Eye technology was invented by the Hawk-Eye company and it is believed it was given the name Hawk-Eye because it keeps an eye on the ball as a hawk keeps an eye on its prey. Due to their invention, the Hawk-Eye company was able to receive a FIFA GOAL LINE TECHNOLOGY LICENCE being the first company to receive this.

The Hawk-Eye technology has been applied in several sports which include football, cricket, tennis ball, rugby, volleyball, and horse racing.

8.3.1. How Hawk-Eye Technology Is Applied

In football: Football is a sport where a ball is passed by foot from one person to another. A lot of disagreements may occur when a player scores goal. The hawk-eye technology works by installing about movement around the goal post. If you are watching a football game you will see how the goal was scored. The TV channel will repeat the process in a slower motion and show the viewers how it occurred. This recording is taken by these cameras. Hence, if the players dispute the goal, they are what actually happened. These cameras are able to record the entire movement of the ball when it is being passed around by the players. Its accuracy cannot be questioned since the technology is very accurate. The use of the Hawk-Eye technology in football has assisted the broadcasters to avoid the need to rerun decisions that may be in question (Baca, 2014).

In tennis: Tennis is a game which involves either two or four players where they use rackets to strike a ball over a net that is stretched across a court. It mostly goes by the name lawn tennis since it is played on a lawn. The Hawk-Eye technology started being used in the year two thousand and two in lawn tennis and has been widely used since then. In tennis it does not go by the name Hawk-Eye technology but it is referred to as Electronic Line Calling (ELC). The Hawk-Eye technology in tennis involves following the players' indents. Hawk-Eyes smart production services uses cameras that track the players as they play and a software called intelligent production that shows the live output workflow that ensures the tournament to be covered fully. By using the Hawk-Eye technology in the tennis game, it enables the game to be covered and how the ball is passed during the game. It also allows the funs to test their power and skills against the world's greatest. It has been used in over eighty million tournaments and its results have been favorable (Baca, 2014).

In rugby: Hack eye technology is now being used in the rugby games. Rugby is also known as the rugby union that is a sport with its origin in England and it spread to other countries and nations. It is a sport that involves running with the ball in the hand. It is a tough game that requires people with a lot of energy. The equipment's used are the rugby union football. By using the Hawk-Eye technology in rugby, it has enabled the rugby officials to make decisions that they may have not seen before and therefore it leads to a fair rule. Since rugby is a rough game, in case an individual is injured during the game rugby can also help the individual to seek treatment since the videos that have been recorded with the Hawk-Eye technology and clips can be given to the doctors which help them to identify the cause of the injury and they can identify the injured spot hence the player can seek treatment. The main type of Hawk-Eye technology used in rugby is the Hawk-Eyes smart replay technology. This enables the rugby union to have the capability to replay the game.

8.3.2. How Hawk-Eye Technology Is Integrated in Sports

Hawk-Eye technology allows the people officiating the game to be able to make key decisions hence reduce the possibility of them interrupting the game. During the game if a game is being played that does not involve the Hawk-Eye technology, there will be a lot of interruptions when the officials want to determine who has scored the goal and how the goal was scored and also a lot of disputes may arise on this account but when the Hawk-Eye technology is introduced then the officials can easily determine who the points goes to and in case of any disputes they can also rewind to avoid this. The Hawk-Eye technology therefore saves time and helps the officials to reduce disruptions and they make accurate and quick decisions (Fister et al, 2018).

The Hawk-Eye technology also makes the decisions to be more accurate and it brings fairness to the players. When the Hawk-Eye technology is being used the game is played more fairly since the cameras are able to trace the movement of the ball and if a goal is scored it shows clearly who scored the goal and hence the decisions made are more accurate than before.

Lastly, by using the Hawk-Eye technology it enables broadcasters to broadcast the game being played. It is impossible for all football funs to attend a football match since they may be held far away or they may be expensive and a football stadium cannot sustain all the funs and hence the Hawk-Eye technology comes hand in hand to assist this situation since with this the game is recorded and it can be broadcasted to the fans. This enables the fans to have the opportunity to watch the game at the comfort of their homes.

8.4. SPORTS EDUCATION

Sports education is an institutional model which associates the sports that is taught in PE with to the wider sporting culture. Sports education involves studying about sports. Initially, sports education was studied manually with the use of books but with the coming up of computer science it has led to the introduction of computers which has led to improvement in the sports education. Computers and other related technology are used in sports science in the following ways: Learning of sport science online, E-books concerned with sport education, visual simulations, finding skills online, YouTube videos and teachings on sport education. These are father explained to bring about better understanding.

8.4.1. Learning of Sport Science Online

Sports science courses are offered online. Online learning is the process in which one acquires knowledge and skills from the internet. Students can be able to access this knowledge and hence computer science is enhanced. Traditionally or in the olden days one would have to attend classes and lectures for them to be taught on specific skills but with the coming up of new technologies through computer science students and other individuals can access knowledge they need to find at the comfort of their homes. They study with the notes offered to them online and watch the videos to improve their understanding and then they do their exams online. Just like any other form of education, Students who learn with the online programmers are also awarded with certificates of merits to prove that they did the course and they can be employed anywhere. It is a better and easier method of study since students are able to study sport science as a part time study and it eliminates the need for students to go to school hence, they can study at the comfort of their homes. It also enables faster form of study and students take a shorter time to study the course as compared to going to school. Students have access to a large amount of information on sports education since they have been given enough resources to use in their study, students can also access education as they find study as they work hence it enables them those students from unstable backgrounds to study as they look for money for their upkeep. Lastly, it enables students to do an additional course that may be a boost to their performance in work (Dabnichki, 2008).

8.4.2. E-Books Concerned with Computer Science

In the past when one wanted to carry out research on a specific topic, they were forced to go to the library and carry out their research by studying books one by one. It would normally take the students a lot of time before they found the books needed for their research. Additionally, reading the large amount of texts was also time consuming. Aside from this, not all the libraries were well equipped with all the necessary books for study. Hence, students carrying out research could fail to get the required information at certain times. Computer science led to the invention of e-books that have brought a revolution in the education sector. E-books are online books that can be accessed through the internet. Most e-books can also be found in the library. Publishers make their books accessible via the internet. Having e-books is advantageous because it saves time that the individuals would take carrying out research. They can now access the books easily using the internet. This has enabled research content to be found especially for students who are in areas that they cannot access the libraries easily ore the libraries and not properly equipped as they can get the books from the internet. Reading with the E-books also enables students to get more information since they give references to the students on where they can carry out more research. It is also cheaper to use the E-books than buying the books physically from the book shops. The use of E-books in sports education has therefore enabled the students to have access to more information at a lower price that is more affordable (Dabnichki, 2008).

Finding skills online: Students learning sports education can find skills through the internet which can also help them to improve their own skills. Most skills are gotten from the internet sources. For example, when an individual download and plays a football game they can improve their skills in football since the games tend to copy everything that is done in the game. Just like the car racing games can help an individual to know how to drive a car it's the same way playing games can help an individual improve in sports. Aside from the game's individuals can also gain skills that are needed through watching others play. When a game is being played normally it is broadcasted in the televisions and can also be aired in the internet. Most funs follow up on these events and they can gain skills that they require through watching the players play for instance if it is a football match they are watching and they notice a player being given a red card for a mistake they have done the player who is watching will be careful when he is playing his match to avoid getting himself a green card too

Virtual simulations: Aside from finding skills online, Virtual simulations can also be used to help players practice. Virtual simulations are mainly used in sports education in the sector of training. Most players during their training they are given devices for examples glasses that is equipped with high tech that makes the match difficult for them. This helps them to be able to conquer any difficulty they may face in a sport or a match. The gadgets can also be computerized such that the player sees obstacles that are not there in real since and this helps the individual to perfect his skills. These gadgets are normally made by the knowledge on computer science and they are widely being used. Virtual simulations in sports has helped making training easier and cheaper. In areas where they may fail to java the accessibility to obstacles in fields, they can easily use virtual simulations which tend to be a cheaper method. The technology used to make the virtual simulations include motion capture technology system which captures the real time 3D course of a moving object. It therefore enables the coming up of easier yet applicable methods of training.

8.5. USE OF COMPUTER SCIENCE AND TECHNOLOGY IN MEDICAL EVALUATION OF PLAYERS

Computer science technologies are used in medical evaluation of players. Before any player is involved in a sport, they have to undergo medical research to determine their health status and also to check if they have taken any substance that may either boost their performance or make them fall ill in their game. In a bid for one to emerge the first for instance in an athletics competition, some malicious runners may take some drugs that may boost their strength and enable them to outshine all the others. This would be unfair to the athletes who don't take the drug and therefore in order to promote equality, players are forced to undergo medical observations. Medical observations cannot be taken by looking at an individual and concluding that they are not fit but there must be the application of a technology that is invented to check if the individual is well and fit. This technology enables the process to be faster and hence many individuals can be checked at a sort span of time. Medical evaluation also enables the players to be screened of any infection or illness that they may be having that may cause them harm when they are playing and hence it reduces the rate at which players fall sick during their game (Dabnichki, 2008).

Computer science is also applicable in medical evaluation in instances where an individual falls sick in the game and the health workers and the first aiders may not know the cause of the illness. When players are playing the whole game is normally recorded and in case of an injury the individual injured can easily be spotted. In case the injury causes so much pain that the individual cannot speak, the videos and clips that are recorded can be given to the doctors, health workers or first aiders to enable them to identify the cause of the injury and the part injured hence the player can get assistance faster.

In case a treatment for a certain illness or injury of a player is not familiar to the health workers and first aiders, they can easily find ways to cure the patient by researching online on ways to cure the illness. Through the computers by research in pages like Google treatment for any type of illness can be found and the causes of the illness and therefore through this the health workers are greatly informed.

8.6. BENEFITS OF COMPUTER SCIENCE AND TECHNOLOGY IN COACHING AND TRAINING

For a sports team or an individual to be successful in the sport that they undertake, they need to have adequate training. Training is important as it ensures that the players are fit. In the training process there are various tactics that are employed to ensure the successful training of the players. The coaches input also assists in the training and preparation of the players for the various games they participate in. Coaching requires planning and coming up with strategies and tactics to use during the match. Technology and computer science have been incorporated to the world of sports to improve the various areas which include training and coaching. Below show how technology and computer science have been used in coaching (Baca, 2014).

8.6.1. Use of Computer Science in Coming Up with Game Plans

Game plans are an important aspect of sport. Having the right game plan will improve the players' chances of being victorious in the match. A game plan is usually showing the position of the players while in the field and the direction they should go. It also indicates the type of strategy that they should employ during the game. Initially, coaches had a hard time as planning involved a lot of paperwork. For instance, in sports like basketball, rugby, and football the coaches were required to draw the game plans for the given match. This would end-up with the coaches having to document every game plan they had in files which is risky as it may be prone to destruction.

This has brought the need for technology and computer science in sports. Technological tools such as computers have been used by coaches in the formulation of game plans. Computer science has been used when coming up with programs used in the drawing of such game plans in the computers. With the use of both the computer and the programs, formulating a game plan becomes easy. Since the game plan is produced in the computer, the aspect of storage is also catered for.

Apart from this, the use of technology and computer science has availed tools such as the digital whiteboards which the coaches use when making the game plans as well as training in the field (Baca, 2014).

8.6.2. Use of Computer Science to Improve Coaching Skills

Coaches need to be skilled and be able to handle the players and manage them properly. As time goes by, they need to sharpen their skills so that they can be in a better position to bring out the best in the players.

Technology and computer science have been useful in helping coaches improve their skills. Technology provides them with resources, such as the internet, where they can access information on the latest trends in coaching. It also provides e-books where they can get more information on what is expected for them as coaches.

The other way in which coaches have been able to use tools such as coaching apps that are availed to them through the use of technology. In such apps, they are able to work on their coaching skills as well as improve their skills in making game plans.

They use tools such as the trainers' tablet to facilitate this.

8.6.3. Use of Computer Science in Decision Making

Coaches are the backbone of sports. They are the ones who makes the decisions and call the shots in terms of the players needed in the team. Coaching revolves around decision making. The coaches make use of technology such as the video technology. The advantage of using this technology is that the coaches are able to make decisions based on what they see. Most of the professional coaches use the videos from the games they have played to make decisions. For instance, by watching the game they are able to identify players who need more training. They are also able to identify the mistakes made during the previous game. This enables them to know what they need to work on as well as the techniques they need to employ. This is referred to as use of game film in decision making (Baca, 2014).

The coaches are also able to make decisions based on data analysis. This is an analysis of the game. They make use of analysis programs to get a comprehensive view on how a game was. This enables them to get more information on player performance. With this knowledge the coaches are able to come up with strategies that will help their teams to win. With the obtained data, the coaches are also able to prepare tasks improving the players' delivery. Technology and computer science are also applied in the training process. Some of the ways it has been used include:

8.6.4. Use of Computer Science in Tracking Player Performance

The players' performance is a really important aspect when it comes to training. By knowing the player performance, the coach is able to decide on the type of training that the player requires. They make use of the sensor technology. The sporting equipment of the players are fitted with sensors. The sensors are usually in the fabrics used in making the clothes. The sensors are linked to a computer which obtains data as the player is training or is playing. This kind of technology is mostly used among the athletes. The sensors pick up data such as the breathing and pulse rate. They also pick up information such as the body temperature and the level of hydration of the athlete (Baca, 2014).

The knowledge on the players' performance. This way the trainers are able to accurately pick the training as per the player's requirements. This way as the players train, they work on their weak areas and put more effort in them and also work on their strong areas. The trainers choose a training procedure that will balance the players require. Apart from gears fitted with sensors, they use technological tools such tracks and timed watches that contain GPS technology.

They are also wirelessly connected to the trainers' gadgets. This way if it is athletes, the trainer is able to know how much distance was covered and the speed of the athlete.

Depending on the speed they are able to work on the progress. This way the athlete will not strain too much and end up injuring themselves.

8.6.5. Use of Computer Science in Improving Communication

Communication is crucial. The players need to have a stable communication with their trainers and coaches. Computer science and technology have facilitated this through the creation of social media platforms such as Facebook, Twitter, Instagram, and Snapchat.

Also, through the revolutionization of communication mediums such as the electronic mail, they are easily able to communicate with each other. For trainers, they use platforms such as YouTube to communicate to the players on the routine they should take up. They usually record the training session then upload it in the internet.

Communication has been made possible through the use of programs and applications such as the fitness apps. These applications are synced up with the trainers' tablet or smart phone.

The programs gain information and send it to the trainers. This way they are able to keep an eye on the players (Dabnichki, 2008).

8.6.6. Use of Computer Science in Reducing Injuries

Injuries are common in the training area. In every sport, there are several counts of injured players more so in very engaging sports such as basketball and football. With the introduction of technology and computer science in sports, the cases of injuries have greatly reduced.

The technology has been used to help players so that they do not end-up doing strenuous training. With the use of technology, the trainers are able to get the players' medical records.

This is important as they will be able to pick out the correct diet for the players. This way the players will be physically fit and will reduce the cases of them suffering from fatigue.

8.6.7. Use of Computer Science in Improving the Players' Movement

This mostly applies for swimmers. For them motion is a very import for them as their sport deals more on motion. Not only swimmers but also cyclists. For cyclists, they use technology that will enable them know how to move faster. The gadget takes record of the position of their bodies giving them feedback on what position they should use. This way they can improve their movement as they carry out the sport. These are but some of the ways in which computer science and technology are used in training and coaching (Dabnichki, 2008).

8.7. USE OF COMPUTER SCIENCE IN SPORTS MANAGEMENT

Management is an important aspect in sport. In many years we have seen several sport teams fail and have been dismembered due to poor management. In the field of sports, management cuts across various fields such as the management of the sports stadium, the players and in sports such as football, management of the football clubs. In order to come up with a good management strategy, computer science has been incorporated into sports management. The following are some of the ways that computer science has been used in management.

8.7.1. Organization of Data

In sports, there are numerous amounts of data that are handled. All these data have to be properly organized for its use. The organization of data will pose quite a challenge for personnel who use outdated process of data organization. Some of them include use of paper which was time consuming and was not effective in terms of storage. This changed with the incorporation of computer science in sports management. Computer science has been used in the creation of data organization programs.

Data organization using computer science deals with the use of computers. This will enable the secure storage of the data. With the use of the programs, there is efficient grouping of data for instance according to the health of the players, their performance and ages among others. With such organized data, it is easier to effectively manage the players (Dabnichki, 2008).

8.7.2. Management of Performance

Performance of the player will determine the success of the team. The trainers are needed to manage the performance of the players. Computer science has been used in managing the performance of the players. This is through the creation of fitness programs that take data concerning the performance of the players. The programs utilize the principle of networking of computer science to link the programs to the tablets or smartphones of the coaches and trainers. This way the trainers get information on their players and can choose a more appropriate training routine to suit the players.

Networking has also facilitated the access to the players' medical records. The medical records will be useful in determining the diet of the players. Computer science provides platforms such as the internet such as the internet where they gain information on first aid practices in case an accident occurs. By gaining the information, the coaches and trainers are capable of managing the players.

8.7.3. Gaining Skills on Sports Management

For one to be able to manage a sports team among others, they need to have good management skills. If the sports managers are not skilled then many problems will be encountered. Computer science has been useful in eradicating this problem. Computer science has been used to facilitate online classes. With such classes, they can be able to learn on the skills that they require in managing the football teams. Some managers use this platform to brush off their skills (Dabnichki, 2008).

Computer science also provides platforms of gaining more information. They include social media platforms such as telegram and Facebook. In such platforms they are able to interact with other managers and get more insight on managerial skills. This way they will be well suited to manage the teams.

8.7.4. Management of Sport Stadiums

There are several sports stadiums more so for sports such as football. All the teams have their own stadium. For such stadiums to run, they require good management in terms of finances and carrying out maintenance practices. Computer science has assisted in the management of the stadiums. There are programs that run a diagnostic in the maintenance practices needed for the equipment present in the stadiums. For instance, the computers and cameras used in monitoring the games. Not only that, the stadiums may undergo some repairs and transformations to make it more suitable for the fans (Dabnichki, 2008).

This requires that the management should have good records of the financial status of the club. Computer science programs are used in the making of financial records used by the managers. They are also used in making predictions and calculations on the total expected expenditure when repairing the stadium.

In conclusion, the incorporation of computer science in sports management has been beneficial. It has assisted in ensuring that the sports clubs and teams run for many years.

8.7.5. Management of Employees

Many people are employed to work in the different fields of sport. The management needs to have information on the individuals they have employed and how many more they need to employ. They use various computer science programs such as Excel to keep records of such. This makes it easier to budget on the salary of the employees. They also use programs to carry out a diagnostic on the performance of the employees to ensure that they meet the set expectation. The employees include the trainers, commentators, and coaches among others (Dabnichki, 2008).

8.8. USE OF COMPUTER SCIENCE IN MARKETING OF THE SPORT

Marketing is also an aspect of sport. People to be knowledgeable on the sport so that they can come watch it. The sport stadiums and clubs run on the money payed by the sports fans as they come to watch the matches and support their teams. It is also used to pay the players. This creates the great need to market the sports. Computer science has been useful in marketing. Some of its principles have been used in creating of websites. The websites give off more information on the sports and the team members.

They also make use of social media platforms such as Facebook, twitter, and Instagram in marketing. By using social media, the players themselves get to take part in the marketing process. They get to engage with their fans and also encourage their fans to spread the word about the sports and invited to the live matches.

8.9. USE OF COMPUTER SCIENCE IN SPORTS ANALYSIS

Sports analysis is an evaluation of various aspects of sports. It may be an evaluation of a player or the performance of a team. It is very crucial as it enables the coach to identify the strengths and weaknesses of the players and the team. It is one of the elements looked into when evaluating they type of players to incorporate in a game. They coach is also able to know which player is an asset to the team, which ones need more training and which player to add to the team (Dabnichki, 2008).

Computer science has greatly been incorporated in the process of sports analysis. It employees the use of other technological tools such as the computers. For instance, video technology is used in recording an entire match. The videos from the match are then uploaded to various software such as Dartfish video analysis software for a complete analysis

This program allows the coach to get a view on things they had missed out during the match. The mistakes in the layout used or the game strategy used. The program has been extensively made such that it allows video playbacks, slow motion and editing as the coaches use it to come up with a new game plan.

These programs carry out individual player analysis. In more sophisticated sports computer science has been used to create software that evaluates the performance of all players. This is mostly used in football where software tools are incorporated into the players' training. As the training process continues, the program picks up data on the player and later in makes a complete analysis of the player (Dabnichki, 2008).

This way the coach is able to identify the strengths and weaknesses of the player. Sports commentators also use the same programs after matches to be able to make a judgment on what they think should have been improved for instance the player layout among other things. Other technologies such as accelerators and GPS have been used to carry out the analysis. The advantage of this technology is that it allows the coaches to carry out analysis based on the criteria they want. The programs allow them to change the criteria they prefer be it speed.

The incorporation of computer science in sports analysis has brought about the term technique analysis. This refers to an analytical method used to evaluate the players as well as the teams. It makes use of all the technologies used in sports such as the Hawk-Eye technology. It is a much better method of carrying out spots analysis. The benefit of carrying out sports analysis is that is enables the coaches to make better decisions (Dabnichki, 2008).

In conclusion, these are some of the ways in which computer science has been incorporated in sports.

8.10. ADVANTAGES OF COMPUTER SCIENCE IN SPORTS

In the past year's technology has been integrated in sports as discussed above. It has led to many advantages and improvements in the field of sports. When the sport sector is compared in the past and now it is observed that in the present the sport sector has shown major improvement and technology is continually being improved on this account. The following are some of the advantages in which computer science has led to improvement in sports: improving sports performance, engaging funs, ensuring safety of the players, democratizing sports and assisting referees in their work.

8.10.1. Improving Sports Performance

With the advancement of technology in the sport sector it is observed that sports have made major improvements. Traditionally training of the players was down using traditional means that did not prove very effective. For instance, when footballers were practicing for their game they were playing naturally which did not prove very effective but with the coming up of technology the practice of the players is done and it is more effective for example some technology makes the players visualize barriers during the game which are not initially there and this helps the players to improve their skills and therefore they can overcome any barrier that they may encounter in their game. When these players go into their game, they will show a better performance and therefore the field of sports is improved.

Technology has also improved sports performance because it has led to coming up of technologies that assist to reduce disruptions of the game. Communication, for example, has been improved in the field of sports by introducing technology and therefore the players can communicate more effectively during the game. With the use of the cameras to record the game it has helped to improve the sports sector because the incidences of the players arguing on who won an oil is prevented as they can be shown from the recording and also it ensures the judges to judge the game fairly as they can easily determine who won the game. Another way that technology has improved sports performance is that the players can get to improve their skills by watching videos of others play and also, they can play games that are invented in the technological devices that are associated with the game itself. When a player wants to improve his skills and they do not have access to people who can train them they can easily train themselves using these technologies. Lastly, technological devices have been invented to keep the players fit and assist them in their fitness journey. Traditionally before the coming up of technology, players did not have the required tools for keeping them fit and since they need to be fit for the game there was a need to come up with better technologies that could improve this situation and therefore with the coming up of improved technologies that help players in their fitness, the field of sports has shown greater improvement (Fister et al, 2018).

8.10.2. Engaging Fans

Watching games and sports is a major recreational activity for many individuals all over the world. Many people want to know who the winner is and how the game is being played. Many fans have their favorite team that they always support. It is impossible for all fans to go to a stadium to watch a game because most stadiums cannot support a large population. Also, it can be very expensive to acquire a ticket and cover all travel costs associated with traveling to another city. Most games today are being aired live as the players are playing and therefore the fans can keep up with the game by watching via their televisions or mobile phones. The games are normally recorded from where they are being played by the cameras.

Fans who may have been busy when the game was being played and missed a certain scene as a result, can easily find the game on the internet and re-watch it at any time. This is advantageous because fans will not miss any game and will stay informed about their team's progress. Another way in which computer science and technology enables fans engagement is new software's have been invented that have enabled funs to make money as they still cheer for their teams. This software refers to the betting apps that engage the fans in predicting the outcome of the game being played and if the outcome comes out as predicted they are awarded some money. This has made many people to have the interest to engage in sports and to know how the games are normally played and therefore an increase in fans engagement has been noted. Social media platforms have also been invented that enable fans to interact with players and get to know about them as they answer questions about them that they have. These social media platforms include

Instagram, YouTube, and WhatsApp. For instance, a player can upload a video of himself doing practice in Instagram and through this the fans may know something about them also the player can post his or her pictures on Instagram and fans and players can engage in a conversation through the technological devices. These has enabled to create fun engagement in the sports sector and has led to more and more people being interested in games and sports (Fister et al, 2018).

8.10.3. Ensuring Safety of the Players

Technology advancement in the field of sport has enabled to ensure safety of the players. Many people avoid going into games and sports for the fear that they may get injured and this has made many individuals not to follow their interests and dreams but with the coming up of technology and it being introduced in the field of technology it has helped to reduce these fears highly and also the players are assured of safety as they engage in the games and sports. Technology helps in the sport sector to ensure the safety of the player as some technological devices are introduced in the jerseys and the attires of the players that they play in to prevent injuries. As compared to the olden days before technology was discovered the jerseys of the players were not that safe and in case the players fell down, they could easily get injured but with the introduction of technology in their garments an improvement has been observed. It is just like how the air bags prevent individuals from getting injured in an event of an accident happening. Most players earn well and they are highly prone to being the victims of a robbery attack or being shot down so that their positions can remain vacant for someone else. Technology has ensured the safety of the players as it has ensured that the cars that the players drive in are equipped with high tech like being bulletproof such that the player can be protected.

Also, most players are dressed in bullet proof suits that may protect the players from the risk of their lives being targeted. Aside from this, the houses of these players are protected by high tech and twenty-four-hour surveillance cameras that ensure that they capture any movements taking place in the building that may rise an alarm. The players may also be equipped with a silenced un that they may use to protect themselves in case of any risk they may face. The safety of the players is also enabled by technology when they are playing and an individual gets injured it is easily noticed and the required measurements is taken to ensure they receive the necessary treatment. The clips taken from the game may assist the first aiders to know the kind of treatment that the individuals require and where they are injured. Lastly, the safety of the players can be ensured as the information that is obtained from the biomedical software that takes note of the movement of the muscles and joints of the players can be used to rate the players' performance output and to analyses possible signifiers, for example, it may show that the player may have imbalance in movement and this helps them to foresee an injury occurring and hence they can prevent it earlier before it occurs eventually. The coming up of technology has therefore aided in ensuring that the players remain safe throughout (Fister et al, 2018).

CHAPTER

9

Has the Transportation Sector Benefited From Computer Science and Technology?

CONTENTS

9.1. INTRODUCTION

Given the technological advancement in our current world, computers have become increasingly important in the transportation system. Computers have been used in the transportation system to enhance transportation in numerous ways. Some of the uses of computer in the transportation system is car navigation, positive train control, mapping, online booking, or weather forecast. Computers brought a positive impact in air, water, and ground transportation. Some of the impacts and applications of computer science in transportation have been highlighted below.

9.2. GLOBAL POSITIONING SYSTEM (GPS)

The US Department of Defense designed a system, called GPS, which is used in navigation. It was formed from the constellation of 24 satellites and ground stations. The US Department is the main financial sponsor of the GPS system. In the beginning, the main reason why GPS was constructed was to help the US military in navigation. Over the years GPS has become used by many agents worldwide in civic duties services without any charges or limitations (Winter, Sester, and Wolfson, 2010). GPS is a form of tracking method that can identify target's exact location. This can be done by installing GPS inside a vehicle and as soon as the vehicle starts moving, GPS will locate its exact location using its coordinates.

Not only does it give the vehicle's exact location, it also tracks vehicle's or person's movement. A network known as the global navigation satellite system (GNSS) is put into use by the GPS. GNSS operates by incorporating a wide variety of satellites that uses microwave signals which are transmitted to the GPS device. This, in turn, gives information about the location, speed, or direction of the moving object. As a result, GPS gives both historic and real-time data on any kind of voyage that the vehicle embarked on.

A special receiver normally processes the satellite signals provided by GPS. The receiver performs a number of functions including tracking the exact location of the vehicle in transit, the velocity of the vehicle, and real-time time metadata. GPS satellites can also calibrate the dimensions in 3D using four satellite signals.

There are 27 earth-orbiting global positioning satellites. 24 of these satellites are operational and the remaining 3 are backup satellites. All satellites move around the Earth in 12 hours and during this time they send radio signals, which are received by GPS receivers. Monitoring stations are located all over the globe in different locations to monitor the position of the moving vehicle. The station processes the signals from GPS devices, which are orbiting around the Earth. People utilizing GPS own the receivers which convert the satellite data to estimate the actual position of the vehicle, its velocity, and the actual time (Stephan et al, 2010).

The concept behind GPS coordinates is based on a simple formula known as the trilateration. The trilateration consists of two elements; one referring to 2D and another referring to 3D coordinates.

The GPS receiver has to know the following data to compute the location of the vehicle. First, it needs to know the specific location traced by at least three satellites orbiting the Earth. Second, it must be able to estimate the distance between that specific location and the moving vehicle. There are numerous receivers that are able to pick up signals from several global positioning satellites at the same time. These radio waves contain electromagnetic energy, which travel at very high speed.

In transportation GPS has numerous functions. For instance, it can be used in logistics to record the position of vehicles as they travel to keep track of valuable assets and other important goods that might be robbed. There are systems which record the exact location and store it. Once they check the location of the vehicle, the information is sent to a centralized database, where they track the movement on a regular basis. This is known as the active tracking or the two-way GPS.

Under certain conditions, the passive global positioning satellite will track the location of the transit and store its data. For example, GPS will record the information or the location of the transit over the past 12 hours. Once the information has been recorded, it will be stored in a memory card. This enables the information to be downloaded and be used for analysis when it is needed. The data can also be automatically downloaded within a given time when requested during the journey.

The real-time system, which is also known as the active GPS tracking system, automatically transmits data to a centralized tracking portal in real time. This is normally the better option for most transport logistics companies as they are able to track the movement of their goods on a real-time basis. This is also used to track the drivers of the vehicles in order for them not to deviate from their given task. In the event that a vehicle is stolen, the police are able to track where it is within an exact location. This has come in handy in enhancing security of vehicles (WINTER, SESTER, WOLFSON, and GEERS, 2011).

9.3. POSITIVE TRAIN CONTROL

Positive train control is a type of a train protection system which functional requirement is used in monitoring and controlling the movement of train. The use of positive train control has significantly improved the safety of railway traffic. Through the use of technical means, train protection systems are used to control the movement of traffic. Train protection system mostly comes in handy whenever the transportation involves high-speed movement or dense traffic of train on the tracks.

Train protection systems have been tested for a very long time. In Europe the test started in the beginning of 1930s and it has always been advanced and modified up to this date. The main objective was how to stop a moving train traveling at a high speed. If this needs to happen, at first a stop order is issued. Without any particular order, the vehicle is allowed to move. The movement of the train is normally stopped in case of non-validation because the positive train control hinders the train movement to a straightforward allowance (WINTER, SESTER, WOLFSON, and GEERS, 2011).

The concept behind positive train control is the movement authority. The authority includes decision on where the train is located, where it is authorized to travel safely, and where it is authorized to make a stop. The equipment and tools implement these orders. This helps prevent unsafe movement of the train. The positive train control then uses the general positioning system of its train in order to work in an either dark territory or a signaled territory. A positive train control has also aided in fuel efficiency of trains. This helps during mechanical failure. The US federal railroad administration outlined the goals of the positive train control. The goals include deploying the nationwide differential GPS as a nationwide uniform and continuous positioning system suitable for train control (Conde and Twinn, 2019).

The background behind the positive train control first appeared around World War II. At the end of World War II, there was little investment in the train industry and at the end of the 1980s there was a delegation where solutions were made alongside the revival of the railway industry. In the 1990 US National Transportation Safety Board involved PTC among its most valuable transportation safety improvements. At that moment, most transportation networks in the US heavily relied on the human resources as there were no technological advancements in the sector. The humans designed safety rules yet still a significant fraction of accidents was attributed to errors made by humans. This was evidenced years later after official reports from the FRAME were made. In 2008 a deadline was set where the positive train control technology was meant to be incorporated into the railway network. This implementation was facilitated after the collision of the Metrolink passenger train and the Union Pacific freight train which led to the death of 25 passengers and numerous injuries. Though there were delays in the implementation of the new technology the technology was completed and the Metrolink commuter rail system in South California was the first passenger carrier to install the technology in its system.

The positive train control has two basic elements in its operation;

- The display of speed and control unit on the train.
- The method that dynamically inform the speed control unit of changing truck or signaling the condition.

There are three additional elements. The first one is the onboard navigation system and the profile database truck that leads to the enforcement of fixed limits of speed. The second one is the data that has a two-way direction link to inform signaling equipment of the trains presence. The last one is a centralized system that directly gives a movement authority and permission to the trains.

There are two methods that are being used in the development of the positive train control. These are:

- The first one makes use of fixed signaling infrastructure for example coded trucks circuits and wireless transponders to make communication with the speed that is on board in the control unit.
- The other method is the use of wireless data radios which are dispersed along the line of transit and is used to transmit information which is dynamic

Through the use of the wireless implementation, the train is able to send its location to the signaling system which will enable its movement. The wireless implementation is less expensive in terms of the cost of equipment. However, it is considered to be less reliable than the use of other communication channels, for example the wireless ITCS systems. In high-density passenger lines, the fixed infrastructure method is more popular because the pulse code cub signaling has been installed. In low-density passenger lines, the use of wireless method is more prevalent and more popular due to the lack of reliance on the wireless communication (Winter, Sester, and Wolfson, 2010).

When it comes to a locomotive, speed control unit should continuously calibrate the train's current speed relative to a speed target some distance away. Normally, the speed targets are usually updated by the data which involves fixed and dynamic speed limits determined by the profile of the truck and the system signals. Positive train control also uses the speed control unit to store a database of truck profiles, which is attached to some sort of navigation system. Along the rail line, the train position is tracked and automatically enforces any speed limitations. By the use of wireless data links, the speed restrictions and limitations are updated before the train departs from its terminal. Braking curves are also calculated using the track data in accordance with the grade profile. In most positive train control systems, the interface is directly connected with the existing signal system. However, other systems may maintain a set of important systems at the central location to keep track of trains (Winter, Sester, and Wolfson, 2010).

Information regarding the status of devices, for example the switch positions, are normally detected and transmitted to the control center by text messages and alarm conditions, which are automatic. Also, the captain in charge can give permissions so that a train can pass through their work areas using a device that is controlled wirelessly.

9.4. MAPPING

Mapping is known as digital photography, where data is collected and formatted into a virtual image. The main objective is to produce maps which are able to give accurate representations of specific areas. Maps give details of major landmarks, such as roads and other points of interest, big companies, stops, and junctions. Mapping also enables one to calculate the distance between roads and places from one point to another. Digital mapping has a variety of applications; but its main use cases are GPSs and automotive navigation systems. The background behind mapping stems from using tradition maps. However, these were inflexible and had to be changed as soon as a new construction occurred. This was a hindrance to many transportation systems and led to the creation of digital maps which can be easily updated. Early digital maps could give a virtual view of roads and buildings in a given geographical setting. Yet, with the help of GPS, digital maps have grown in the past decade and now are able to give live traffic updates, points of interest, and service locations. These updates have enhanced digital maps and have enabled them to be more user-conscious (Conde and Twinn, 2019).

Digital mapping also provides the users with an option to choose between virtual maps or hybrid maps. Also, with the ability to update and upgrade the digital mapping devices, people are able to view newly constructed places, such as roads, buildings, and other landmarks. This leads to the general accuracy of the map. There is software that can be used to create 3D maps. However, such 3D maps require large amounts of data collected over time. Such data can come from satellite images or street-level information. The digital map should be updated often to provide a near accurate location of an area due to the major technological and urbanization of areas.

The main use of digital mapping has been mostly derived from the GPS technology. The GPS is the foundation behind the construction of mapping navigation systems and it has been widely used by companies and individuals in the current world to make tracking of areas and locations smooth and easy (Abduljabbar et al, 2019). Information from the global positioning satellite receiver is obtained to provide the digital mapping program with points of origin. The data provided is then evaluated and analysed. Then, the information is compiled to create a map which provides an easy and efficient way to approach your destination. In technical terms, the device normally works in the following way:

- At least four global positioning satellites that are orbiting the Earth calculate their 3D position. GPD receivers collect and analyse this information.
- The exact points of latitudinal and longitudinal directions from the global positioning satellite are then provided using the GPS coordinates
- Using the coordinates, an output is provided. Normally the range is between 10–20 meters of the actual location and such a distance cannot mislead a user.
- Then, the digital mapping software is fed into the mapping software
- An output, which is a real-time visual representation of the route, is able to move along the path of the driver.
- When the driver is drifting or shifting directions, the navigation system uses the current coordinates to calibrate the road to the destination of the car.

Computer-aided mapping can also be used to map tunnels. In specific situations, such as geometrically complicated situation, the mapping software helped draw the profile used in the construction of tunnels (Conde and Twinn, 2019). Search tunnels can be used in the construction of a pipeline, which is used in the transportation of petroleum. It can be used in the creation of construction or railway tunnels. In the past, the use of computer-aided mapping was used to construct the elliptical cylindrical sections. Computer-aided mapping interpolates geological elements whenever changing geometric conditions are involved. A computer can develop the roof of tunnel in a more accurate and precise way when compared to hand-drawn projections. Once information from the geological components has been recorded using the computer structural diagrams, it can be processed immediately. The computer can also become valuable in providing a 3D representation of the perspective block (Conde and Twinn, 2019).

9.5. ONLINE BOOKING

Over the past few years, booking has been made easier and more convenient. Nowadays, one is able to book a flight or a ticket from the comfort of their living room. The central reservation systems are computerized systems used to store and retrieve information. They are also used to conduct transactions, which are related to air travel, hotels bookings and rental of cars (Winter, Sester, Wolfson, and Geers, 2011).

Computer reservation systems were initially operated by airlines but later on their function was extended by travel agencies. Global distribution systems are used for booking and selling tickets for multiple airlines. Recently the computer reservation systems have been outsourced to the global distribution systems by airlines. This has enabled the consumers to access tickets through the Internet. Not only has the global distribution system enabled the users to book airline tickets, it has enabled them to book hotel rooms or rent cars. This has led to the general enhancement and facilitation of transportation (Winter, Sester, Wolfson, and Geers, 2011). In other economies, the global distribution systems manage railway and ground transportation bookings. The departure control system has enabled the automation in airline management, which involves storing information required for check-ins at airports. About 98% of departure control system normally manages tickets using interfaces from a number of devices which include kiosks for checking installing, online checking, mobile boarding cards and their handling of baggage.

The departure control system can identify, capture, and update reservations from airlines for passengers whose details have been stored. Reservations are normally updated via the departure control system when passengers are checked in or boarded their flight (Winter, Sester, Wolfson, and Geers, 2011).

An interface for immigration control, such as advanced passenger information system, can be paired with the departure control system for visa purposes, immigration, and passenger no-fly watch list. This is used in safeguarding flights and passengers.

In the past, North American countries modified and developed the departure control systems and incorporated them as a part of the reservation system with checking in for flights being initiated directly from the passenger name record. A stand-alone operation application provides weight and balance control that is the load control. Airlines outside North America developed systems in the past that had database which is separated from the departure control system. The re-engineering of airline passenger service systems is being developed by vendors such as SITA. This is a new generation of departure control system is being developed. In this new system, a common database is being used and where all the services such as reservations check-in and others can be maintained and can be monitored from one database. This helps in giving a consistent view of passengers' information (Winter, Sester, and Wolfson, 2010).

The first automated booking system was installed in 1946 in American Airlines. The electromechanical reservoir was being experimented. The magnetronic reservoir was then introduced and it was temporary storage. The system was a success and sooner or later it was being used by many Airlines in the United States. It heavily relied on human operators to actually check the lookups ticket. Agents were needed to call a booking office whose operators ordered the team managing the systems and then read the results using a phone. There were no direct ways in which the operators were able to give out the information.

In 1950, the world's first seat reservation system for trains was designed. The ticket reservation system was planned and designed by the Japanese National Railways Institute, now the railway technical Research Institute. They named it the MARS-1train ticket reservation system. It stands for magnetic electronic automatic seat reservation system. It was designed by Hosaka, Yutaka Ohno, and others at the Japanese National Railways Institute in 1958. The MARS-1had the capability of reserving seats positions for people and it was controlled by a transistor computer which had a central processing unit. There was a later version of MASS which used the MASS 501 system and it was introduced in the year 2002. The Mars one was able to indicate whether seats in the train were vacant or they were reserved by the use of registering order to fasten the process of searches and to accelerate the updating of the seat patterns, communication with terminals, printing reservations and cathode ray tube displays (Winter, Sester, and Wolfson, 2010).

The record containing a passenger name plays an important role in computer reservation. This record contains the details of a passenger or a group of passengers who are traveling together. The concept of passenger name record was introduced for the sake of interlining passengers. The travel websites create passenger name record, which is used when the passenger books an itinerary. An example of such a global distribution system is Travelport. This type of passenger name record is known as the master passenger name record and is normally linked to the itinerary. The record locator identifies the particular database in the passenger name record. In the event that not all records on the travel is provided by the holder of the master passenger name record. his or her copies of the data is normally transmitted to the computer reservation systems of the airline. The computer reservation system then checks for copies which are original of the passenger name records in their system and will manage the remaining part of the itinerary which they are supposed to be responsible for. Sharing of the passenger name record is enabled because most Airlines have their customer reservation systems hosted by the global distribution system (Winter, Sester, and Wolfson, 2010). Originally passenger name records were introduced for the purpose of air travel and airline systems but nowadays it is also used in airport transfers and Train trips.

Before booking is done, there are five components that the passenger number record must have. These include: passenger's name, any details of the passenger for the travel agent or airline office, ticketing details, a common travel leg for all the passengers listed, and finally the name of the contact person. Other data, for example pseudo city code, will automatically be booked. All data is retained in the history. A customer reservation system will give a special alphanumeric record locator once the booking has been completed. This alphanumeric record locator will not change in future. This can only change if the multi-person passenger name record has been broken. A unique record locator is then created by the booking airline for them to be placed in the booking record and this depends on the legal agreement that was done between the customer reservation system and the airline that is involved. The unique record locator is then transmitted to the customer reservation system and it is stored in the booking. In the event that the travel agency and the airline use the same customer reservation system, this means the record locator will also be similar in both.

For the passenger name record to be accurate, some information is desirable by the airlines and the travel agency to make sure there is efficiency in the booking process and travel. This information includes:

- Details regarding the fare though the amount may be suppressed but the type of fare will be indicated and any limitation and restrictions that may be imposed in the tickets during booking.
- The amount of tax that will be levied from the relevant authorities.
- The form of payment that is normally used. This is important in that there are times that wrong payments can be done and this will restrict any refund if the ticket is not utilized.
- Other contact details and this can include the phone number of the agency, it's address, additional phone numbers; the passengers address and the intended place of landing of the user.
- In the case there is an unaccompanied child or an old passenger, age details comes relevant to the travel agencies and Airlines.
- The type of seat requested
- Data that shows how frequent the passenger flies.
- Special service requests for example the requirements of the diet, wheel chair assistant or any other request of such nature.
- Optional services instruction. This is information that is sent to a particular airline or all Airlines and it enables the booking agency to provide better services. This information can involve contact details, ticket numbers airline staff on load and upgrade priority codes and other details such as passenger language and any details regarding disability.
- The remarks from the vendors. This involves the comments and any other specifications that have been made by the airline and it is normally generated automatically during the booking process. This normally includes the record locator of the airline, replies to special requests and other advices on ticketing time limits. Normally the agency and the airline send such information to each other.

Recently, many states require the airlines to ask for further information and such information might be used in the event that there is investigation happening and the government wants to trace criminals or terrorists. This information includes the gender of the passenger, the passport details, that is, nationality, the number and the date of expiry the place of birth. If previously given to the Passenger by the US authorities, a re-address number is required and any other available billing information. The customer reservation system normally identifies the elements of the passenger name records internally by a one-character code. As opposed to using a graphic interface, this code is used when creating a passenger number record through a direct entry into a terminal window. Some of the codes which are standardized across all the customer reservation systems are; the name, the segment information which includes the number of booked seats, the status code and the class of the fair, related public number record identification, other identification such as customer reservation system username and rule, other airline service information, host airline SSR or OSI, remarks received and recorded, ticketing information, ticket time limit and contact phone numbers.

9.6. WEATHER FORECAST

Weather forecasting is very important in the transport industry. Weather affects and influences travel patterns, security, and many other factors. Therefore, it is important for weather forecast to be discussed. Computers have brought significant technological advancement in weather forecasting as it gives out tools and methods that can help predict weather forecasting more accurately in a precise manner which has led to the general improvement in the transportation sector (Winter, Sester, Wolfson, and Geers, 2011).

Currently in our modern world the Marine sector, aviation sector and land sector in transportation is using their own approach to determine weather patterns, to predict weather and to deal with the effects of high impact weather on the efficiency, safety, and the continuous nature of transportation with their operations. Different sectors also use different types of data source to customize their weather forecast analysis. Transportation mainly involves movement of commodities and movement of people and the movement of people in communities in our current world is highly integrated and it has a multimodal nature. For us to investigate the impact of weather on the performance of the transport system there is the need for researchers in a meteorological department to integrate the two things, that is, commodities, and people in a seamless manner.

Research done recently suggest that land transport network has less regulation and harmonization when it comes to the integration of meteorological services delivery. Air transport and marine transport has a more developed integration of meteorological service delivery and this needs to be discussed and rectified in order for land transport to also have a greater integration since it is also important. Land transport has a greater vulnerability as compared to aviation and maritime Transport and this is evidenced by the recent statistics that were collected. Data from the United States show that road accidents related to weather results in an average of 6000 deaths in a year with more than 40 billion US dollars in loss. Weather forecast also affects their transport in ways that are more regulated though they still have a greater impact in revenue generation and service delivery. Challenges such as traffic delays have impacted a lot of economic losses as 10% of the economic impact of weather-related highway losses have been recorded in the recent past in the air transport. Weather-based integrated service delivery has been introduced in the transport sector so as to lead to efficiency and control. It optimizes the results of the network in response to adverse weather conditions. They include common situational awareness and comprehension with information and decision support services. The main objective of this is to lead to an integrated service delivery which has the capability to function across multiple transport modalities (Winter, Sester, Wolfson, and Geers, 2011).

For instance, when one is moving goods or commodities from one place to another, it is necessary for the meteorological department to consider the effects of the adverse weather conditions If a journey is complex, the meteorological department needs to consider the weather impacts at the different times and multiple locations throughout the journey. This is a complicated process in that it is important to keep in mind that these weather conditions can be heavy rainfall or snow might have very different effects at the different points and for different users.

The effects of adverse weather conditions in the transport sector has been well-researched. It remains a significant problem in quantifying and mitigating these effects across sectors that are made multiple, across various scales of space and time and across different geopolitical boundaries. For such problems to be solved, various considerations need to be addressed and they include the identification of particular requirements, the optimization of weather, the measurements involved in rail and road and air transport, usage, and blending multiple forecasting techniques which include numerical weather prediction also the improvement of communication and delivery of messages and finally integrating seamlessly across multiple transport sectors. With the introduction of integrated service delivery, there will be a reliability quality and relevance in analyzing weather information. The service will need to be customized in order for it to fit the needs of different transport sectors which might include; companies that deal with tracking airline bus and shipping, the user of transport, for example, the general public, companies that deal with postal services and companies that supply medicine, etc.

For attainment of eligible degree of integrated service delivery, there is need for advancement in meteorological observation in terms of analysis tools and their applications, in models and frameworks of weather forecast in approaches that are unified across transport modes and also changes in culture on either sides that is providers of weather and the stakeholders of the organization. This change can be initiated by basically giving a situational awareness across the different transport sectors in the event there is a high-impact weather event that will probably bring about challenges. With this the challenges that are weather related that may come about between the interconnections using the multimodal integration and among stakeholders will need to be discussed and addressed and this is the most vital challenge in the procedure. Using the first step, the multimodal integration challenge can be well focused on by user groups and this will lead to the facilitation of creating a strategy that will be used in a development, testing, and reporting of required activities best which will be translated to other end user groups. In land transport, the integrated services will heavily rely in the advancement of the number of meteorological tools and its capabilities which include the atmospheric and surface state measurement type of systems, the data assimilation procedures and numerical weather prediction frameworks are also important. These features could improve in the resolution of special and temporal elements and the accuracy of forecast of atmospheric conditions and also it might accurately help in determining the type and rate of precipitation. The integrated meteorological service delivery program will be affected by technical, cultural, and climatic changes and below are some of the examples of which service provider will have to stay in check on the changes; the technology involved with computer science is bringing about paradigm shifts in the transport industry. End users and the system managers will benefit, in that, vehicles will be able to sense weather patterns as they will be installed with weather sensing platforms which will result in a real-time mobile observation capability which will enhance weather analysis and forecasting. This is an example of vehicle-to-vehicle and vehicle-to-infrastructure technology (Abduljabbar et al, 2019).

Also aerial and marine systems that are unmanned have been introduced. These systems will be a climate and weather observation platform. These unmanned systems will have a great potential for providing additional opportunities in order for gaining comprehension of weather and climatic conditions specifically in the zones that are difficult to be accessed with conventional systems of measurement. When this system continues to evolve, the availability of a time conscious observation of the lowest few miles of the atmosphere as well the observation of both inside and outside the sea will be a more common thing. Search advancements will enable the proper analysis and evaluation of the impact of adverse weather conditions in land transport. Due to the heightened availability of observational tools and computational resources alongside the advancement in statistics and modeling numerically, there will be an improved weather and climate information gathering techniques for end-users. Furthermore, the expansion of these techniques for data mining and machine learning (ML) will come in handy as it will propel the modification of new weather-related products and services. With the integration of transport data for example traffic flow and the conventional weather data which involves observation and forecasting, there will be the introduction of new weather-related impact-based capabilities which would be used in analyzing weather and will lead to the general efficiency in transportation (Abduljabbar et al, 2019).

Throughout the history, researchers experimented with many techniques to foresee weather efficiently and accurately. Nopw, it is possible to accurately predict the weather in days and even months in prior to the event. This has been propelled mostly by computer science. The use of computer models became widespread mainly throughout the late 1950s as the first weather satellite was installed.

This came with many changes in the metrological department and the overall beneficiaries which in our case is transport. The types of computer models that are used in forecasting mainly depends on the climate type and the weather conditions. Some of the computer models HR used in weather forecasting have been listed and explained below;

Climatic models: This type of framework is basically used to predict climate change that will have a huge impact in the Earth. Climate is defined as the mean conditions of weather in a specific geographical area for a period of time of about 30 to 40 years. Climate models use a mixture or current data and statistical data to come up with a technical reasonable prediction the CFS is among and the most commonly used climatic framework that is used in predicting planetary scale weather conditions, for example, El Nino hurricanes and tsunamis*Mesoscale models:* Most meteorological departments utilize mesoscale frameworks to commonly predict local weather. In meteorological slang, mesoscale is defined as the atmospheric condition that ranges within a distance of 2 to 20 km. Climate and synoptic frameworks normally luck sufficient resolution to predict localized conditions of weather such as a single cellular thunderstorm and a tornado.

Dynamic models: Dynamic models is the most unique and sophisticated framework that is used to predict weather. It mostly uses costly tools that leads to its advancement the dynamic model is modified and can be able to use advanced fundamental equations of the atmosphere to forecast weather changes based on current weather conditions despite their level of efficiency dynamic models framework can cause errors during the onset of running. According to the findings of National Hurricane Centre GFS and CMC are some of the dynamic frameworks that are mostly utilized in the country.

Statistical model: This framework fundamentally gives the experts in the meteorological department precise weather predictions. Statistical frameworks use historical data to help them get a better understanding of the next condition. This type of framework is commonly used when they are tracking mid-latitude cyclones and tropical cyclones. If the dynamic framework agreement is not bringing sense and reason, meteorologist usually use statistical frameworks to give out better predictions.

Despite computerized models being a safe and effective tool that is used in weather forecasting there is still no pinpoint accuracy. Computer models are normally less in efficiency mostly during the preliminary runs.

9.7. THE AUTOMATIC CONTROL OF URBAN ROAD TRAFFIC (UTMC PROGRAM)

The urban traffic management control started as a government research program and its main objective in the United Kingdom was to help in the development of a more open approach to intelligent transport systems in urban areas. The urban traffic management control development group now manages the initiative and this initiative represents both local transport authority and the systems in the industry. Urban traffic management control has been manufactured and designed in a way that it integrates and enables different applications which are found in the modern traffic management system to communicate and share data amongst each other (Abduljabbar et al, 2019). Due to these data that was considered to be disparate from multiple sources such as automatic number plate recognition cameras, variable message sign (VMS), car-parks, traffic signals, air quality monitoring stations and major electrical data can now be consolidated into one central database. The whole idea behind the development of urban transport management control was to optimize road networks so as to create a stronger intelligent system that has the capabilities of handling current and future management requirements.

The program was initiated in 1997. The first phase of the construction mainly put emphasis on particular applied research roles on both the technical and operational issues. In 2001 the second phase began and it was the phase that was used to demonstrate the consolidation and integration of the results that was gotten from the first phase. McDonald's provided key systems in the introduction of a full-scale demonstrator project which took the urban traffic management control approach and the research was undertaken in Preston. A development group was created in 2003 and the group comprised of local authorities and other suppliers and them together with the support of the DFT they would overlook the development of urban traffic management control. Ever since the introduction of urban traffic management, control sets of standards have been adopted appropriately which are not over constraining and it allows users, suppliers, and other integrators of the system to plan and supply system costs in an effective way in the open market. This has enabled the local authorities to interpolate the network and this makes the standards essential. A group called the urban transport management control specification and student groups was formed and its function was to ensure there is responsible urban traffic management control technical framework and it was continuous so as to meet the demands of the local authorities currently and in the future. The function of the specification and standard group was to oversee the maintenance and the upkeep of the urban transport management control technical particulars both the local authorities and the suppliers community are the members for the local securities are the ones who control.

The full range of urban transportation management controls and the specifications and standards group work together closely in ensuring that technical requirements have been achieved.

Technical research and standard development activities are funded from time to time by the commission but mostly the commission operates solely through the coordination of the input freely provided that suppliers and their uses involved. For shared data, that is where standards are set by the specification group, that is, they are communicated between applications in the urban transport management control system or between the urban transport management control system and an external system. This communication can occur in the following ways; keeping the definitions of the current urban transport management control objects and availing them to users, receiving of submissions for prospective new urban transport management control objects, the coordination and consultation as necessitated, the facilitation of contacts between object developers, advising when changes that are needed to prospective new urban transport management control objects and finally the registration of new urban transport management control objects.

There are a couple of activities that might aid the market in the initiation of the traffic management of unit. Annually, a conference is held and normally papers and articles are published in major industrial journals and normal workshops. The objectives and goals of this article is to focus on the main agenda that is the technical and operational themes. A campaign was run in 2006 to demonstrate the compatibility of products of the urban transport management controls to a village of suppliers in London.

9.8. VEHICLE COMMUNICATION

Researchers started to perform experiments regarding vehicle communication. Intelligent transport is the next transformational invention in the engineering department and an area that has been gaining momentum over the past few years. All different transport entities vehicles, bridges, traffic lights, roads everything will communicate and cooperate exchanging information with each other, improving safety and efficiency of the transport system. In our current road systems about 60% of accidents and fatalities could be avoided in the event that the driver is given a warning half-a-second earlier before the crash happens. This technology is achievable if vehicles that are traveling will be able to send data of their speed and location every tenth of a second to other vehicles on the road. The technology can be achievable though there are many difficulties that the system has to tackle and some of the difficulties it needs to tackle is the need for an intense rapid verification and control of error. This becomes a challenge in that every package of data, for example, an email the part of the package will involve acknowledgment and shaking and a recovery error.

9.9. DATA SHARING AND INTEROPERABILITY

Most of the aspects regarding the data management in the transportation sector should be carefully considered. New ideas and experiences should be freely shared to advance the traport technology. Conference presentation and journal publications are good ways of exchanging such ideas and experiences. These experience will come in handy during the process of analyzing and study of real-life information. Data does not have to be collected again if it can be retrieved or supplemented easily. The transportation systems and communities are being encouraged to undertake such activities that are related in the exchange of transportation data sets. Some of the activities that are encouraged to be taken are;

- Determining the types of data that might be vital in terms of usage during planning designing operating and creating safety and maintenance of the transportation facilities. One should learn how to classify the data.
- Determination of the format and the standard that will be used in the publication of the datasets for instance the data saved should be standardized in terms of publishing. Not only that but the data should contain a description of how it was collected and the function of its collection that is what and how to use them and where to get them and many other descriptions.
- The standards that will be used in the dissemination of data should be defined.

After the integration of systems have been neglected, the next objective is interoperability. Some of the questions we need to ask ourselves regarding interoperability is what is the definition of interoperability? is interoperability practically achievable? how does interoperability differ from compatibility, interfacility, and substitutionability?, what is the role of standards in achieving it?, which standards are we going to use?, what is the difference between component-level interval interoperability and system-level interoperability? where are the early examples of interoperability in transportation?.

Other futuristic applications of computers in transportation involves the analyzing of aging and disabled drivers, vehicle, and highway automation, information dissemination, collision warning, and avoidance systems and intelligent vehicles.

CHAPTER

10

How Has Computer Science and Technology Changed the Environment

CONTENTS

10.1. INTRODUCTION

It is evident that computers have considerably made major changes in the lives of human beings. It is very hard for us to ever imagine or lives without computers. They have been able to provide means that help in making the lives of people easier and much more comfortable. Computers have led to the provision of many opportunities for people to keep in touch and they have also provided job opportunities.

These days, people are even able to use cars that have been computerized and do things for one end of the world from the other end. All in all, computers have proven to be an electronic brain that the humans can depend on. They are important in very many fields and that does not leave out the environment.

The world as we know today has many different problems occurring within at a time. The environment is under threats from many different factors including the climate. Climate change has become one of the major issues affecting the environment as of today. Many organizations are working on finding out ways to reduce the level of global warming. Computers have advanced to a level that allows us to utilize them to make some of these changes.

Figure 10.1: There are many different ways in which computer science and technology can be integrated into different aspects so as to improve the environment.

Source: http://myelectronicsblog.blogspot.com/2008/12/green-computers-and-computing.html.

The number of natural disasters that are occurring in the world have increased by four times since 1970. This is mostly due to a rise in the global temperature that or happens annually. In addition to the rise in the global temperature, there has also been an increase in air pollution, forests being cut down and also bush fires, greenhouse omissions have increased, carbon dioxide omissions have also increased, and many other contributors to the state of the environment now as we know it.

These changes in the environment are affecting many different aspects including the fishing farming, crop farming, livestock farming, etc. all of which are very important in providing both a livelihood and food for the growing population. This being said there are many scientists who are working to reduce or reverse the effects that have occurred, and they are using supercomputers to do so. Below we will discuss all the different ways in which computer science and technology can be utilized in the environment.

10.2. REDUCING THE LEVEL OF PLASTIC POLLUTION

Every year, around 14,000,000 tons of plastic is dumped in our water bodies. In comparison, one can imagine a fully filled garbage truck dumping all its trash into the ocean every single minute. There has been production of plastic in the last decade that is much more than what has been produced in the whole of the last century. This plastic takes around 500 years for it to degrade.

Figure 10.2: Plastic pollution is becoming one of the major threats to marine animals today. Many fish are dying from either getting trapped in plastic waste, or swallowing plastic waste which is indigestible. This can greatly affect our food source.

Source: https://www.nrdc.org/stories/10-ways-reduce-plastic-pollution.

This is very detrimental to our environment considering the fact that most of the plastic that is produced, and that we use, can only be used once. This includes straws, plastic water bottles, plastic plates, plastic spoons, forks, etc. Considering how deep we are in the hole, it is important for us to consider and state some ways in which computers can be of help when it comes to cleaning up the plastic in the world, as well as prevent any more plastic pollution. Below are some of the ways computer science and technology can help in reducing and eliminating plastic pollution.

10.2.1. Using Social Media and the Internet

We can find any information we need at any time due to the help of the internet. The internet has provided us with a way to communicate with people all over the world in seconds. There are many applications and social networks that give us this opportunity.

It is important to acknowledge that there are over 5 billion people that use social networking sites and applications. It is important to use these sites to create awareness on the major matters that we need to communicate on. Things that people care about and things that they should care about.

There are many campaigns that have been run on social media platforms. An example can include the campaign that was done by UNEP. They did a campaign on Twitter called #BeatPlasticPollution, which was targeting the population, and trying to get people to stop using plastics.

This has been a great method. On top of them raising awareness, they were able to raise money and get people together for the organization of events all over the world on informing the population on the negative effects of plastics and how to avoid this (Zaib, Hassan, and Khan, 2019).

Social media has also been used to post images on the effects that plastics have brought to our environment. These photos may help in drawing a larger audience due to the severity of the issue. It appeals to the softer side of the human being.

10.2.2. Monitoring Ocean Plastics Using Satellite Observation

There is a non-profit organization that deals with the development of technologies that are advanced that help in eliminating the plastic that is in the ocean. It is called The Ocean Cleanup.

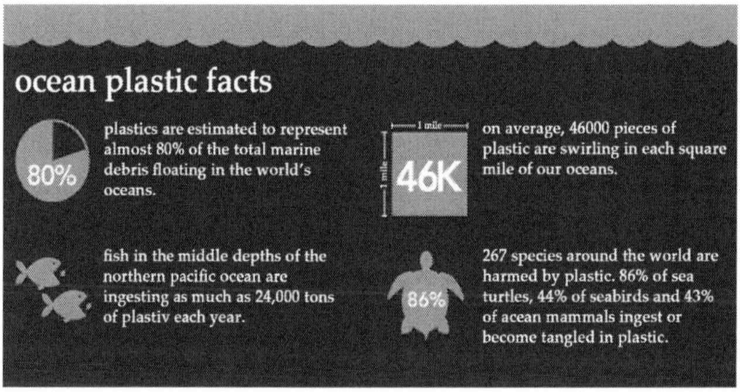

Figure 10.3: Above are some of the facts about plastic pollution and how it affects our oceans.

Source: https://twitter.com/plasticbank/status/491642358602006528.

They use satellites to receive images of the ocean, as well as machine learning (ML) so as to ensure that the ocean is cleaned up, so as to get rid of the large amount of plastic in the ocean; roughly 5 trillion pieces. They have been able to make this estimation through their satellite observations which has helped them see the garbage patches that are found in the ocean. They are working in making sure that they have collected around half of the garbage in the ocean in the next five years (Zaib, Hassan, and Khan, 2019).

After working for around 3 years, they were able to give some feedback on the work that they have done. They have been able to collect, count, sort, characterize, and categorize 1.2 million pieces of plastic. They have been able to process terabytes of aerial images and also data. This information is at the time being reviewed scientifically. They however, have been able to ascertain the public that they will make a huge change and also provide a lot of information to scientists that can help in reducing the plastic in the ocean. Despite the fact that they have done a lot of research and made many discoveries, they have not yet finished and still have a lot to do.

More research work is being planned in the next few years to monitor the progress of the cleanup and provide useful data to improve the technology that is used for this cleanup.

They deal with research and also engineering as their core principles to eliminate this threat. Plastic waste is killing many fish species in the ocean. However, the problem is that these marine species are important in both maintaining the integrity of our environment and providing food to the large population (Zaib, Hassan, and Khan, 2019).

Additionally, the European Space Agency will utilize their satellites to detect and track the large amount of plastic from space with the goal to identify areas that are most affected by this problem.

10.2.3. Understanding Natural Systems Using Artificial Intelligence

There are certain reports that have been filled by the World Economic Forum on great opportunities for promoting conservation of the earth. One of these is being able to harness artificial intelligence (AI) for the earth which will help in ensuring that key technologies will mature such as ML and big data.

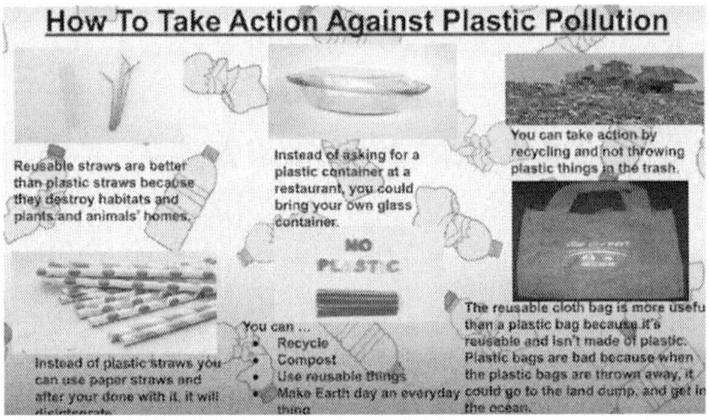

Figure 10.4: These are some of the ways that people can be educated on to take action against plastic pollution.

Source: https://twitter.com/hashtag/5thgradeexhibition?src=hash.

This means that climate scientists will be able to use the developed computing power as well as better designed agricultural algorithms to fully understand the environment, as well as ensure optimization of the interventions by being able to model and predict the patterns of the climate using climate informatics. It also helps in promoting improved coordination amongst those who are doing the research allowing them to have sharing and analyzing of important information when it comes to plastic pollution (Zaib, Hassan, and Khan, 2019).

10.2.4. Visualization of Data and Big Data

Big data refers to fields that work on treating manners used for analyzing, extraction of information in a systematic manner from, or also end up dealing with information sets that are too big or complicated to deal with while using the traditional application software that is used for the processing of data.

This field is important in making measurements as well as keeping track of the resources on earth. While utilizing ML as well as visualization of data, big data is able to help us to make decisions that are better informed. The biggest problem in this sector are the things that are not known. There are many organizations that have come to the conclusion that the main reason we have a problem with the management of plastic waste, is because we do not have the ideal information we need to avoid it. Very few countries in the world measure and well document their plastic waste.

10.2.5. Blockchain

There is a plastic bank that provides digital tokens that are secured using blockchains for exchanging plastics that have been recycled. They do this aiming at ensuring that people who recycle their plastics are rewarded. This helps to do two things at the same time: reduce the amount of plastic trash, as well as eliminate poverty. The plastic bank has partners that helps in the implementation of this scheme which is aiming at meeting the growing demands as well as securing the transactions that are running on it (Cerny, 2011).

Figure 10.5: Blockchain technology cannot have its data modified.

Source: https://www.enisa.europa.eu/news/enisa-news/enisa-report-on-blockchain-technology-and-security.

There are many different organizations that are aiming at using block chain technology to change the current condition of the climate right now. So as to beat plastic pollution, there is a need for sustainable models that will help in the implementation of these aspects and also research that should be done into the technology so as to ensure that the technology being developed is effective enough to help in combating this problem.

10.3. USING ROBOTS TO TRACK THE QUALITY OF WATER

It is not easy to clean up or avoid an oil spill in an ocean or a river. However, technology has made it easier to detect such spills. Visually, it is easier to see the spill in the ocean because it covers a relatively large area. Unfortunately, it can have a negative impact on lot of animals and plants that live nearby. It is, however, harder to detect other different types of water pollution because they are not that easy to notice yet because a lot of damage.

Sewage that has not been treated, runoff from agricultural activities, and wastes from heavy metal industries create a dangerous pollutant mixture that may often be invisible. Scientists regularly monitor water quality to decide whether the body of water is safe for fishing, swimming, and even drinking. This however, requires the scientist to travel to the locations where they will be able to test the waters. Traveling to the site is not only expensive, but also requires a lot of time for the collection and processing of the samples. The hole analysis cycle can take as long as even three months (Cerny, 2011).

Figure 10.6: This is the eel-like robot that helps track of water quality. They have sensors that are able to direct them as well as collect data.

Source: https://thenewstack.io/eel-like-aquatic-robots-use-living-sensors-zero-water-pollution/.

In an effort to make this process easier, researchers in certain countries have invented robots that can monitor the quality of water for them. Switzerland has created one such robot called Envirobot. It is eel-shaped and moves through the water to collect and analyse water samples in real-time.

This robot is autonomous and can decide on the route it wants to take in response to certain aspects. Therefore, it can track and locate the source of pollution.

There are several advantages that come with operation of such robots in comparison to sending scientists to the sites. It makes it faster and the information is deployed easily in case it is needed immediately for analysis.

The Envirobot was designed to be similar to a number of generations of robots that had been created earlier generations and they are based on a swimming motion that is natural. The manner in which it is constructed allows the scientists to have the ability for attaching or detaching segments of the robot as required. They are not designed to accomplish certain tasks that are specific, but are also designed to study and learn from animals.

The robots have models that are watertight and independent containing their own motors that are powered by batteries. These segments are connected using 2 data bus networks, and the head of the robot is connected to Wi-Fi and antennas from the radio, a computer that has been embedded, and a GPS receiver.

These robots have sensors that help in the collection of data on the temperature of water, the amount of oxygen in the water, the salinity, and also the pH. In addition to this, they also have biological sensors that are sophisticated and utilize living organisms for the detection of toxins.

Most of the methods that are used to detect chemicals only detect certain compounds, however, these biological sensors are able to detect a wide range of things such as the quality of water being good or bad.

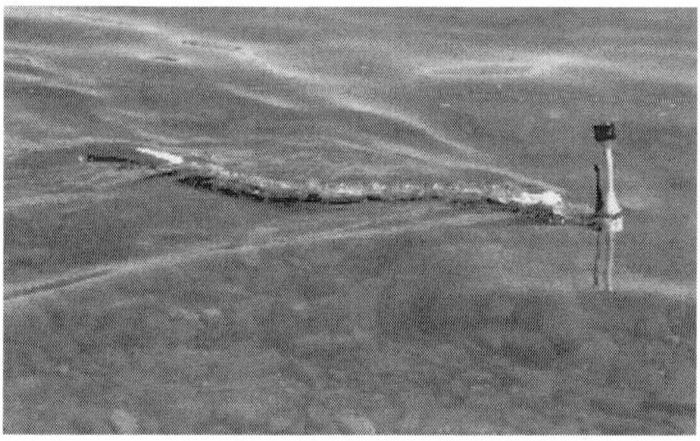

Figure 10.7: It uses electricity to move in the water as it collects data on the water quality. It is able to note any unwanted materials in the water such as heavy metals.

Source: https://ideas.ted.com/this-amazing-robot-swims-like-an-eel-and-detects-pollution/.

The segments that have the biological sensors contain certain tiny chambers that fill up with water as the robot is swimming. This allows for the robots to analyze specific organisms such as water fleas that are in the water, so as to detect contaminants that they react to, which helps to provide a bigger picture on the quality of water.

In the laboratory setting, these sensors work very well; however, it is difficult for the scientists to make them small so as to fit in the robot, and also find a way for their information to be transmitted to the laboratory computers which needs an electrical signal. They also allow for bacteria that has either frozen or dried to be reconstituted as the water enters the chamber. These bacteria are then able to have reactions to any mercury compounds that are present in the water by the emission of a light, which then and undergoes measurement using a luminometer and the signals and then transmitted to the robot (Cerny, 2011).

As of now, this bot is able to fulfil the recording and visualization of data for up to one hour in one single route. This fully depends on the condition of the weather and the battery life of the bot. All the information that is collected by the robot undergoes logging in the computer that it has on board; however, the researchers are also able to monitor this information in real time from a remote place.

Scientists are able to confirm that this robot has performed specific missions that have been successful in Lake Geneva whereby, they have been able to navigate deeper waters and pursue the course it has been programmed to do, and thereafter return to the shore. They are however, also programmed in a manner that allows them to use a probability mode for the determination of their own course. It is able to take a sample from any position in the water and thereafter decide where it should travel to next, which helps in taking the scientists to where the pollutants are coming from (Cerny, 2011).

There is still a lot of research that is being done to improve the accuracy of the robot, and the future versions are expected to dive into deeper waters and collect samples from there.

All this gives the scientists much more time to concentrate on the matters that are much more challenging and important because the robots then do all the physical sampling and measurements. Some of the more important matters include making decisions on what to do to respond to the data that has been collected, or the development of measures to end the pollution that is happening (Cerny, 2011).

10.4. CREATING CHEAPER WIND ENERGY

In some areas the wind speed exceeds 40 mph, such as those in the Pacific North. Due to windy conditions, these areas are popular amongst paragliders, wind suffers, and now even enthusiasts for sustainable energy.

Figure 10.8: Wind energy is a clean and safe way of providing electricity to a large area. It is also safe for the environment and very effective. Its efficiency however, depends on the condition of the weather.

Source: https://www.scientificamerican.com/article/how-does-wind-energy-work/.

There are already wind turbines set up in those areas and are able to ensure a generation of up to 4500 MW of power. This is almost equal to more than five 800 MW nuclear power plants. It is however, hard for engineers to optimize this power due to the unpredictable nature of the wind.

Those who operate these utilities need predictions of the wind power that are reliable due to the long amount of time that it takes for the nuclear power plants to start up and cool down. If by any chance the power of the wind floods the grid without their knowledge, there is wastage of energy.

It is however, complicated to also predict the conditions of the wind and make forecasts of hampers due to the many natural artefacts that are surrounding the gorge including mountains, coastal areas, canyons, etc. which may bring up many different effects that are complex. It would be easier to promote the integration of wind energy into the grid, as well as reduce the costs of electricity, by using forecasts that are much more accurate.

There are two hourly models of updating forecasts of the atmosphere that have been developed by the national center for environmental prediction that are able to predict wind power. These however, are mainly developed for the simulation of weather on flat terrain. There is a need for models that have finer grid spacing so as to resolve the features of the wind that are in topographies that how much more complex such as the gorge.

So as to achieve this, scientists can boost the accuracy of these models so as to allow them to run at larger grid spaces of around 750 m. This will help in the collection of extensive data of the real world so as to test and validate the model. Scientists were able to place more than 21 sensors of the environment in the gorge, for the recording of the conditions of the wind every 10 minutes over a certain period of time.

These sensors are then able to send the information that they have collected to the scientists, where they undergo assimilation into a representation of the atmosphere in 3-D. And allows them to run experimental models of the initial conditions.

Figure 10.9: There are simulation kits that have been developed to ensure the better prediction and decision making when it comes to wind energy.

Source: https://www.energy.gov/eere/wind/articles/simulation-toolkit-promises-better-wind-predictions-increased-farm-production.

They are created in a manner that allows them to simulate large amounts of events of the weather at model resolutions that are very high. They can also aid in forecasting weather conditions that are difficult to focus. They are working on developing these models to make the information collected more accurate.

Some of the research has shown that scientists will be able to simulate a whole year of weather conditions while emphasizing mostly on the conditions of the wind in the gorge so as to compare the models that exist right now with the newer ones that they would be able to develop that have physical parameters that have been improved. It has however, been difficult for the engineers to predict the conditions of the wind accurately, due to certain complications that they have encountered.

One of the greatest challenges that they face, is the determination of the section of the model forecast system that is responsible for the differences that are noted between the observations and the forecasts.

They are focusing on improving the physics of the model; however, they have noted that there are errors that occur due to having inadequate states of the atmosphere or dynamics (Cerny, 2011).

These models are required to work synergistically with other components so as to improve the weather forecasting skills, mostly for higher speeds of wind that are 60–160 m above ground level. Researchers are working hard to ensure solid improvements in the forecasting of wind.

The next upgrade of the operation version of the existing forecast models that are updated hourly, will have implementation of these improved components.

Improving the forecast of wind has the potential to reduce and limit the utilization of energy reserves that are expensive, such as coal, as well as reducing the amount of greenhouse gas emissions which can help in reducing negative climate changes. This will help in saving people money and also improving the air quality that people breathe.

10.5. REDUCTION OF THE CONSUMPTION OF URBAN ENERGY

60 to 80% of global greenhouse gas emissions are due to the existence cities. Cities also lead to the consumption of 80% of the energy supply globally. Buildings in the city, both residential and commercial, need lighting, ventilation, air conditioning, heating, and many other important appliances. It is however, difficult for city officials to make analyses, visualizations, and even translations of the data from 20,000 plus buildings into recommendations of policies and programs.

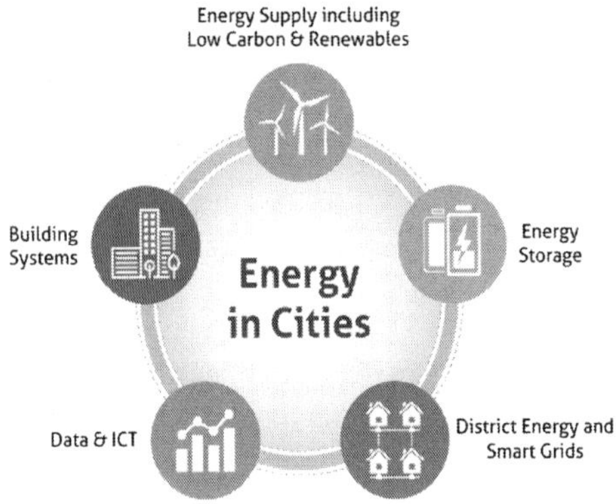

Figure 10.10: To ensure that urban energy systems are sustainable, they need to meet the needs of the growing population.

Source: https://www.apuea.org/index.php/urban-energy-systems/introduction-to-urban-energy-systems2.

There has been development of benchmarking that is aided by computers and helps in measuring the actual energy consumption of a building against a performance baseline, and also helps in deriving data on how the buildings are in comparison to other buildings that are similar and also the most likely impact of improvement on energy efficiency. The employment of methods that are data driven can be used to enable an urban building planning that is sustainable. This helps in taking out the guesswork from the energy management of the municipal.

As of right now, more than half of the global population reside in the cities. This movement of people from rural areas to the cities is causing a major threat to the governance of the urban areas, infrastructure, and even management of the environment. So as to deal with these issues, researchers have been working at the development of solutions that are data driven and integrated.

3% of the global total land surface is occupied by cities in some bun areas. They however, account for 58 to 80% of the world's greenhouse gas emissions, while still consuming 78% of the resources that are natural and 81% of the world's supply of energy. There are many cities in the United States that are developing methods that will allow them to understand the performance of energy in buildings, for the identification of opportunities that will help in reducing the usage of energy.

In the United States, they have enforced laws that mandate for buildings to collect and disclose data on their use of energy. This is what is referred to as energy benchmarking. Using these methods has helped the United States to save 7% annually which is approximately $10 billion in lowered costs of energy. The collection and recording of data is done using computers (Zaib, Hassan, and Khan, 2019).

There is however, a problem, for many municipalities, with the translation of this information into insights that are actionable and also identification of the buildings that are considered better candidates for interventions of energy efficiency. The benchmarking initiatives that have been implemented have provided results that show that it is not enough to enact benchmark laws so as to save and conserve energy.

Figure 10.11: Conserving energy in the cities is important in lowering the high costs that are spent annually on electricity.

Source: https://www.shutterstock.com/search/how+to+conserve+energy?section=1&measurement=px&sort=popular&image_type=all&safe=false&search_source=base_related_searches&language=en&saveFiltersLink=true.

As of now, there are a number of tools that the government use to accurately and quickly ensure translation of benchmarking information into recommendations for policies and programs that promote effective energy efficiency. These tools also help for the tracking of the implementation of these recommendations.

New York City enacted a law that requires those who own buildings that are more than 50,000 feet to ensure that they report information on the consumption of energy to the city so as to have benchmarking of the performance. This was aiming at ensuring that the people who make policies have enough information for the development of programs and policies that promote energy efficiency within the municipal (Zaib, Hassan, and Khan, 2019).

There is a need to improve the energy efficiency of buildings in the United States so as to achieve energy independence. Researchers have therefore developed programs that will allow the officials in the cities to make analysis, visualization, and translation of this information in an easier manner, so as to create policies and programs that will help in ensuring that energy is efficiently used.

As of today, most of the officials in the city use ad-hoc analysis modules and have constraints to the issuance of yearly reports that are static, and these fail to promote policies and programs for energy efficiency. There is a lot of information that needs to undergo generation, on the energy use of buildings by the benchmarking laws, and it is the work of the scientists to find methods that will help the policymakers use that information in an effective and efficient manner.

That has been development of a method that is data driven and novel integrated so as to meet this need. This method has helped to analyze any benchmarking information that has been collected successfully. This method involves making analysis of the relationships that are there between the characteristics of buildings that are high dimensional and the energy use that is obtained from a building, based on their benchmarking mandates of the government, and use this to make sure that there is a separation between the impacts of errors that are random from sources that may not be efficient. There is a program that has been designed in this manner.

This program has been developed in a manner that allows for it to make a comparison with local peers so as to ensure the calculation of its optimum maximum level of efficiency, instead of making a comparison with a specific target building with different building in the nation. This allows the policymakers as well as a urban planners to have a visualization ranks that are assorted, of building buildings that are efficient in energy as well as the amount of energy saving potential that they have. These tools have been designed in a manner that allows for the running of large numbers of simulations for the determination of the saving potential of energy (Zaib, Hassan, and Khan, 2019).

This has also helped for the accurate calculation of energy efficiency levels for buildings in the city so as to ensure the maintenance of interpretability that is needed for the facilitation of designing policies and programs in the municipal. The two objectives can be linked with the data science.

Data science has helped in the building of scalable processes, due to recording of data such as the size of the building, and even data on the dates in which there is delivering of fuel oil to the buildings each month. This allows the city of officials to efficiently and effectively examine the buildings in a collective manner so as to discover any patterns that have been hidden of the characteristics and use of energy.

Figure 10.12: It is important for cities to look for alternative sources of energy that are renewable. This will help in cleaning up the environment, which is very important if we are going to stop climate change.

Source: https://www.nationalgeographic.org/activity/non-renewable-energy-resources/.

The server has a high generalizability that allows for easy application two different cities that may have different laws on benchmarking. Due to the increased rate of urbanization, this benchmarking method that is data driven is meant to play a major role in ensuring the sustainable use of energy from urban buildings that are energy intensive and it is also important in ensuring that we meet the goals of global emissions.

There is a current need for the improvement of energy efficiency of buildings so as to achieve energy independence. This means that buildings need to use the exact quantity of energy according to need, and eliminate any urban energy consumption that is not necessary.

There are certain laws that can help in reducing the gaps in information that bring up issues when it comes to investing in improving the efficiency of energy use.

This research on benchmarking has acted as a representation of the first step towards integrating analysis that is data driven and supporting their use of sustainable methods to promote energy efficiency, so as to eliminate challah that are affecting the management of urban operations (Zaib, Hassan, and Khan, 2019).

10.6. USING DRONES TO SAVE TREES

There are many aspects that are affecting the trees in the world today. Examples include bush fires that are burning down large population of trees or illegal deforestation by people or drones. Climate change has led to the threatening of many of these forests and this can be a major threat to the global population.

It is important for scientists to address these issues so as to prevent any further damage than what has already occurred.

The global temperature is rising each year and for every 1°, there is a reduction of the stream flow by 5 to 7%, which leads to a negative effect for the trees.

Researchers are struggling with these numbers and trying to innovate ways in which they will be able to deal with this major threat.

The first ever cloud resource that is used for research in science and engineering was developed. It is called Jetstream.

This is a form of drone. It is fully supported by the National Science Foundation. Jetstream can run large instances and at the same time ensure the tests are parallel which helps in the completion of processes in 1/10th of the amount of time it would take when using the normal laptop computers (Pires, 2007).

Figure 10.13: Drones are being used to survey forests, so as to catch situations on time, so as to be able to reverse them before they become irreversible.

Source: https://sociable.co/technology/how-drone-technology-sows-restoration/amp/.

One of the greatest benefits that this resource offers is being able to ensure the development of geographic information systems that are interactive and these can be accessed by scientists all over the world, no matter where they are. This gives researchers the opportunity to make analysis of information that they gather, as well as creation of models in a fast and more effective manner. There is an application that is a Web-open map for the drone, and this app can run on Jetstream, allowing for the uploading of images that have been taken from aerial systems that are small and unmanned using a connection to Wi-Fi or 4G on a mobile phone so as to make models that are in 3-D. This helps in providing actionable data that is useful, and this data is provided in real time.

These drones also allow for the scientists to work with spatial data infrastructures that are scalable, which is very beneficial in the times to come for computational science considering the fact that the sets of data become large and much more complicated (Pires, 2007).

Using these drones can help in providing spatial data infrastructure that is utilitarian and horizontally scalable to the community of life sciences. Researchers have the ability to use these drones to promote the extension of their analytical capabilities and also in answering research questions that were previously and unanswerable. There are some researchers that are scared of using these advanced computing networks; however, this specific equipment comes with the opportunity for training of new users to the system. Cyber infrastructure is an aspect that many researchers fear working with due to an assumption of how complex it is to learn the code.

This being said, there are applications that are available which provide online tutorials for newer users, so that they are able to pick up the basic coding at a fast rate, as well as understanding skills in geographic information systems so that they can use them in their research.

This resource is very important, considering the many negative effects that are leading to the destruction of our forests (Pires, 2007).

10.7. SAVING ENDANGERED SPECIES

There are major advancements in technology, as well as innovations that have occurred, due to our normal human tendency, which has helped in formulating solutions for ensuring that certain species on earth are not endangered or do not become extinct.

There are many different types of technology, low-tech, and even newer technology, that are being used as a wide variety of scientific and technological concepts that will help in the preservation of endangered species. Below is a discussion on some of the ways we can save endangered species.

10.7.1. Using Better Methods to Map and Visualize

When Google invented Google earth, it was mostly used as a way to create maps or to find directions; however, it has proven to be more useful than that. It has become a major tool that is being used in conserving and preserving habitats and species.

There are many new species that have been found by researchers who are using Google Maps to browse the globe. There are also many different organizations that are using Google Maps as a tool to map and visualize endangered species and their habitats so as to make illustrations of the common aspects that threaten their survival. This software has helped in preventing and reducing any dangers that may lead to the endangerment and extinction of these species. It is important to protect these species as they are a major key to ensuring the survival of the human population (Dominik and Jacek, 2014).

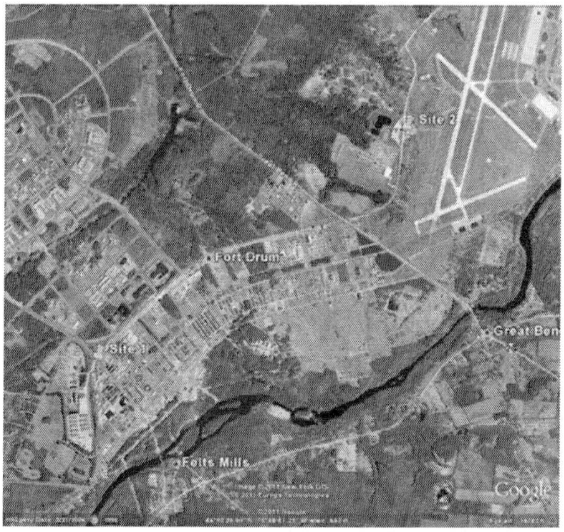

Figure 10.14: Google maps provides a satellite view of the global landscape, which can aid in the visualization of local habitat. Using these images, we can keep track of changes to the habitat and its survival.

Source: https://www.researchgate.net/figure/Satellite-map-of-Sites-1-and-2-From-Google-maps_fig21_278003909.

10.7.2. Using Computerized Collars on Species That Are Endangered

Biologists have been able to create smart collars that utilize accelerometer technology as well as GPS for the tracking of locations of wild animals and also annoying how they are moving when they are hunting. These collar helps in showing the biologists all the moves of the specific animal that has the collar. Biologists believe that being able to know exactly what the specific species is doing at a time can help in allowing them to understand the species in a better manner and therefore also allow the biologists to make predictions on their behavior in addition to lowering the number of conflicts between humans and animals, therefore leading to the revolution of the manner in which we manage and interact with these species.

10.7.3. Photography and Videos Are Controlled Remotely

Being able to record and get close-ups of the details and characteristics of these animals in their natural habitat can help in allowing us to learn about what they need and what the threats to the endangered species are. This however, can be difficult due to having to get close to the animals and have an access that is clear without being seen by the animals. There are certain technologies however, that have helped in making this even easier. One of them is called The Beetle Cam, through which we can observe other species. These technologies have allowed us to take images that are clear, and these would have been hard to do without these high-tech equipment. The equipment can be controlled from wherever the biologist is.

10.7.4. Monitoring the Sounds of Wildlife Remotely

There is a new computer technology that has been created by certain researchers that helps in the listening to certain bird sounds at a time, which helps in making identification of species that are in the specific environment and also being able to notice if any changes occur because of loss of habitat and also changes in the climate. This technology helps in providing an approach that is automated to monitor the species of birds, instead of the researcher going all the way to the field to observe the birds directly. The researchers also believe that these methods can not only be used bird species, but also for many other different species in the forest such as frogs and insects and maybe even mammals in the marine.

Figure 10.15: Above are the components of the remote monitoring system that can be used for the monitoring of wildlife.

Source: https://www.researchgate.net/figure/Components-of-remote-monitoring-system_fig5_49968076.

10.7.5. Remote Controlled Sampling

When researchers want to take samples from huge animals such as whales and sharks, they have been able to come up with a manner to utilize helicopters that are controlled using a remote to make it happen.

This however, can be difficult because it can lead to injury during collection of the samples of the tissue, or contact that is invasive with the animal. Apart from having to collect blood from the whale, the researchers can be able to collect tissue samples from the blow-hole air, which is equipped with snot from the whale.

The researchers were able to come up with a method that is not invasive and it involves being able to hover a remote-controlled helicopter, that is 3 feet, over the pod of the whale, with petri-dishes that are strapped onto the helicopter, so as to be able to collect the samples after the exhaling of the whale.

10.7.6. Being Able to Text Elephants

In Kenya, scientists are using a different version of the smart collar to track elephants, so as to reduce the level of conflict between the elephants and the humans.

This collar that is used on the elephants has a mobile SIM card that is able to send text messages with the location of the animal so as to track their locations and movements. In the future, researchers are hoping to design them in a manner that allows the SIM card to alert the farmers that are in the area if there are elephants that are moving towards their farms in the form of a text message.

10.7.7. Fish Hooks That Are High-Tech

This is also referred to as a SMART (selective magnetic and repellent-treated hook) hook and it is a high-tech fish hook that is magnetic. These hooks are being used to keep certain fish species away from fishing lines.

These hooks have been created with a coating that is metallic and is able to produce a certain voltage when it is immersed in sea water. These can then be noted by sharks because they are very sensitive to electrical fields that are present in water.

This will help in keeping the sharks away from the fishing lines that are meant to be used on other fish species.

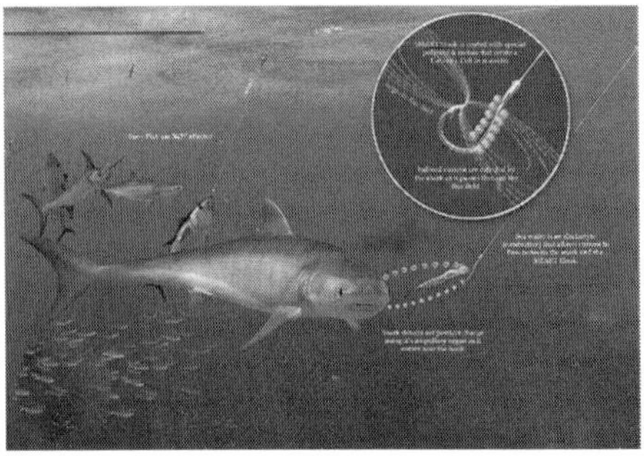

Figure 10.16: SMART hooks are helping in preventing ghost fishing as well as fishing unwanted species. This helps in protecting endangered species that may get trapped on long lines, such as sharks.

Source:-http://www.sharkdefense.com/other-research/smart-hooks/.

10.7.8. Sequencing of Genes

This involves being able to isolate the endangered species that are not affected when they are threatened by certain diseases, so as to breed them. This is now being boosted by technology. Scientists are now able to use high-tech machines that can be used for gene sequencing in preventing the extinction of fish species due to certain fatal diseases such as the devil facial tumor disease.

10.7.9. Beehive Fences

Due to some innovative thinking, there has been easier interaction between elephants and human beings in certain countries. This is due to the help of the honeybee. This involves making a fence using beehives that have been connected together using wires. This has proven to be effective in preventing elephants from crossing certain boundaries especially considering the fact that they can be a huge nuisance and destroy crops that are meant to be for human consumption and creation of livelihoods.

10.7.10. Measurement Tools That Are Controlled Remotely

Being able to get close to some species for observation, such as sharks, so as to get measurements that are precise for efforts to conserve and research is quite hard to do without certain tools. There has however, been development of certain tools that are high-tech, that have been used to study sharks, such as the stereo camera. These have helped in allowing the scientists to make these measurements very accurately, without having to get into contact with the animals at any point.

10.7.11. Drones for Ensuring Conservation

Figure 10.17: Drones are becoming very popular, despite the fact that they are quite expensive. They are being used to observe animals and take photos so as to avoid having a researcher going to the field themselves.

Source: https://www.ranthamborenationalpark.com/blog/drones-human-cry-safeguarding-wild/.

Drones are not only used in the military, but also in the observation of wildlife and marine animals. Scientists have been able to develop a drone equipped with sensors, cameras, and GPS for the mapping of certain activities, such as deforestation. These drones are quite expensive but they are worth because they help monitor and track long-term changes. At the same time, they provide valuable data and real-time video feeds.

10.7.12. Making Predictions for Wildlife Using Analytics

IBM created a new software for collecting wildlife data, such as the animal location and its well-being. The goal is to identify the most important aspects to focus on when it comes to the wildlife conservation. This software can help save many endangered species.

These advancements in technology allow us to live in a very exciting time. We can use different methods to conserve the environment and protects animal species that are endangered. The common theme is to utilize the possibilities that involve data gathering in order to identify better methods to monitor these animals.

10.8. USING COMPUTER SCIENCE TO FIGHT CLIMATE CHANGE

Computer science can play a major role in managing and preventing climate change. Technology has allowed us to collect large amounts of data that is helping in the innovation of new methods almost every single day. In the future, there will be only a few things that computer science cannot fix.

One of the main ways in which we can fight climate change is through utilization of cleaner energy systems (Zaib, Hassan, and Khan, 2019).

Computer science has helped in the analysis of data so as to allow us to specialize in the development of systems that will help us with these issues. There are many scientists who are very optimistic about what the future holds due to the daily developments of technology.

There is a lot of work that needs to be put into energy software before computer science can save the world.

This work not only needs to be done on certain algorithms, but also in the software industry as a whole. Computer scientists who are developing for energy have a lot of work to do.

There are many ways in which computer science can help us fight the changes in climate and below is an explanation of a few of them.

10.8.1. Development of a Software That Can Be Used to Educate the Public on Consumption of Energy

There is a need for improvement in energy related software. There is a need to create informative software so as to inform the public in matters to do with the conservation of energy.

This is probably one of the greatest opportunities that computer scientists have. This involves modernization of the grid.

Figure 10.18: Above is an example of an application that is used to educate the population on different monkey species, including those that are endangered.

Source: https://en.unesco.org/news/great-apes-app-wins-mobilewebaward-best-environmental-mobile-application-0.

So as to have future that is clean, it is important to ensure that the consumers of electricity are knowledgeable on their responsibilities in the conservation of energy. This can be achieved in a number if ways. For one, it is possible to create an application that can educate the population on conservation of energy.

This application can help in showing the electricity consumption in a household for every single month. There can also be another application that helps in informing the population on the impact of greenhouse gas emissions that are emitted every day in different states and even countries. There can even be an application that informs the population on certain actions that they can carry out as consumers of electricity and also how to track their own consumption. Another person can create an application that can be used to educate the population on the benefits that they provide if they used renewable energy or less energy.

There is a lot of change that is expected in the coming years due to the development of technology. This change however, cannot occur if the consumers of electricity are not on board. This is why educating the population on conservation of energy is very important (Zaib, Hassan, and Khan, 2019).

10.8.2. Development of Software's That Are More Robust in Making Decisions and Also Predictive Software

Computer scientists can develop software that helps them in making identification of certain trends in data so as to promote better decision making. This is referred to as decision making and predictive software. This software is designed to predict climate changes from analysis of data that is provided by sensors or weather stations, so as to use this analysis to make more informed decisions on certain aspects such as agriculture. These softwares can be quite complex, and there are many aspects that still require improvement.

Computer scientists have stated that it is almost impossible to create a predictive software that is perfect, due to the complexities that are involved in climate change. This means that there is a lot of work that needs to be done in this sector.

The reason thus software is difficult to create is due to the fact that is not possible to account for the many different variables in the climate or even in the electric grid. This means that the scientists should be working in creating a software that is able to evolve. This will allow for it to continue learning by itself as time goes.

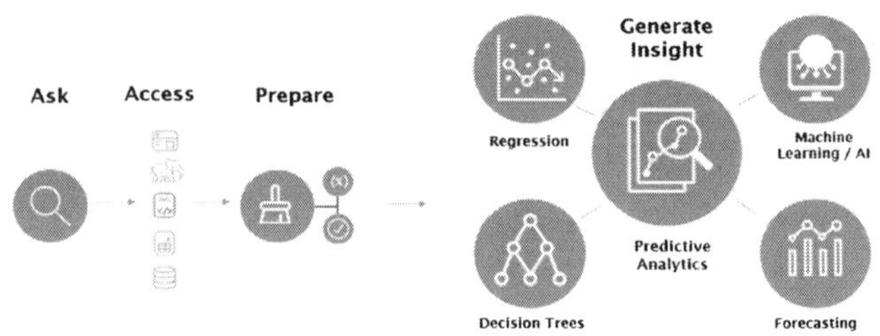

Figure 10.19: Above is an illustration on the manner in which predictive analytics occur.

Source: https://www.datawatch.com/data-fabric-save-a-stitch-in-time-with-predictive-analytics/.

Systems that are able to learn in an automatic manner are called ML systems. Due to the large sets of data on the internet, these systems will be able to predict and even make decisions based on the data they receive. As of now, there is a lot of amazing work that has been done by researchers in predictive software; however, there is a need for softwares that will have better performance and visualization and even being able to better utilize energy data so as to help systems in learning.

10.8.3. Developing Software That Is Better Customized for Collaborative Multidisciplinary Research

So as to fight against climate change, there is a need for everyone to work together. Different disciplines are needed to provide insights so as to increase the progress rate in fighting climate change. We do not have much time to waste on this matter (Cerny, 2011).

Being able to model climate is a process that is computationally intensive and it needs a wide range of data and physical atmospheric models that are quite complex so as to be able to collect accurate information on the factors that are leading to climate change. This being said, it can only be achieved if well knowledgeable numerical programmers come together to perform this work while having atmospheric scientists to help in the production of insight.

Despite that fact that there is already existence of collaborative research software, there is a high demand for software that is well customized. Without a platform that is custom made for multidisciplinary research, it would be almost impossible to model climate change. It would be very hard and complicated. It would make the process much more efficient if they design a software that is specially designed to consider what the scientists want (Cerny, 2011).

These facts are all required if there is going to be effective collaboration in the researching of energy. Another collaboration that can occur is between computer scientists and economists. For the creation of these predictive and decision-making models, there will be a need for programmers that are detail oriented to work with those who are knowledgeable in economics and creation of policies so as to design decision making tools that are accurate.

10.8.4. Improving Cyber Security in Large Company Networks

Not having proper cyber security can prevent networks that are large and well connected from taking off. These days the risk of getting hacked is much higher than it used to be. All companies need to view cyber security as their major priority. This important in order to avoid having their information leaked online or otherwise used without prior authorization.

Figure 10.20**:** Cyber security is one of the major threats in the world today.

Source:-https://www.edie.net/amp-news/8/Cyber-threats-and-climate-change-ranked-as-key-business-concerns-by-Allianz/.

Without cyber security, it can be possible to hack into the company's system. Large connected networks need to have compulsory security.There are many hackers with malicious intent and can take ownership of valuable data and share it with external parties. As a result, we need to be aware of cybersecurity and should invest into research focused on tackling these problems.

10.8.5. Donating Money to Environmental Organizations

The internet has made it possible to facilitate online financial transactions. Examples include shopping or donation of money to organizations that are working to improve environmental conditions. There are many factors that are affecting the environment and most of these factors have different roots.

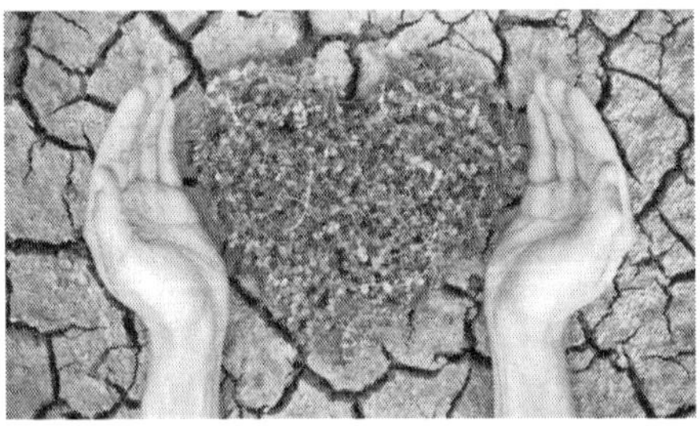

Figure 10.21: Donation can be done online with the click of a button on your mobile phone. Technology has made it easier for us to give back to the environment that has given us so much.

Source: https://www.mnn.com/lifestyle/responsible-living/blogs/21-environmental-charities-you-should-know-about.

When floods occur, people are displaced from their homes. When droughts happen, people in those areas lack food and water. When forest fires happen, people are also displaced from their homes. There are many negative outcomes that can occur due to drastic climate conditions.

It is important for people to donate money to people and organizations that need it. There are many environmental and financial websites that raise money for wildlife conservation.

The pace of technological inventions is very fast. People buy new or upgrade their existing devices very often. Once we make such upgrades, we can denote an old device to organizations that need it for scientific collaboration or research.

If the computer is less than five years old and still working well, it is possible to donate these computers to low budget scientific operations or non-profit organizations that are working on conserving the environment. This can be done online where you can use your mobile phone to order a courier who will deliver the computers to the organizations in need (Zaib, Hassan, and Khan, 2019).

References

1. Baca, A., (2014). *Computer Science in Sport: Research and Practice* (pp. 18–82). London: Routledge.
2. Bernhard, P., & Dirk, B., (2007). *Visualization in Medicine: Theory, Algorithms, and Applications* (pp. 1–11). Netherlands: Elsevier.
3. Bhatt, C. M., & Peddoju, S. K., (2016). *Cloud Computing Systems and Applications in Healthcare* (pp. 1–77).Pennsylvania: IGI Global.
4. Bodomo, A. B., (2009). *Computer-Mediated Communication for Linguistics and Literacy: Technology and Natural Language Education: Technology and Natural Language Education*(pp. 9–95). Pennsylvania: IGI Global.
5. Cerny, T., (2011). Competitive and collaborative approach towards a more effective education in computer science. *Contemporary Educational Technology* (pp. 163–173).
6. Dabnichki, P., (2008). *Computers in Sport* (p. 323). Southampton: WIT Press.
7. Daoliang, L., & Chunjiang, Z., (2019). *Computer and Computing Technologies in Agriculture XI: 11th IFIP WG 5.14 International Conference, CCTA 2017, Jilin, China, August 12–15, 2017, Proceedings, Part 2* (pp. 1–94). Berlin: Springer.

8. Daoliang, L., & Yingyi, C., (2014). *Computer and Computing Technologies in Agriculture VII: 7th IFIP WG 5.14 International Conference, CCTA 2013, Beijing, China, September 18–20, 2013, Revised Selected Papers, Part 2* (pp. 1–79). Berlin: Springer.
9. Deborah, M., & Charles, S. P., (2016). *Understanding Computers: Today and Tomorrow, Comprehensive* (pp. 2–48). Boston: Cengage Learning.
10. Edward, H. S., & Leslie, E. P., (2013). *Medical Informatics: Computer Applications in Health Care and Biomedicine.* Berlin: Springer Science & Business Media, 3–76.
11. Gallier, J., (2011). *Geometric Methods and Applications: For Computer Science and Engineering* (pp. 1–65).Berlin: Springer Science & Business Media.
12. Hausser, R., (2013). *Foundations of Computational Linguistics: Man-Machine Communication in Natural Language* (pp. 1–89).Berlin: Springer Science & Business Media.
13. Hwa, Y. J., Mohammad, S. O., Neil, Y. Y., & James, J., (Jong Hyuk) Park. (2013). *Advances in Computer Science and its Applications: CSA 2013* (pp. 1–65).Berlin: Springer Science & Business Media.
14. Iztok, F., Iztok, F. Jr., & Dušan, F., (2018). *Computational Intelligence in Sports* (p. 277). Berlin: Springer.
15. Jacob, T. S., & Chee-Keng, Y., (2016). *Algorithmic and Geometric Aspects of Robotics (Routledge Revivals)* (pp. 1–43). London: Routledge.
16. James, G. A., & Stephen, J. J., (2012). *Use and Impact of Computers in Clinical Medicine* (pp. 2–86).Berlin: Springer Science & Business Media.
17. Jennifer, P., Helen, S., & Yvonne, R., (2015). *Interaction Design: Beyond Human-Computer Interaction* (pp. 8–62). New Jersey: John Wiley & Sons.
18. Kaushik, A., Kumar, A., & Biswas, P., (2019). *Handbook of Research on Emerging Trends and Technologies in Library and Information Science* (p. 434).Pennsylvania: IGI Global.
19. Kenneth, S. P., & Jean, K., (2012). *Applications of Computer Technology to Dynamical Astronomy: Proceedings of the 109th Colloquium of the International Astronomical Union, held in Gaithersburg, Maryland, 27–29 July 1988* (pp. 19–98).Berlin: Springer Science & Business

Media.

20. Kim, G. J., (2015). *Human–Computer Interaction: Fundamentals and Practice* (p. 163). London: Taylor & Francis Group.
21. Kurosu, M., (2017). *Human-Computer Interaction. User Interface Design, Development and Multimodality: 19th International Conference, HCI International 2017, Vancouver, BC, Canada, July 9–14, 2017, Proceedings, Part 1* (pp. 3–94). Berlin: Springer.
22. Lajpat, R. A., Liwang, M., & Terry, A. H., (2016). *Agricultural System Models in Field Research and Technology Transfer* (pp. 1–71).Florida: CRC Press.
23. Li, D., (2008). *Computer and Computing Technologies in Agriculture, Volume II: First IFIP TC 12 International Conference on Computer and Computing Technologies in Agriculture (CCTA 2007), Wuyishan, China, August 18–20, 2007* (pp. 737–833).Berlin: Springer Science & Business Media.
24. Management Association & Information Resources. (2014). *Computational Linguistics: Concepts, Methodologies, Tools, and Applications: Concepts, Methodologies, Tools, and Applications* (p. 1727).Pennsylvania: IGI Global.
25. Maria, L. C., & Ian, T., (2019). How artificial intelligence is making transport safer, cleaner, more reliable and efficient in emerging markets. *Thought Leadership* (pp. 1–8).
26. Mehta, D. K. (2017). Business administration and computer science degrees: earnings, job security, and job satisfaction. *American Journal of Business Education* (pp. 1–8).
27. Michael, J. W., Jeffrey, D. S., Kamal, M. A., & Ashok, N. S., (2012). *Advances in Machine Learning and Data Mining for Astronomy* (p. 744).Florida: CRC Press.
28. Pires, J. N., (2007). *Industrial Robots Programming: Building Applications for the Factories of the Future* (pp. 1–92).Berlin: Springer Science & Business Media.
29. Rusul, A., Hussein, D., Sohani, L., & Saeed, A. B., (2019). *Applications of Artificial Intelligence in Transport: An Overview* (pp. 1–24). www.mdpi.com/journal/sustainability (accessed on 19 March 2020).
30. Sally, L., & Xiong, H., (2011). *Advances in Computer Science, Environment, Ecoinformatics, and Education, Part II: International Conference, CSEE 2011, Wuhan, China, August 21–22, 2011.*

Proceedings, Part 2 (pp. 1–89).Berlin: Springer Science & Business Media.

31. Sankowski, D., & Nowakowski, J., (2014). *Computer Vision in Robotics and Industrial Applications* (pp. 1–71). Singapore: World Scientific.
32. Segall, R. S., & Cook, J. S., (2018). *Handbook of Research on Big Data Storage and Visualization Techniques* (p. 917).Pennsylvania: IGI Global.
33. Sergio, C., Diego, R. R., & Milan, P., (2019). *Data Science for Healthcare: Methodologies and Applications* (p. 367). Berlin: Springer.
34. Sheikh, J. Z., Raqeeb, U. H., & Omar, F. K., (2019). Green computing and initiatives for environmental issues. *International Journal of Computer Science and Mobile Computing*, *6*(7), 49–55.
35. Stephan, W., Monika, S., & Ouri, W., (2010). *Towards a Computational Transportation Science* (Vol. 39(3)). New York, SIGMOD Record.
36. Sutcliffe, A., (2013). *Human-Computer Interface Design* (pp. 6–81). Berlin: Springer.
37. Vetulani, Z., (2011). *Human Language Technology. Challenges for Computer Science and Linguistics: 4th Language and Technology Conference, LTC 2009, Roznan, Poland, November 6–8, 2009, Revised Selected Papers* (p. 578).Berlin: Springer Science & Business Media.
38. Winter, Sester, Wolfson, & Geers. (2011). Towards a computational transportation science. *Journal of Spatial Information Science* (pp. 119–126).
39. Zhang, Dan, Wei, & Bin. (2018). *Novel Design and Applications of Robotics Technologies* (pp. 1–66).Pennsylvania: IGI Global.

INDEX

I

J

K

L

M

N

O